LET THERE BE
LIGHT

Making Sense of the

Creation/Evolution

Controversy

Jay Seegert

LET THERE BE
LIGHT

Jay Seegert

ICON
PUBLISHING GROUP

First printing: November 2012

For information contact:
Icon Publishing
Customer Service: +1 877 887 0222
P.O. Box 2180
Noble, OK 73068

ISBN: 978-1-62022-028-3

Cover and Interior by Brent Spurlock, Green Forest, AR

Printed in the United States of America

Please visit our website for other great titles:
www.iconpublishinggroup.com

I would like to dedicate this book to my wife and children, however, I have an even better idea.

I am actually dedicating this book to all those who will be reading it; but more importantly, I am reaffirming my dedication to Christ and expressing sincere gratitude to my wife, Amy, without whose support I would not be in full time ministry today. She is my biggest cheerleader and I have matured significantly in my Christian walk as a result of her support and Spirit-led insights.

I am also very thankful for my son and daughter, Taylor and Tori, who are truly a gift from God and also a great inspiration and encouragement to me. I pray that God will continue to mature me on my journey as He enables me to be a protection and provider for them in all areas of their lives.

TABLE OF CONTENTS

Preface

I t is ironic that I should write a preface for my own book. I seldom read prefaces when found in other books because I am too eager to get into the "nuts and bolts" as quickly as possible. However, the point I make in this brief introduction is poignant and foundational to the rest of the book so I am glad you are taking the time to review its message.

When judging art, it certainly is not a straight-forward exercise based simply on the dimensions of the painting or the quantitative amounts of color used. It goes much deeper than that. These details might play some role in the final evaluation, but there are other factors that are much more crucial in making an overall assessment.

In a similar fashion, the creation/evolution controversy is not really just a matter of listing the facts on both sides of the argument and making a decision. If it were, the verdict would have been in a long time ago and all scientists would be in agreement. The fact that there are extremely intelligent and knowledgeable scientists in both camps is evidence that it can't just be about the facts. There's something much broader and more fundamental lurking behind the scenes. I wish it were as simple as just reviewing the facts, because it would have been much easier to write this book. I would start out with chapter 1 being "The Origin of the Universe," in which I would list the associated facts. Chapter 2 would be "The Origin of Life," in which I would list those facts, and so on. What this book will provide is a much greater understanding of "the bigger picture" within which lies the key to truly making sense of the controversy.

WHAT'S IN IT FOR YOU?

I realize that not everyone is like me (and that's a good thing), and how you respond to this book will largely be dependent upon who you are and where you're coming from. You most likely fall into one of the following general categories:

Already There. . .
You may already firmly believe in the biblical account of creation and are hoping just to refine your understanding, strengthen your faith and learn a bit more regarding how to defend your belief in the inspiration of Scripture. Given that there are even varying views among Christians regarding the creation account, I believe this book will help you sort through these different positions and be more confident as to which is the most biblically and scientifically sound point of view.

Not Quite Sure. . .
Maybe you lean towards the biblical account of creation, but aren't fully convinced or don't know where to start in defending your belief. This book is sure to greatly improve your understanding of the creation/evolution controversy and bolster your confidence in Genesis and Scripture as a whole.

Fairly Skeptical. . .
Perhaps you greatly doubt the biblical account of creation and feel that the theory of evolution is well-substantiated by science. You may, however, at least be open to hearing what the other side has to say so that you can make an even more informed judgment one way or the other. I give you a lot of credit for your intellectual integrity and pursuit of the truth. This book will definitely help you better understand the arguments for the Genesis creation account.

Seasoned Skeptic. . .
It just may be that your mind is made up and virtually nothing will change it. That's fine. The intent of this book isn't really to prove anything. It merely lays out the case for the accuracy of the biblical account of creation and enumerates various problems, both scientifically and biblically, within the theory of evolution.

If you find yourself in this category, I am honored that you are even taking the time to read this and truly wish there were more in your camp that were as open as you apparently are to examining something from the opposition. It is my hope that reading this book will cause you to reexamine your own beliefs and challenge you to think of things that you may have never considered before. It can only help.

Independent of which category you find yourself in, I appreciate you taking the time to read this book and pray that you will also make as much effort to read God's Word, which promises "*to never return void*" (Isaiah 55:11). He rewards those who diligently seek Him (Hebrews 11:6)!

Chapter One

In the Beginning: A Good Place to Start

 It was twenty-six years ago that I found myself wandering through the halls of the Biology Department at the University of Wisconsin-Whitewater. I was in my fourth year of college, but it was my first year at Whitewater. I had attended John Brown University (a Christian college in Arkansas) for the first three years, studying mechanical engineering. As much as I enjoyed my time at John Brown, I decided to switch majors to physics, and John Brown only offered a minor in physics. I was faced with either giving up my interest in physics in order to stay at John Brown or change schools altogether. I opted for the latter and transferred to UW-Whitewater which was much closer to where I lived in southeastern Wisconsin.

Why was I wandering the halls of the Biology Department? That's where my story begins.

I was raised in a strong Christian home and believed everything I had ever been taught in church about the Bible. Even in college, I still had the same viewpoint and was not really challenged about any of my beliefs while attending a Christian college. However, transferring from a small Christian university (about 800 students at that time) to a fairly large state school (over 10,000 students) changed my life forever.

When I arrived at the state university, I found that all of my science professors (physics, geology, thermodynamics, etc.) were evolutionists and some were very vocal about their anti-Christian views. I assumed they had a lot of evidence for their beliefs; after all, they were scientists, right? I, on the other hand, was a very shy, soft-spoken, undergrad student who believed in creation just the way the Bible teaches. It was then that I finally realized that although I knew *what* I believed, I didn't know *why*. This was a very uncomfortable position to be in, but like it or not, that's where I was. The life-changing element originated from the fact that for the first time in my life I was challenged to defend what I believed, specifically regarding the Genesis creation account and the authority of God's Word. During this time, it struck me that if the book of Genesis was accurate and true in all it taught, there must be a lot of supporting evidence. Conversely, if evolution was not true, theoretically there shouldn't be any real evidence for it. With this bit of logic forever imbedded into my gray matter, I began my own personal quest to find this "evidence for creation" and more importantly, reasons to trust in the inspiration of Scripture.

I wasn't able to find any of this information in the university library or even in the city public library. Fortunately (and looking back, I believe divinely orchestrated) a man from the church I attended in my home town had already done a fair amount of research on this very subject while pursuing his PhD in medical physics. He was more than happy to loan me whatever I needed. I was overwhelmed by the sheer volume of information I found and my excitement grew with every page I turned.

At this point in my life, I was also very naïve. I had visions of grandeur that once I shared this newly found information, my professors would respond by saying something like, "Wow, I never knew about all this information; I guess creation really is true!" Needless to say, that's not the response I received. Looking back, being older and somewhat wiser, I have a much better understanding of their actual reaction, which was one of irritation, revulsion and annoyance. I did not realize it at the time, but I was indirectly and unintentionally telling them that they had been completely wrong their entire lives about the origin of life and the universe. This was quite an offense to them, especially coming from a simple undergrad college student. It wasn't my intention to condescendingly point out that they were wrong about their views, but rather to draw their attention to the fact that there was a lot of scientific information in direct opposition to the positions they so confidently held and that the alleged supportive evidence was extremely questionable or outright invalid. Unfortunately, because of the human psyche (fallen nature), they did not focus on the actual arguments, but simply reacted emotionally to the "attack" on their beliefs.

What does all this have to do with roaming the halls of the Biology department? As a member of the Physics Club, each student was required to give a speech on some topic related to physics. I was extremely shy and hated speaking in front of anyone, for any reason, but had to think of some topic to present during one of the meetings. The talks that were given by students usually lasted only ten minutes and were followed by a mere two or three questions. You didn't have to be an expert in the subject; you just had to do enough research in order to deliver your presentation. I initially considered doing a talk on lasers, because I thought they were fascinating and had recently read a few articles on the subject, but God had something else in mind. I had just started my research into evidence for supernatural creation and strongly felt that God was leading me to give a talk along those lines. I was scared to death knowing how controversial it would be and how much my professors would most likely challenge me, possibly making me look like a fool in front of all my peers. Nonetheless, I felt compelled that it was the right thing to do.

As I was preparing for my talk, I realized that if I did not address the best evidence for evolution somewhere in my lecture, it would not be a very effective presentation. I had one problem: I had no idea what those evidences were! I needed to quickly remedy the situation, so I stopped in to see one of my physics professors. Here's a summary of our conversation (I'll never forget it):

Me: "Can you tell me what the best evidences are for evolution?"

Prof: "I don't know."

Me: "But you believe in evolution, don't you?"

Prof: "Yes."

Me: "But you don't know what any of the evidences are?"

Prof: "No."

Me: "So you just take other scientists' word for it?"

Prof: "Yes."

I was very surprised to hear his responses and they did not make sense to me. I was under the impression all scientists who believed in evolution and publicly proclaimed it would know *why* it was true. I realize that there will always be things that we accept as being true even though we ourselves can't personally defend it, but I thought it should be different with an issue as significant as the origin of life and the universe, especially coming from a PhD scientist.

Not having had much success with my physics professor, I decided to ask my geology professor the same questions. I was confident he would know, because he not only believed in evolution, he was very vocal about it in his class. He promoted it often, ridiculing the Bible at the same time, getting the other students to laugh about how silly the Scriptures were. Again, the same results; he didn't know either. He did, however, suggest that I ask the biology professors, because in his words, "they teach this stuff every day." Although I was deeply disappointed that he could not address the issue, it at least made sense to follow his advice and seek out someone from the Biology Department.

So I soon found myself wandering the hallways in the biology department. I did not have any biology classes while at Whitewater, so I wasn't quite sure where to go or whom to ask. It wasn't long before one of the professors noticed me walking aimlessly through the halls and asked if he could help me. I simply told him that I was going to be giving a talk on evolution and creation, and that I was trying to find out what the best evidences were for evolution. He didn't know either, but he said there were two other biology professors just down the hall and maybe they could help. Again, I was a bit surprised and disappointed, but at least he was being friendly and willing to assist me.

We got to their office and found the two of them sitting at the same desk working on something together. The professor who brought me there knocked on the open door to get their attention. They both turned around and one of them said, "Can we help you?" The professor at the door said, "this young man is trying to find out what the best evidences are for evolution." They immediately asked, in a very defensive tone, "Why do you want to know?" They did not know me from Adam (no pun intended), but I told them the same thing I had told the initial professor; that I was going to be giving a talk on evolution and creation and was trying to find out what the best evidences were for evolution. They immediately started arguing with me and it didn't take long before it was apparent that I was a believer in the Genesis creation account and a skeptic of evolution. At one point, I turned to the professor at the door to say something and when I turned back around, the two professors had gone back to working on whatever it was that they were doing when we first arrived. The professor who brought me there kindly said to them, "Can you at least answer his question?" to which they replied, in a very unkind tenor, "We have nothing more to say to you!"

Their blunt response left me shocked, disappointed, embarrassed, confused and disillusioned. I honestly did not understand the reason for their response. I didn't then, but I do now. My experience over the past twenty-six years has shown me that the vast majority of those who believe in evolution either don't know any real evidences or are afraid to state exactly what those evidences are for fear of having them easily rebutted. (By the way, I have another very powerful story regarding an additional confrontation with a college science professor that I share in chapter 14, so be sure to look for it when you're there!) I also have come to realize that the creation/evolution debate is not really a scientific debate, but a spiritual issue.

> The man without the Spirit does not accept the things that come from the Spirit of God, for they are foolishness to him, and he cannot understand them, because they are spiritually discerned (I Corinthians 2:14, KJV).

Because of this truth, I have become much more sympathetic towards those who are skeptical of the creation account and Christianity in general. No matter how great the evidence is that we may present, they often just don't see it. We need to be Christlike examples when we confront others, being "wise as serpents, and harmless as doves" (Matthew 10:16, KJV). A key point is that if our beliefs are based on our own human reasoning, they are subject to change over time as we learn more and more, and see things differently with each passing year. We will develop this thought much further throughout the rest of this book.

Romans 1:18-25 is a very powerful passage that contains a lot of insight related to this issue.

> The wrath of God is being revealed from heaven against all the godlessness and wickedness of men who suppress the truth by their wickedness, since what may be known about God is plain to them, because God has made it plain to them. For since the creation of the world God's invisible qualities—his eternal power and divine nature—have been clearly seen, being understood from what has been made, so that men are without excuse. For although they knew God, they neither glorified him as God nor gave thanks to him, but their thinking became futile and their foolish hearts were darkened. Although they claimed to be wise, they became fools and exchanged the glory of the immortal God for images made to look like mortal man and birds and animals and reptiles. Therefore God gave them over in the sinful desires of their hearts to sexual impurity for the degrading of their bodies with one another. They exchanged the truth of God for a lie, and worshiped and served created things rather than the Creator—who is forever praised. Amen. (NIV)

Here are a few selections from this passage, including brief comments:

- *who suppress the truth by their wickedness*—It is actually man's wickedness that is causing the suppression of truth. When we think of "wickedness" we tend to focus only on those things that are more morally vile and extreme, but it can also include simple disobedience to God and subconscious rejection of Him altogether.

- *since what may be known about God is plain to them, because God has made it plain to them*—God has made Himself plain or clear to them, *so that men are without excuse.* No amount of rationalization (no matter how academic it may seem) will serve as an excuse before God.

- *their thinking became futile and their foolish hearts were darkened.* In this state, it is no wonder that they have drawn erroneous conclusions regarding the origin of life and the universe (and that they are so often very resistant to things of a spiritual nature).

- **they claimed to be wise, they became fools**—Many in the academic world are very vocal regarding how wise they are, but in God's eyes their reasoning is nothing short of foolishness. (I Corinthians 3:19, NIV—"For the wisdom of this world is foolishness in God's sight. As it is written: 'He catches the wise in their craftiness'.")

- **Therefore God gave them over in the sinful desires of their hearts**—God allowed them to wallow in the natural consequences of their actions, which made them even more entrenched in their depravity, leading to all sorts of sexual immorality.

  Aldous Huxley (grandson of Thomas Huxley, who was nick-named "Darwin's Bulldog") stated, "I had motives for not wanting the world to have meaning: consequently, assuming it had none, and was able without any difficulty to find reasons for this assumption. . .The philosopher who finds no meaning in the world is not concerned exclusively with a problem in pure metaphysics; he is also concerned to prove there is no valid reason why he personally should not do as he wants to do. . .For myself, as no doubt for most of my contemporaries, the philosophy of meaninglessness was essentially an instrument of liberation. The liberation we desired was simultaneously liberation from a certain political and economical system and liberation from a certain system of morality. We objected to the morality because it interfered with our sexual freedom."[1]

- **They exchanged the truth of God for a lie, and worshiped and served created things rather than the Creator**—Most evolutionists today are much more enamored with the *creation* (i.e., the natural world) than they are with the *Creator*. We can spend untold amounts of time and energy fighting to save some bug that might go extinct or trying to secure human rights for gorillas and apes, all the while aborting millions of human babies—and it doesn't even phase us. It can also lead to extreme forms of environmentalism. We should certainly take care of the world God has given to us, but it should not take precedence over our relationship to our Creator or each other.

Each person's worldview greatly affects the way they view "evidence." Consider the following two statements, each made by a very brilliant scientist:

Victor Stenger (American physicist, adjunct professor of philosophy, University of Colorado and professor emeritus of physics and astronomy, University of Hawaii):

It is hard to conclude that the universe was created with a special, cosmic purpose for humanity.[2]

Owen Gingerich (Harvard astronomy professor and senior astronomer at the Smithsonian Astrophysical Observatory):

A common sense and satisfying interpretation of our world suggests the designing hand of a super-intelligence.[3]

Both of these men are looking at the same evidence yet coming up with diametrically opposing conclusions. The explanation lies not in the evidence, but in their dissimilar starting points, their worldviews, which will be explored further in following chapters.

With all this in mind, the remaining chapters of this book are not simply recitations of scientific facts supporting the biblical creation account or disproving evolution. It certainly does include those elements, but it is much broader in scope and will hopefully equip you to respond to this on-going controversy that has such a profound effect on one's beliefs and subsequent ability to decipher truth from myth.

APPLES AND ORANGES: DEFINING EVOLUTION

Before we can have a meaningful discussion about the creation/evolution controversy, we need to briefly define our terms. I am reminded of the skeptic who felt the Bible could not possibly be true, if for no other reason than the fact that it talks about the Israelites wandering in the wilderness for forty years, the whole time carrying around the ark (presumably Noah's) on their shoulders! The issue clears itself up after we see from the context that the ark being referred to was not Noah's ark, *which would certainly stretch the imagination beyond reasonable limits*, but the ark of the covenant, two completely different things.

The word "evolution" is used in many different contexts with a variety of intended meanings. *The Oxford English Dictionary*, which is the standard reference for word usage in the English language, enumerates twelve different definitions for "evolution," some of which are as follows:

- Unfolding, opening out, emergence.

- Growth according to inherent tendencies.

- Rise or origination of anything by natural development.

- The process of developing, or working out in detail, what is implicitly or potentially contained in an idea or principle.

- Biological development.

- Formation of the heavenly bodies.

- Origin of species.

We even speak of the "evolution of the Corvette," but it has no real connection to biological evolution, especially since in this case, each model was carefully and purposely designed and crafted by intelligent automotive engineers. On the other hand, the "evolution" that we are discussing has no intrinsic purpose or design, as evidenced in the following quotes:

1954 Corvette

> In the evolutionary pattern of thought there is no longer either need or room for the supernatural. The earth was not created: it evolved. So did all the animals and plants that inhabit it, including our human selves, mind and soul as well as brain and body. So did religion.[4]

1965 Corvette

> Let me summarize my views on what modern evolutionary biology tells us loud and clear: there are no gods, no purposes, no goal-directed forces of any kind.[5]

For our purposes, we will be focusing on the generally accepted meaning used by most educational institutions and academics, which is along the following lines:

2007 Corvette

First, a fairly complex definition:

> Biological (or organic) evolution is change in the properties of populations of organisms or groups of such populations, over the course of generations. The development, or ontogeny, of an individual organism is not considered evolution: individual organisms do not evolve. The changes in populations that are considered evolutionary are those that are "heritable" via the genetic material from one generation to the next. Biological evolution may be slight or substantial; it embraces everything from slight changes in the proportions of different forms of a gene within a population, such as the alleles that determine the different human blood types, to the alterations that led from the earliest organisms to dinosaurs, bees, snapdragons, and humans.[6]

Second, a much simpler definition:

> Common ancestry and descent with modification.[7]

I think we'd all agree that the second definition is a bit easier to comprehend. It basically states that all life has descended from a common ancestor through numerous modifications (and implies a time-frame of multiplied millions of years).

YE OLDE "BAIT AND SWITCH"

A number of years ago there was a sales technique used that was very crafty, but also fairly effective. It was called the "Bait and Switch" technique. It worked along the following lines. A retail store would advertise an incredible deal on a specific product, let's say a flat panel computer monitor. The consumer, seeing the ad and feeling it is an unbelievable buy, rushes to the store immediately not wanting to miss out on the incredible bargain. That's the "bait." However, once they get to the store, the salesperson says something like, "You know, we just ran out of those monitors, but if you liked that  one, you're really going to love this model over here!" after which he shows the customer a unit that costs more, is not as high quality and makes a lot more profit for the store. That's the "switch." The store owner had no intention of selling what was advertised. Fortunately, this technique is now illegal. Unfortunately, something similar is used (intentionally or unintentionally) by evolutionists when it comes to discussing evolution.

In the context of our discussion, the "bait" is when students are told that evolution is an absolute fact, and the "switch" occurs when it comes time to discuss the actual evidence. When they state that evolution is a fact or that it is beyond questioning, they are referring to the belief that non-living chemicals produced a living single-celled organism that learned how to replicate itself and eventually produced every other life-form on this planet, including people. (We call this concept "molecules-to-man" evolution. I highly recommend using this term when discussing evolution with others.) However, when they speak of the undeniable evidence for this dogmatic belief, they focus on the simpler, broader definition of evolution which merely refers to "change" or "modification" of various species. The problem is that while these changes are actually very real (and not denied by creationists) they are not the kind of change required by the molecules-to-man of evolution. We'll discuss this in much greater detail in chapter 6.

One piece of advice when discussing the creation/evolution controversy with a skeptic is to first ask what they mean by "evolution." Too often what happens is that the skeptic thinks that any kind of change in the living world represents evidence of evolution. In their mind, change = evolution. When you state that you don't believe in evolution, they think that you are denying "change" and conclude that you are crazy and in complete denial of reality. This situation is quite understandable, because at that point you are talking about two different things! You think of evolution as being a single-celled organism spontaneously arising from non-living chemicals and subsequently changing into every other life on the planet through a series of undirected accidental mistakes (mutations) and natural selection. They, however, are simply focusing on changes in living organisms, which as a matter of fact does occur and has been observed. So in their mind, for you to reject evolution is to deny real-life changes that scientists have observed and confirmed over and over. Therefore, make it clear that you are talking about the descent of all living creatures from a common ancestor, which itself was the result of the spontaneous appearance of a single-celled organism from non-living chemicals. That should save one or both of you from wanting to pull your hair out! It will also aid in having a potentially fruitful conversation.

THE "EVOLUTION OF EVOLUTION": FROM WHENCE DID IT COME?

Now that we've defined "evolution" let's briefly discuss "from whence it came."

Just after the creation of Adam and Eve, the entire earth's population (a whopping total of two) would have been considered "creationists." They probably didn't belong to any local creationist organizations or attend any conferences, but they were definitely devout believers in creation. Today, with a slightly larger population (just over 7 billion), this is not the situation. Although many polls indicate that a fairly high percentage of the general public believes that God created life and the universe, it is safe to say that many do not, including a fairly high percentage of scientists.

So where did the idea of evolution come from? One of the biggest misconceptions about evolution is that it was "invented" by Charles Darwin back in the latter 1800s. While it is true that he published his book *The Origin of Species* in 1859, which aided greatly in the popularization of evolution, the concept of evolution had been around long, long before his time.

As far as we can tell, organic evolution was postulated by the Greeks as early as the 7th century BC. It is very likely that Greek philosophers borrowed/modified their evolutionary ideas from the Hindus, who believed in a state of perfection called "nirvana" that was achieved by souls transforming from one animal to another.

Darwin's writings were greatly influenced by his predecessors, as is evidenced in the following quote:

> Evolution, meaning the origin of new species by variation from ancestor species, as an explanation for the state of the living world, had been proclaimed before Darwin by several biologists—thinkers, including the poet Johann Wolfgang Goethe in 1795, Jean-Baptiste de Lamarck in 1809, Darwin's grandfather, the ebullient physician-naturalist-poet-philosopher Erasmus Darwin, and in Darwin's time anonymously by Robert Chambers in 1844.[8]

What can be said about Charles Darwin is that he was the central figure responsible for popularizing evolutionary concepts that eventually led to the modern theory of evolution, primarily through the writing and publishing of *The Origin of Species* in 1859. Richard Dawkins (one of the world's leading evolutionists—whom we will further reference later in this book) stated that "Darwin made it possible to be an intellectually fulfilled atheist."[9] The point being that prior to his time, the theory of evolution lacked any substantive academic credibility. (I personally believe that it still lacks credibility and we will spend the rest of the book developing this very point.) It is interesting to note, however, that even with the publication of *The Origin of Species*, the ideas put forth by Darwin were not initially accepted by the scientific community as a whole, much less the church.

The Scopes Trial

In 1925 (sixty-six years after the publication of *The Origin of Species*) the public school system in the US was still teaching origins based primarily on the biblical account of creation. It was in this year that one of the most famous trials in American history occurred. If you want to get a fairly good picture of what actually happened in this trial, you could watch the movie/play *Inherit the Wind*, with just one caveat: conclude just the opposite of most of what is presented. This play was not intended to be an historical account, but most viewers are not aware and assume that they are "learning a bit of history." It is much more like propaganda and indoctrination.[10]

The phenomenon of "learning truth" via movies is all too common in our day, including among Christians. Think of how many people learned about the history of the Jews, not from reading the Old Testament, but from watching Charlton Heston as Moses in epic film *The Ten Commandments*.

The famous Scopes Trial (nicknamed the "Monkey Trial") centered around the alleged violation of the Butler Act, which made it "unlawful for any teacher in any of the. . .public schools of the state. . .to teach any theory that denies the story of the Divine Creation of man as taught in the Bible, and to teach instead that man has descended from a lower order of animals." Contrary to popular belief, it was not a trial about the validity of either creation or evolution, but simply whether or not the teaching of Mr. Scopes had actually violated this law.

John Scopes

John Scopes, a high-school coach who happened to have substituted for the biology teacher during the last few weeks of the school year, was accused of teaching evolution. He was convicted and later acquitted on a technicality. There are numerous elements to this historical event that are significant, but I wish to point out only a few.[11]

William Jennings Bryan, prosecuting attorney, foolishly agreed to be cross-examined by defense attorney Clarence Darrow (an agnostic) regarding his belief in the Bible and its associated miracles. Bryan should have seen this as being clearly irrelevant to the reason for the trial, but was apparently temporarily naïve and took the stand, nonetheless. One factor that aided in Bryan's compliance was that Darrow agreed in turn to be cross examined by Bryan regarding his personal agnostic and evolutionary views. Both men were great orators, but Bryan did a fair amount of damage to his own cause when responding to Darrow's question about the meaning of the "days" in Genesis 1. Darrow asked if Bryan believed that God created everything in six literal days and Bryan responded by claiming that the Bible never asserts such a notion. When further asked about the phrases "evening and morning were the first day" and "evening and morning were the second day," etc., he responded with "I do not see that there is any necessity for constructing the words, 'the evening and the morning,' as meaning necessarily a twenty-four hour day." This opened the flood-gates to reinterpreting the Bible based upon whatever the current scientific theories are, undermining the authority of Scripture. Chapter 10 discusses the details behind what a "day" actually means in Genesis 1.

At this point, it seemed to at least some of those in attendance that there was reason to doubt the inspiration of the Bible and the historical nature of many of its miraculous events, because Darrow had his chance to attack these claims. But Bryan would have his chance to show the weakness of Darrow's agnostic and humanistic views as agreed, right? Wrong. Darrow, in an unprecedented masterful move, actually asked the judge to instruct the jury to find John Scopes (his own client) guilty of teaching the descent of man from apes, thus eliminating the need for Bryan to cross examine his own views.

The Butler Act was eventually repealed in 1967 (Epperson vs. the State of Tennessee). Currently, the only legally permissible view allowed in the public school science classroom is the random and purposeless process of evolution. (See chapter 12 for further details on the battle within the public school system.)

It is interesting to note that in Darwin's day, the predominant teaching was that of biblical creation, which prompted him to state in *The Origin of Species:*

> A fair result can be obtained only by fully stating and balancing the facts and arguments on both sides of each question.[12]

Darwin felt that it was unjust to only present one side. Ironically, today the tables have been turned and we still have only one side being presented, but it is the Darwinian view that shares the stage with no one.

WHY ALL THE FUSS?—"LET'S JUST FOCUS ON JESUS"

So why does the whole creation/evolution issue even matter? Aren't there more important things to be concerned about, like abortion, homosexuality, divorce, world hunger and racism? Isn't pleasing God and telling others about Jesus all that really matters?

If we can't trust the Bible regarding what it tells us about the beginning, how can we be so confident that we can trust any other part, including those passages concerning Jesus? Put another way, if we can't trust the Bible's history, how can we trust it concerning spiritual matters? The trustworthiness of the Bible's spiritual truths are premised on its historical accuracy. I heard a story of a mother and her nine year old daughter who were in church one week and heard the pastor tell the congregation that, "You can't take Genesis literally; it doesn't really mean what it says." Afterwards, the young girl sincerely and innocently asked her mother, "If we can't trust Genesis, when does God start telling the truth?" Wow—how powerful! That's a good question.

Virtually every major doctrine we hold as Christians is founded directly or indirectly in the book of Genesis.

- *The Doctrine of Sin*. What is sin? Well, God created Adam and Eve and they were perfect, but they disobeyed God. That was sin (cf. Romans 5:12).

- *The Doctrine of Death*. Why is there death in the world? Because God created Adam and Eve, they were perfect, but they disobeyed God and that brought death and a curse into God's perfect world. Death is the direct consequence of sin (cf. I Corinthians 15:21-22).

- *Marriage*. Why is marriage one man with one woman? That's hotly debated in this country today and around the world. The answer: because God created Adam and Eve, and He said it was to be one man and one woman for life (cf. Matthew 19:4-6)!

- *Clothing*. Why do we wear clothes, other than it gets cold out once in a while, depending on where you live? Because God created Adam and Eve, they were perfect, but they disobeyed God and that brought death and a curse into God's perfect world. Clothing was just a temporal covering for their sin (cf. Genesis 3:21).

- *Work*. Why do we work? Because God created Adam and Eve, and told Adam to till the ground, to work the land. He was commanded to do this even before he sinned. Work is a good thing. . .ordained by God, but it got a lot harder after sin entered into the picture (cf. Genesis 2:15, 3:18-19).

- *The Last Adam*. Jesus is referred to as being the "Last Adam." If the first Adam wasn't real, what does that say about the last Adam (cf. I Corinthians 15:45)?

- *The Gospel Message*. What is the gospel message? We'll cover that shortly.

RESISTANT TO THE MESSAGE

If you were to take a stroll through an impoverished neighborhood and hand out free lottery tickets or $100 bills, you would not likely run into any resistance from the local residents.

Likewise, if you visited a beach on a very hot summer day, giving away free bottled water, you would be surprised if your offers were not well-received. You might also think that if you approached a gospel-preaching church, offering a free creation seminar, that you would be enthusiastically welcomed with open arms. Sadly, all too often this is not the case. Why is this true?

There are a number of reasons that this has become all too common of an occurrence, including the following:

- Some pastors and church leaders have observed creation presentations that were overly dogmatic, condescending and/or arrogant and not very gracious.

- Some have observed creation presentations that were so deep and highly technical that it just didn't seem appropriate for a general church audience.

- Some feel that the church should focus on discussing spiritual issues, while science education is for the school systems to handle.

- Some feel the whole issue is too controversial, too divisive and overall not all that important. They believe that we should just be focusing on Jesus.

The first two concerns are issues directly related to the specific presenter and not the message itself. We all know that you can deliver the right message in the wrong way and also the wrong message in the right way. The last two concerns have much more to do with misconceptions about science and the Bible than any actual issues with the message itself. We'll take a minute to delve a little deeper into these two concerns.

SEPARATION OF CHURCH AND STATE SCIENCE

Astronomy, geology, biology, anthropology; if you are hearing about these subjects, you certainly aren't in church, are you? These are areas of science, which is what we learn about in school, right? That's the feeling of many within the church today, including many pastors. I would agree that if the Bible doesn't talk about a certain subject, then we shouldn't make too big of a deal out of it. You have probably heard people proclaim that "the Bible is not a science textbook!" They're right! My response to this is that I'm glad it isn't, because science books have to be constantly updated and re-written as we make new discoveries! What we do find in the Bible, however, is a framework for properly understanding science. Make no mistake: the Bible does address these areas.

Astronomy. Psalm 33:6 (NIV) states, "By the word of the LORD were the heavens made, their starry host by the breath of his mouth." This is a commentary on astronomy. God created the universe, including the stars and galaxies. We don't expect that natural processes can generate these objects. We also read in I Corinthians 15:41 that "There is one glory of the sun, another glory of the moon, and another glory of the stars; for one star differs from another star in glory." When this verse was written (~ 54 AD), we had very limited knowledge of the heavens and most stars looked virtually identical—just small specks of light off in the distance. The apostle Paul was actually stating something that seemed to go against "common knowledge," that is, everyone could see for themselves that the stars were basically all the same, with a few being a bit brighter or dimmer than others. With today's advanced technology, we now know that each star does appear to be unique! The Bible teaches us about astronomy!

Geology. Genesis 6:17 (NIV) states, "I am going to bring floodwaters on the earth to destroy all life under the heavens, every creature that has the breath of life in it. Everything on earth will perish." This helps us better understand what we actually observe when we are looking at the earth's geology. As a matter of fact, we see numerous sedimentary layers containing billions of fossils all over the earth. Those are just the raw facts. How did they get there? We weren't there to see it so we have to guess. On one hand, we might guess that they formed by the same slow, gradual processes we see today. However, the more we examine this hypothesis the more highly improbable it seems. On the other hand, we could consider the Genesis flood account and conclude that they were produced catastrophically in a relatively short period of time during this monumental event. After all, that's exactly what we would expect to see if there truly was a flood as described in Genesis. The Bible helps us understand geology!

Biology. Genesis 1:24a (NIV) states, "And God said, 'Let the land produce living creatures according to their kinds.'" This helps us understand the diversity of animals and other life forms on the planet today. We see a great variety, but creatures are always reproducing after their same kind, just like the Bible describes. This is obviously contrary to current evolutionary thinking which believes that one kind eventually changes into something very different. Once again, the Bible gives us a framework with which to better understand the world around us. Its explanatory power far exceeds that of evolutionary models.

Anthropology. Genesis 2:7 (NIV) states, "Then the Lord God formed a man from the dust of the ground and breathed into his nostrils the breath of life, and the man became a living being." This precludes mankind evolving from an apelike creature over millions of years. Regarding Eve, Genesis 2:21-22 (KJV) tells us that "the Lord God caused a deep sleep to fall on Adam, and he slept; and He took one of his ribs, and closed up the flesh in its place. Then the rib which the Lord God had taken from man He made into a woman, and He brought her to the man." This completely goes against evolutionary models which really struggle explaining the origin of the sexes, male and female, which we will touch on a bit later. Yes, the Bible even addresses anthropology!

These are just a few of the numerous examples where the Bible directly addresses major areas of science, and comments on the origin and history of life and the universe. Since the Bible addresses these areas, as Christians, we should understand them as being wholly inspired by God and not simply relegate teaching in these areas to the educational system, especially not the public school system which eliminated God and the Bible in the early 1960s. Lest anyone misunderstand me, I am not recommending that we teach particle physics or cell biology in church, I am simply referring to understanding the "big picture" which largely involves something we call "historical science" (a point to be further developed later in the book).

A CONTROVERSIAL MESSAGE

Some assume that because controversy exists when considering the topic of creation, there is ultimately no way of knowing the truth. This has led many to respond by saying something like "Why does it really matter how or when God created everything, as long as we believe that He is ultimately the "Creator"? Let's just focus on Jesus—that's all that really matters." I cannot tell you how many times I have heard similar statements from many well-meaning pastors, church leaders and laypeople. In fact, just recently the pastor of a large local evangelical church stated from the pulpit "Whether a day is a thousand years or however long it took doesn't really matter. We just need to get to the gospel where it really counts."

In my over twenty-six years of ministry experience, I have found that most churches resistant to speaking-out on creation from the pulpit, are hesitant primarily because of how they feel this issue is perceived by others, inside and outside the church. In particular, they feel that if they take a stance on the creation account, it will appear as if their church rejects science and is out-of-touch with reality, still living in the dark ages. The Ben Stein movie, *Expelled: No Intelligence Allowed,* depicts this phenomenon within the scientific community. Those who would dare question evolution (let alone speak of biblical creation) are more often than not castigated, ostracized and relegated to ranks of the "unwashed masses." The resultant effect is that many scientists who question evolution remain very quiet about it throughout their professional careers. Thankfully, many are taking their chances and speaking out in spite of the significant threat to their livelihood.

There's an interesting corollary passage in Scripture, found in John 12:42-43 (NIV). "Yet at the same time many even among the leaders believed in him. *But because of the Pharisees they would not confess their faith for fear they would be put out of the synagogue;* for they loved praise from men more than praise from God" (emphasis added). These "believers" were too worried about getting or maintaining the approval of those around them, particularly the academics of their day. Sounds all too familiar with what we see today. There truly is "nothing new under the sun" (Ecclesiastes 1:9).

Many church leaders are also very aware that there are other views (held by some highly-respected Christians) that allow Genesis to be interpreted in a way such that modern astronomy, geology and biology can be accommodated. This is very comforting to them, knowing that they are in "good company" if they directly or indirectly teach one of these views, or ignore origins altogether, implying that: (a) it doesn't really matter, (b) everyone has to decide for themselves, or (c) that you can't really know for sure. In addition, they often ask, "Why risk causing division over something that shouldn't really matter that much?" There is seldom any challenge from the congregation, because of the general pervasiveness of biblical illiteracy. The typical Sunday morning attendee has similar reasoning that the "solution" most likely involves some sort of compromise and that it ultimately isn't all that relevant to begin with. I do not intend to paint too broad of a stroke here, implying that there are not many diligent students of Scripture within the church, because there certainly are. However, in general, the level of biblical literacy continues to decline. Too many Christians obtain their beliefs based on what they hear from church leaders, read in a book by a Christian author or see in a Christian video, as opposed to coming from personal knowledge of God's Word through the aid of the Holy Spirit. This is a challenge I face in my own life. I truly enjoy reading what others have written and watching well-produced Christian DVDs, but I continually have to make sure that I am personally spending time in God's Word, so that I do not go too far astray.

After speaking with one pastor regarding a potential engagement, he stated that it just wouldn't fit in with their plans right now. I told him that I completely understood and asked about something for the more distant future, such as anytime within the next year or two. Sensing from him that he really didn't even want to schedule anything at all, but not having the courage to be direct, he responded by saying that it really doesn't fit their "model." I politely requested to ask a few additional questions in order to help me better understand where he was coming from and the general mindset of the church leadership. He graciously agreed, so I proceeded. My main question was in regard to the fact that surveys have shown that over 60% of Christian students end up walking away from their faith before leaving college.[13] I said that when the students in his youth ministry enter college, they will very likely be confronted by highly intelligent professors who will tell them that the Bible is certainly not the Word of God, being full of errors and contradictions, particularly with its mythical creation account and global flood story, both of which science has utterly disproved. They will also be told that Christianity is just one of many religions, which are all ultimately of human origin and that Christianity is actually to blame for most of the world's atrocities. I then asked how his church was preparing them to deal with these types of faith-shaking confrontations. His answer: "We're not, we're just telling the students about Jesus." I was a bit surprised, but I thought to myself, "OK, now he's going to say something like, 'You know, maybe it would be a good idea to have you come in and speak to the students about these issues.'" Sadly, he was still not interested.

We often hear things that sound great on the surface, but when analyzed a bit further, just don't measure up. One example is that "the facts of nature are like a sixty-seventh book of the Bible." It would seem logical to think that if God created the universe and everything in it, then the "facts of nature" should be just as true as the "facts" revealed in His written Word. I would actually agree that the facts of nature are just as true as God's revealed Word, but this can often be misleading. The problem is that we don't always know what the "facts" of nature are. You may be aware that "facts" in and of themselves are devoid of meaning and must all be interpreted by some type filter in order to have any real meaning (e.g., a filter such as a "worldview" or presuppositions in the case of origins, ethics and morality). Fairly often various scientists will have diametrically opposing opinions regarding the exact same "facts." Then there's the whole question of how we even determine whether or not something should be considered as "fact." To all of that, add the realization that we are all mortal humans who were not there at the beginning, we make mistakes, sometimes even lie and are studying a fallen, cursed world (which is not the way God originally created it), all of which makes determining "scientific facts" about the past a bit tricky at best. Therefore, elevating the "facts of nature" to the same level as God's written Word would not be the wisest thing to do and can potentially be very dangerous.

Another statement that at first blush sounds laudable and is directly related to the topic at hand, is: "Let's just focus on Jesus." What Christian in their right mind would argue with that? I certainly wouldn't, but I would also want to explore it a bit deeper and not simply accept its usual intended meaning, which in the context of this book is, "Don't get all caught up in debating what the Genesis creation account actually means, just focus on telling others about Jesus."

My response, which I work on conveying in a very gracious manner, is that if we are going to focus on Jesus and the gospel, let's look into it a bit deeper. The first question is always, "Who is Jesus?" The normal response is, "He's the Son of God, the Savior of the world." I agree, but long before he was our Savior, he was our Creator (cf. John 1, Colossians 1, Hebrews 1). If we are truly going to focus on Jesus, we'd better understand who He is, as well as understand the foundation for the gospel message.

I usually continue with a series of semi-rhetorical questions (listed below with their typical associated answers):

"What is the gospel message?"—That Jesus died, was buried and rose again.

"Why did He die?"—To pay for the sins of the world.

"Why did He have to do that?"—Because we are sinners.

"What is sin?"—Disobedience to God.

"Why do we sin?"—Because Adam sinned and it affected all of us.

"Who is Adam?"—He was the first human created by God in the garden.

"Alright, so we're sinners, but why did Jesus have to die?"—Because Adam's sin brought death into the world and the penalty for sin is death.

"So then the gospel is directly related to the creation account?"—Yes, I guess so.

After thinking through this line of reasoning, there is a general consensus that the gospel is related to the creation account, but most people don't make that connection on their own.

It is interesting to note that Jesus Himself taught that Adam and Eve have been here from the beginning of creation, which has huge implications for the creation/evolution controversy, but we'll touch on that further in chapter 10.

Jesus also said, "You are in error because you do not know the Scriptures or the power of God" (Matthew 22:29, NIV). It has been my own personal experience that whenever I am wrong about a biblically-related issue it is generally because I don't truly understand God's Word, at least not to the extent I should. Pastors have been given the responsibility of teaching God's Word to their congregations. I personally encourage each one to study the Genesis creation account and come up with their own personal, Holy Spirit-directed conviction of Scripture, rather than relying on the supposed expertise of other Christians who claim authority in some area of science and teach that the Bible is perfectly compatible with current thinking in modern origins science.

Another pertinent quote of Jesus is, "If you believed Moses, you would believe me, for he wrote about me. But since you don't believe what he wrote, how are you going to believe what I say?" (John 5:46-47, NIV) The words of Moses in Genesis 1 and 2 are no less inspired than those of Jesus in the New Testament.

Lastly, Jesus warns us in John 3:12 (NIV), "I have spoken to you of earthly things and you do not believe; how then will you believe if I speak of heavenly things?" While the Bible does not give us all the details in modern "scientific lingo," it is still completely accurate in all that it asserts and can be used confidently as a framework for understanding science and origin issues today!

When the church doesn't address Genesis specifically, it is telling the congregation (the body of Christ in general) that since this issue is so difficult to grasp that not even pastors can really figure it out, there's no way the average layperson has a chance. And since it is apparently so challenging to sort out, it must not be very important to God, otherwise He would have worded it differently, but He didn't so we shouldn't really worry about it or bother with it. This reveals a very low view of the inspiration of Scripture.

It all comes down to a choice each of us has to make. Do we trust God and His inspired, inerrant Word or do we yield to the temporal theories of many of today's scientists, who do not have a biblical worldview nor do they have a proper reverence for God and his Holy Word?

It is better to trust in the Lord than to put confidence in man (Psalm 118:8, KJV).

ENDNOTES

1. Huxley, Aldous, "Confessions of a professed atheist," *Report: Perspective on the News*, 3:19, 1966, p. 8.

2. Stenger, Victor J., *God: The Failed Hypothesis—How Science Shows That God Does Not Exist*, Prometheus Books, 2007.

3. Floyd, Chris, "Eyes Wide Open: An Interview with Owen Gingerich," *Science and Spirit*, http:// science-spirit.org —last accessed August 20, 2012.

4. Huxley, Julian, *Essays of a Humanist*, Penguin Books, UK, pp. 82-83.

5.   Provine, William G., Cornell University—Provine, W.B., Origins Research 16(1), p.9, 1994.

6.   Futuyma, Douglas J., *Evolutionary Biology,* 3rd ed., Sinauer Associates Inc., Sunderland, MA; (1998), p.4.

7.   National Center for Science Education web article: http://www2.ncseweb.org/evolution/education/defining-evolution, last accessed 9/15/10.

8.   De Vries, A., *The Enigma of Darwin*, Clio Medica 19(1-2):136-155, 1984; p. 145.

9.   Dawkins, Richard, *The Blind Watchmaker,* Norton & Company, Inc. 1986, p. 6.

10. "Inherit the Wind: An Historical Analysis," http://creation.com/inherit-the-wind-an-historical-analysis, last accessed 9/15/10.

11. Ibid.

12. Darwin, Charles, *Origin of Species*, Sixth Edition, London, John Murry, 1876 , p. 2.

13. http://www.barna.org/barna-update/article/16-teensnext-gen/147-most-twentysomethings-put-christianity-on-the-shelf-following-spiritually-active-teen-years?q=leave+church+college, last accessed 9/16/10.

Chapter Two

The Evidence:
Hold On...Not So Fast!

CONSIDER THE FOLLOWING:

- A cockroach can live for over a week without a head.

- The Incas measured time by how long it took to cook a potato.

- A bookshelf consisting of ten books can be rearranged 3,628,800 different ways.

- Mozart was five years old when he wrote, *Twinkle, Twinkle Little Star*.

- "Ukulele" means "jumping flea" in Hawaiian.

- Grocers got their name because they sold food by the gross.

- The 1900 Olympic Games included croquet, fishing, billiards and checkers.

- Giraffes have no vocal cords; they communicate with their tails.

So what do we call this type of information? Trivia. What exactly is trivia? Generally speaking, it is any piece of information that, while being at least somewhat intriguing, is of little or no consequence to our daily lives.

If you're anything like me, you enjoy occasionally hearing a few pieces of trivia, but almost never remember the details for more than a just a little while. From time to time you'll meet someone who has somehow managed to retain every piece of trivia they've ever heard and can be quite the life of the party (but it can also be quite annoying). Here are a few pieces of trivia that for whatever reason I still remember, even though it's been over twenty-five years since originally hearing them:

• Wilma Flintstone's maiden name was Slaghoople.

• Betty Rubble's maiden name was McBricker.

• The next-door neighbors on the Brady Bunch TV show were the Dittmeyers.

Why am I talking about trivia at this point? I am convinced that when we spout off a list of scientific facts allegedly supporting creation we are in danger (at least in perception, if not reality) of simply disseminating trivia. Not that the information itself is necessarily trivial or inconsequential, but it loses its impact without a larger context. To simply share evidence of a "creative agent" still leaves the door wide open for belief in any kind of god or supreme being (or even alien life). The God of the Bible is just one of many options at that point. We'll delve into this a bit deeper in the chapter on intelligent design.

Even if we are successful at helping someone turn away from atheism, it doesn't necessarily put them in a much better position regarding their eternal destiny. Eternal life is granted not to those who simply believe in God, but only to those who believe in the God of the Bible, repent of their sins, placing 100% of their trust in the death, burial and resurrection of God's Son—Jesus Christ. Simply believing in God (or a god) might be a good start, but if that's all the farther it goes the seeker is still hopelessly lost. (See chapter 13 for further discussion.)

I'd be the first to admit, however, that it certainly does make for interesting headlines when a famous atheist finally "sees the light." One relatively recent example is that of Antony Flew (British philosopher, 1923-2010). He has arguably been the world's most infamous atheist, but in 2004 he shocked the world by announcing that he believed in God. Flew subsequently wrote a book entitled, *There is a God: How the World's Most Notorious Atheist Changed His Mind.*[1] Another example is that of Fred Hoyle (British astronomer and atheist for most of his life—and the one who coined the term "big bang"). He did a "180" in 1981 expressing his belief in "god."

While I am encouraged anytime I hear these types of stories, we don't want to read too much into them, especially not to use it as any kind of evidence for the truth of Christianity. If so, what are we to make of the instances where supposed Christians (or religious people) become atheists? By our own (misguided) logic, that would be evidence *against* Christianity. One interesting example of a "reverse-conversion" is that of Charles Templeton (1915–2001). He was a co-founder of Youth for Christ International and a co-evangelist with Billy Graham. He was listed among those "best used of God" by the National Association of Evangelicals in 1946 and actually exceeded Graham in his popularity and apparent effectiveness.

One of the primary contributing factors in his turning to atheism was his questioning of God's Word, specifically the Genesis creation account. (I don't believe that it's wrong to have questions about the Bible. I have many questions myself, but when we question its inspiration or authority, it is a very slippery slope.) Templeton placed what he felt was solid science in authority over Scripture. In a conversation with Billy Graham, he stated:

> But, Billy, it's simply not possible any longer to believe, for instance, the biblical account of creation. The world wasn't created over a period of days a few thousand years ago; it has evolved over millions of years. It's not a matter of speculation; it's demonstrable fact.[2]

In 1996, he wrote a book entitled, *Farewell to God* (the source of the above quote). It also elucidates the progression of his thinking, going from merely questioning the complete trustworthiness of the Bible, to his out-and-out rejection of the biblical God altogether.

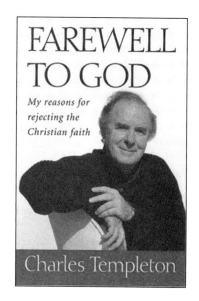

> I believe that there is no supreme being with human attributes–no God in the biblical sense–but that all life is the result of timeless evolutionary forces. . .over millions of years.[3]

Templeton died in 2001 with no sign of any change in his atheistic/agnostic thinking.

Ultimately, Christianity must stand on its own merits and not on who "buys into it" and who doesn't. There will always be skeptics who end up embracing it as well as others who apostatize who were once counted as being among the faithful.

SCIENCE: SETTING THE STAGE

According to Stanford University physicist, Leonard Susskind:

> Two stories are possible. The first is creationist: God made man with some purpose that involved man's ability to appreciate and worship God. Let's forget that story. The whole point of science is to avoid such stories.[4]

Is that the point of science—to rule out anything having to do with God? Anyone who knows anything about the origin of modern science and how it truly operates would not make this claim.

One of the most critical elements necessary to making sense of the creation/evolution debate is to have a proper understanding of science itself. Without it, there's no way of knowing whether science is a friend or foe of any particular view. We'll take a brief look at this issue from a semi-technical point of view and then from a much broader, conceptual view. (Many readers at this point may be somewhat less than excited when considering this section, but it will be easy to understand, fairly brief and crucial to further discussion of the debate in general.)

Modern science, as a formal entity, had its beginnings in seventeenth century England. What comes as a surprise to many is that most scientific disciplines today were founded by Bible-believing Christians. A few notable examples are as follows:

• Chemistry—Robert Boyle

• Genetics—Gregor Mendel

• Modern Physics—Galileo Galilei

• Observational Astronomy—Galileo Galilei

• Physical Astronomy—Johann Kepler

• Calculus—Isaac Newton

• Dynamics—Isaac Newton

• Oceanography—Matthew Maury

• Paleontology—John Woodward

• Thermodynamics—Lord Kelvin

• Electronics—John Ambrose Fleming

• Computer Science—Charles Babbage

• Scientific method—Francis Bacon

These scientists (and numerous others) were studying God's world with the purpose of learning more about their Creator and His creation, viewing life and the universe through "biblical glasses." Since God is a God of order (I Corinthians 14:33), they fully expected to discover evidence of this order when surveying His creation. They logically expected to be able to find patterns, regularities and "laws" that governed how nature operates. On the other hand, if the universe were truly the result of random, undirected events, there would be no reason to expect such order or regularity.

In their minds, some physical phenomenon would turn out to be the result of the laws of nature established by God, not needing any sort of special miraculous explanations. One example would be how water is converted from a liquid state to a solid when it reaches a temperature of $32°$ F (at standard atmospheric pressure). Natural law is certainly sufficient to explain this phenomenon. Therefore, there is no reason to believe that God is miraculously intervening in each instance to carry out this conversion. At the same time, other phenomenon might be quite beyond the realm of natural law, in which case it might require supernatural involvement. One important point to note is that just because we are not able to explain certain occurrences by natural law, it does not necessarily mean that they require supernatural intervention. It may simply mean that we do not possess accurate or adequate knowledge in those areas. Scientific conclusions should be based on what we do know rather than on what we do not know. It is fairly common for an evolutionist to say something like the following: "Just because we have not been able to show how inorganic chemicals could naturally combine to form a living cell doesn't mean it didn't happen. I'm sure we'll figure it out some day." They have every right to believe in chemical evolution, but at this point it is strictly a *statement of faith*, not at all supported by any evidence and should not be presented as a scientific statement (much less a scientific fact) in any academic setting.

In the early days science was generally defined as "the search for explanations for the natural world around us." We observed the natural world (i.e., nature; matter and energy) and tried to figure out how it operates. They were typically more concerned about "operation" than "origin," believing as a presupposition that God was the one who created it to begin with. In fact, science used to be referred to as "natural theology," meaning the study of God (theology) through nature.

However, since science had its beginnings, the "rules of the game" have been stealthily and strategically changed. The new definition reads more like "the search for *natural* explanations for the world around us." God, or any such supernatural entity, has been ruled out right from the beginning. No matter what the evidence seems to indicate, no non-natural elements will be allowed to be part of the equation, as evidenced in the following quote by Kansas State University immunologist Dr. Scott Todd:

> Even if all the data point to an intelligent designer, such an hypothesis is excluded from science because it is not naturalistic.[5]

D. James Kennedy made this comment on the exclusion of God and His word within the scientific community:

> Calvin said that the Bible—God's special revelation—was spectacles that we must put on if we are to correctly read the book of nature—God's revelation in creation. Unfortunately, between the beginning of science and our day, many scientists have discarded these glasses, and many distortions have followed.[6]

What Calvin (French theologian and primary figure in the Protestant Reformation) was saying, is that if you want to correctly understand God's world, you must look at it through the lens of God's Word. This is how most of the initial scientists carried out their experiments—with the belief that God was the ultimate author of all life and the entire universe. Since that time, however (the beginning of modern day science), many scientists have moved away from such a presuppositional belief, leading to many errors in their conclusions.

The claim is often posited that Christians base everything on faith, whereas scientists are purely objective and solely rely on the evidence to lead them. (Note the subtle secondary implication here; that you are either a Christian or a scientist, but not both.) Sadly, all too many Christians don't know how to respond to this claim. The following quote from Boyce Rensberger reveals the truth of the matter:

> At this point, it is necessary to reveal a little inside information about how scientists work, something the textbooks don't usually tell you. The fact is that scientists are not really as objective and dispassionate in their work as they would like you to think. Most scientists first get their ideas about how the world works not through rigorously logical processes but through hunches and wild guesses. As individuals they often come to believe something to be true long before they assemble the hard evidence that will convince somebody else that it is. Motivated by faith in his own ideas and a desire for acceptance by his peers, a scientist will labor for years knowing in his heart that his theory is correct but devising experiment after experiment whose results he hopes will support his position.[7]

Whether someone is a Christian, Muslim, Buddhist, atheist, agnostic, etc., they all start with some type of presupposition or worldview, which can, and usually does, greatly affect their interpretation of the world around them. What are presuppositions and worldviews? A presupposition is something that is believed without proof or at least as a starting point, before proof is sought after or discovered. A worldview is a presupposition (or set of presuppositions) specifically regarding life and the universe.

Here's an example of a presupposition/worldview from Dr. William B. Provine, professor of biological sciences, Cornell University:

> Let me summarize my views on what modern evolutionary biology tells us loud and clear. . .There are no gods, no purposes, no goal-directed forces of any kind. There is no life after death. When I die, I am absolutely certain that I am going to be dead. That's the end for me. There is no ultimate foundation for ethics, no ultimate meaning to life, and no free will for humans, either.[8]

One interesting note about this quote is that it implies that his stated belief is specifically not a presupposition, but rather a logical conclusion from nature (i.e., modern biology). He says that this is what "modern evolutionary biology tells us loud and clear." He claims that this is an unavoidable conclusion of nature and not just his own opinion. In reality, there is absolutely nothing in biology (or any other field of science) that indicates "There are no gods, no purposes, no goal-directed forces of any kind" or "no life after death." Science cannot address issues such as intent, purpose, value or ultimate meaning. As powerful as it can be (within its confines) science is not as all-encompassing as some would like you to believe. For instance, can science tell us whether Chinese food is better than Italian or Mexican? My answer to this question changes depending on the mood I'm in and is ultimately a subjective question that science cannot address.

Here's another presuppositional statement, but slightly different than Provine's:

> I want atheism to be true and am made uneasy by the fact that some of the most intelligent and well informed people I know are religious believers. It isn't just that I don't believe in God and naturally, hope there is no God! I don't want there to be a God; I don't want the universe to be like that.[9]

This is an example of a very strong worldview statement, without pretending to claim that it is driven by the facts. He is honest about his personal affinity for this view as opposed to it being a foregone conclusion of science.

And then there's Richard Lewontin (professor of biology, emeritus—Harvard University, Alexander Agassiz professor of zoology in the Museum of Comparative Zoology, emeritus). He was quite transparent regarding his worldview/bias:

> Our willingness to accept scientific claims that are against common sense is the key to an understanding of the real struggle between science and the supernatural. We take the side of science in spite of its failure to fulfill many of its extravagant promises of health and life, in spite of the tolerance of the scientific community of unsubstantiated just-so stories, because we have a prior commitment to materialism. It is not that the methods and institutions of science somehow compel us to accept a material explanation of the phenomenal world, but on the contrary, that we are forced by our *a*

priori adherence to material causes to create an apparatus of investigation and a set of concepts that produce material explanations, no matter how counterintuitive, no matter how mystifying to the uninitiated. Moreover, that Materialism is absolute, for we cannot allow a Divine Foot in the door. . .

It is said that there is no place for an argument from authority from science. The community of science is constantly self-critical. . .It is certainly true that within each narrowly defined scientific field there is constant challenge to new technical claims and to old wisdom. . .But when scientists transgress the bounds of their own specialty they have no choice but to accept the claims of authority, even though they do not know how solid the grounds of those claims may be. Who am I to believe about quantum physics if not Steven Weinberg, or about the solar system if not Carl Sagan? What worries me is that they may believe what Dawkins and Wilson tell them about evolution."[10]

Finally, one from Aldous Huxley:

I had motive for not wanting the world to have a meaning; consequently assumed that it had none, and was able without any difficulty to find satisfying reasons for this assumption. The philosopher who finds no meaning in the world is not concerned exclusively with a problem in pure metaphysics, he is also concerned to prove that there is no valid reason why he personally should not do as he wants to do, or why his friends should not seize political power and govern in the way that they find most advantageous to themselves. . .For myself, the philosophy of meaninglessness was essentially an instrument of liberation, sexual and political.[11]

Again, a strong statement with the inherent admission that it was driven by desire, not evidence.

We need to be aware of such statements and be able to see them for what they are, rather than accepting them as something that cannot be argued against simply because it came from the mouth of a scientist. Worldviews have a very significant influence on how evidence is treated. Many scientists are strongly motivated and driven by what they want or hope to be true and are very hesitant to accept any evidence that would appear to be contrary to their cherished beliefs.

In actuality, worldviews and presuppositions are not bad. In fact, they are quite necessary. It is virtually impossible not to have some type of worldview. So the key question isn't whether or not you have a worldview, but rather, how reasonable is the one you have?

Both Christianity and atheism posit worldviews. However, I am fully convinced that Christianity represents a set of logical presuppositions that are soundly consistent with actual history and true science, as opposed to atheism which is "consistently inconsistent" in these areas. Christianity and atheism alike both require faith, which in many people's minds often seems quite contrary to common knowledge. They assume that Christianity (and other various religions) is largely, if not solely, faith-based, while atheism is a rejection of faith and strictly an embracing of science. This is far from the truth.

It's interesting that the Bible itself never attempts to prove or defend God's existence. It simply states that He exists, and that He always has and always will. This is an example of a presupposition that is found in Scripture. Christians accept this presupposition as well as the fact that God created the entire universe. Hebrews 11:3 tells us that "By faith we understand that the universe was formed at God's command, so that what is seen was not made out of what was visible." This does not mean that we have no evidence, because we in fact have a mountain of evidence that is consistent with the validity of the Christian worldview and its presuppositions.

Atheism accepts by faith that God (or a god) does not exist, although many atheists would deny they invoke any kind of faith. It may come as quite a surprise, but science is actually quite incapable of proving that God does or does not exist. Science only deals with the physical world of matter and energy. Since God, by definition, is outside of these entities, scientists cannot conduct experiments that directly test God's existence in anyway. Is there something wrong with science? No, it can produce some amazing results, but it is also limited in scope. Does that mean there is no "evidence" for God's existence? No, not really. I believe there is a lot of evidence for God's existence—things that truly only make sense if God exists. However, none of these things constitute proof in the strictest sense, scientifically speaking, because science is all about interpretation. There will always be people who interpret such evidence in ways opposite of that which a theist might. For much more on proof for God's existence, please see appendix B (Presuppositional Apologetics). I guarantee it will be worth the trip (and no science is required)!

You may read various scientific articles or books claiming to contain "proof" that God does or does not exist. Once again, however, science does not possess any tools that are capable of truly proving God's existence or non-existence. Let's look at it in a bit simpler fashion. God (by biblical definition) is a non-physical being, having no physical characteristics (mass, size, temperature, etc.). Science, on the other hand, is only capable of dealing with the physical world—with things of a physical nature. Therefore, science cannot *directly* comment on the existence of God. What it can do, is make an attempt at determining whether or not something we do observe can be satisfactorily explained by the laws of science which we have previously discovered. Why does Styrofoam float? Is it some miraculous event that occurs, dumfounding the world's most brilliant scientists? Of course not. We have a fairly thorough understanding of buoyancy principles and they are sufficient to account for what we observe. On the other hand, we see life, but have not discovered any laws or principles of science that can account for its origin. In this case, science would be providing supportive evidence for God's existence, but certainly not proof. It's not proof, because we cannot say with certainty that science will *never* discover some sort of principle that naturally explains its origin. (I do not personally believe that they will ever discover a natural explanation for the origin of life, but how could I even begin to prove that?) So while there are numerous things in science that are strong evidence for God's existence and for His involvement in creation, none will ever constitute absolute proof. If science was capable of providing such evidence, but had failed to do so, that would be something to worry about. However, such is not the case.

The converse is true as well; science is incapable of proving that God does not exist (for the same reasons mentioned above). Here's the challenge: go out and find the twenty thickest books claiming that God does not exist, and I guarantee that you will not find in any of those books, even one single piece of scientific evidence against His existence! How can I be so confident? Here's why. Since scientists cannot directly prove or disprove the existence of God, all they can really do is try to argue against the existence of a "god" as they define Him. After trying to show that there are supposedly natural explanations for many things that appear to be exquisitely designed, they focus on evidence for the non-existence of a god who would never for any reason ever let anything "bad" happen to "good" or "innocent" people. This is not proof that God doesn't exist. At best, it is only circumstantial evidence for the non-existence of that kind of god, but it says nothing about God as described in the Bible. I have yet to meet even one casual atheist who doesn't have *personal* problems with the concept of God or His possible existence. I believe (just my opinion) that in the vast majority of cases the atheist's beliefs are driven by much deeper, more personal issues, rather than mere objective scientific arguments. Again, for a more thorough defense for the existence of God, see appendix B.

With all of this in mind, let's take a quick look at the meaning of "science" before heading into the scientific arguments regarding the validity of the Genesis creation account.

The key factor here isn't really focused on getting a handle on a technical definition, but understanding that there are different types of science. There are a variety of definitions, but for the most part they are generally quite similar. A typical definition of science would look something like this:[12]

a. knowledge or a system of knowledge covering general truths of the operation of general laws, especially as obtained and tested through scientific method;

b. such knowledge or such a system of knowledge concerned with the physical world and its phenomena.

It is not the intention of this book to quibble over which of all the definitions is most accurate. The differences among the various definitions generally do not affect the creation/evolution debate. What is vital to understanding, however, is that science comes in two "flavors"—operational and historical.

Operational science (also called "observational" science) typically deals with things that can be done in a laboratory, performing multiple, repeatable tests, which also allows for potential falsification of one's initial hypotheses. It is responsible for creating things such as lightning-fast computers, space shuttles and finding cures for diseases. It may be surprising, but creationists and evolutionists rarely argue over operational science.

The other type of science is "historical." Historical science (sometimes called "origins science") deals with events that occurred in the unobserved past, are not repeatable, and cannot be directly tested in the present. The big bang falls into this category. We were not around to observe this event. We cannot repeat it in the present and cannot test it directly. We can only make guesses and assumptions as to whether or not it occurred and how it might have happened. Interestingly, God's original six-day creation also falls into this same category. We were not around to observe this event, we cannot repeat it in the present and cannot test it directly. Scientifically speaking, we can only make guesses and assumptions as to whether or not it occurred and how it might have happened. If, on the other hand, the Creator of the universe chose to give us a written record of what He did (i.e., the Bible), we could know a lot more detail. We could also know for certain, because the Bible is the inspired Word of the one who was there in the beginning, created it all and does not lie. That's exactly what the Bible claims to be and there exists a wealth of evidence to support such a claim. (See chapter 8 for further details.)

Having spent over a quarter of a century speaking and researching on this subject, I am fully convinced that the creation/evolution controversy is ultimately not a *scientific* debate, but rather a *spiritual* issue. The Bible states:

> But the natural man receiveth not the things of the Spirit of God: for they are foolishness unto him: neither can he know them, because they are spiritually discerned (I Corinthians 2:14, KJV).

We've all been in situations before where we are talking with someone about something seemingly obvious, but they just can't see it. (And the reverse can be true as well.) It's really not about the evidence—it's about one's worldview.

WORLDVIEWS AND INTERPRETING FACTS

It is a commonly held belief that creationists and evolutionists each have their own unique bodies of evidence. In this scenario, the debate is mainly a matter of each side presenting their "facts." In a perfect world, whoever has the most compelling facts wins. Case closed. It's certainly not nearly that simple. If that were the case, the scientists would have the debate, make a decision and all be united from that point on. In reality, nothing is ever really that simple, but if it truly is just a matter of raw scientific facts, it should be just about that straight forward.

This goes hand-in-hand with the idea that "the facts speak for themselves." However, this is another widespread myth. Every fact that you have ever heard of must be interpreted by some type of explanatory filter, presupposition or worldview. As alluded to previously, a worldview is the sum total of what we believe about the most critical life-issues (e.g., origins, meaning, purpose, destiny, etc.). A more formal definition would look like the following:

> A worldview is a set of presuppositions (assumptions which may be true, partially true or entirely false) which we hold (consciously or subconsciously, consistently or inconsistently) about the basic make-up of our world.[13]

Here's something that may come as a real surprise: contrary to popular belief, all scientists, whether they are evolutionists or creationists, have the exact same facts! They're living on the same earth and looking at the same dirt and same DNA. The main difference is *how* they look at (or interpret) the facts or evidence, which is strongly influenced by their worldview. In reality, facts don't even become evidence until they are interpreted. What's even more interesting is that often the same facts are claimed as evidence by each side!

Consider the following raw fact: There are many sedimentary layers in the Grand Canyon. No one would deny that. However, an evolutionist (and anyone else who believes that the earth is billions of years old) would look at those layers through a filter or worldview partially or solely shaped by man's theories and conclude that it would have taken millions and millions of years for those layers to form. A creationist, looking at the layers through a filter or worldview based on Scripture, could say, "That's exactly what I would expect to see: layers catastrophically laid-down all over the earth as a result of the global flood of Genesis." They are looking at the exact same facts, but arriving at very different conclusions.

Another example would be the fact that there are definite similarities between human and ape skeletons. An evolutionist would look at the similarities through a filter or worldview of man's theories and conclude that this is proof (or at least strong evidence) that humans evolved from ape-like creatures. A creationist, looking at the similarities through a filter or worldview based on Scripture could say, "I would expect to see some similarities, because they were designed by the same designer, they are living on the same planet and are eating similar foods." Once again, they are looking at the exact same facts but coming up with two very different conclusions.

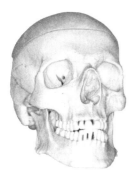
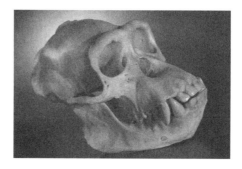

We are led to believe that while Christians are completely biased by their *a priori* belief in the Bible, scientists, in stark contrast, are completely unbiased, simply making observations and following the evidence wherever it leads. The reality of the situation is quite different, as discussed in the following quotes:

. . .corruption and deceit are just as common in science as in any other human undertaking.[14]

. . .that there's an agenda other than pure science at work here.[15]

But I would also reject any claim that personal preference, the root of aesthetic judgment, does not play a key role in science. True, the world is indifferent to our hopes—and fire burns whether we like it or not. But our ways of learning about the world are strongly influenced by the social preconceptions and biased modes of thinking that each scientist must apply to any problem. The stereotype of a fully rational and objective "scientific method," with individual scientists as logical (and interchangeable) robots, is self-serving mythology.[16]

Science. . .is not so much concerned with truth as it is with consensus. What counts as 'truth' is what scientists can agree to count as truth at any particular moment in time. . .[Scientists] are not really receptive or not really open-minded to any sorts of criticisms or any sorts of claims that actually are attacking some of the established parts of the research (traditional) paradigm—in this case neo-Darwinism—so it is very difficult for people who are pushing claims that contradict the paradigm to get a hearing. They'll find it difficult to [get] research grants; they'll find it hard to get their research published; they'll, in fact, find it very hard.[17]

Another important point to keep in mind when considering evidence is that no matter what facts we might present as support for the Genesis creation account, a serious, committed skeptic will always come up with (or at least try to come up with) a way to explain away the evidence or interpret it in a way that fits with his or her worldview. We'll discuss this phenomenon further in chapter 14.

A PROPERLY BALANCED WORLDVIEW

With all that said, I certainly do not wish to give the impression that evidence does not matter at all. Without evidence, all anyone has is a blind faith. There would be no compelling reason for anyone to accept what we believe and there would be no overtly tangible reason for us to hold-fast to our own beliefs, other than sheer will or volition. However, I Peter 3:15 explicitly states that we should have reasons for what we believe so that we can give hope to those around us:

But in your hearts revere Christ as Lord. Always be prepared to give an answer to everyone who asks you to give the reason for the hope that you have. But do this with gentleness and respect (NIV).

I believe that when we seek God sincerely with all that we have, He truly does reward us with greater and greater understanding of not only His character and holiness, but His creation as well. I think we're ready now to start looking at the actual evidence, so let's do just that.

ENDNOTES

1. Flew, Antony, *There is a God: How the World's Most Notorious Atheist Changed His Mind*, HarperCollins, New York, NY, 2007.

2. Templeton, C., *Farewell to God*, McClelland & Stewart, Inc., Toronto, Ontario, Canada, p. 7, 1996.

3. Ibid., p. 232.

4. Susskind, Leonard, *The Cosmic Landscape—String Theory and the Illusion of Intelligent Design*, L. Brown and Co. (2006), p.196.

5. Todd, S.C., correspondence to *Nature* 401(6752):423, 30 Sept. 1999.

6. Kennedy, D. James, & Newcombe, Jerry, *What if Jesus Had Never Been Born?* (Nashville, TN: Thomas Nelson, Inc. Publishers, 1994) p. 102.

7. Rensberger, Boyce, *How the World Works*, William Morrow, NY, 1986, pp. 17-18.

8. Provine, William B., *Origins Research*, 16, no. 1 (1994): 9.

9. Nagel, T., *The Last Word*, Oxford University Press, New York, 1997, p. 130.

10. Lewontin, Richard, *Billions and Billions of Demons* in New York Review of Books, January 9, 1997, p. 31.

11. Huxley, A., *Ends and Means*, Chatto & Windus (1937) p. 270.

12. Merriam-Webster On-Line: http://www.merriam-webster.com/dictionary/science.

13. Sire, J., *The Universe Next Door*, IVP, p. 107, 2004.

14. Broad, W., and N. Wade, *Betrayers of Truth: Deceit and Fraud in the Halls of Science*, London: Century Publications, 1982, appears on the dust cover.

15. Wells, Jonathan, *Icons of Evolution*, Regnery Publishing, 2002.

16. Gould, S. J., "In the mind of the beholder," *Natural History*, 103(2), 1994, p. 15.

17. Richards, Evelleen, *Lateline*, 9 October 1998, Australian Broadcasting Corporation.

Chapter Three

Something from Nothing: The Origin of the Universe

If you are a fairly normal, well-adjusted human being you most likely do not seriously question whether or not the universe actually exists. It seems more than obvious that it is indeed real and that we are here observing it. It does remind me, however, of a story I once heard. There was a Christian speaker giving a talk to a large state university audience regarding the tenets of Christianity. In the middle of his lecture a student rudely jumped up and shouted, "How do I even know I exist?" The speaker gently lowered his glasses, looked directly at the student and replied, "And whom shall I say is asking?" Brilliant! That gets right to the point, doesn't it? If the student doesn't really exist, then he didn't actually ask the question and therefore, there's no question to be answered. If, on the other hand, he really did ask the question, he obviously must exist!

One of the most fundamental questions we can ask about the universe (assuming that it truly does exist) is "Where did it come from?" Is the universe just the product of random forces of nature or was it actually designed, implying an inherent purpose to life itself? If it really was just an accident, what exactly is "nature" and where did it come from? How did nature exist without the universe? If it was actually created, who (or what) was the creator and just as importantly, where did he/she/it come from?

These are all very pertinent questions and we will attempt to address each of them in this chapter from both scientific and theological perspectives.

THREE OPTIONS

When considering the existence of our universe we only have three options to ponder: (1) The universe has always existed, (2) it was created by someone or something outside of itself, or (3) it created itself. Of these possibilities, the third option seems more instinctively absurd than the others. It is readily obvious to most people, even those with no formal training in science, that something cannot create itself. In order for something to create itself, it would have to be able to do something. In order to be able to do something it would first have to exist. It's the classic Catch 22.

It comes as no surprise that for much of recorded history there were two dominant views: the universe was either created by God (or at least a god or gods), or it has always existed. Those of a non-religious persuasion were, in essence, forced to choose the eternal existence view, not wishing to evoke any kind of supernatural entity. Most others had no problem believing that a supernatural power created the universe. It seemed intuitive and, after all, that's exactly what the Bible says: "In the beginning God created the heavens and the earth" (Genesis 1:1, NIV).

One theory that attempted to avoid a beginning involved the concept of an oscillating universe. In this scenario, the universe experiences a series of oscillations, each beginning with a "big bang" (expansion stage) and ending in a "big crunch" (contraction stage). After having spent fifteen years in an attempt to find support for this theory and the eternality of the universe in general, Robert Jastrow (founding director of NASA's Goddard Institute for Space Studies) made an interesting statement regarding his disbelief in this idea:

> This is an exceedingly strange development, unexpected by all but the theologians. They have always accepted the word of the Bible: In the beginning God created heaven and earth. . .[But] for the scientist who has lived by his faith in the power of reason, the story ends like a bad dream. He has scaled the mountains of ignorance; he is about to conquer the highest peak; [and] as he pulls himself over the final rock, he is greeted by a band of theologians who have been sitting there for centuries.[1]

In essence, he was admitting that the theologians had been correct all along, in as much as they believed that the universe did indeed have a beginning.

With the continued advancement of science it was becoming more untenable that the universe could be eternal. The second law of thermodynamics argues against it because it indicates that everything (left to itself) is continually running down hill, becoming more disordered, running out of gas so-to-speak. If the universe were truly infinitely old, there would not be any energy or order remaining, yet we see high concentrations of energy and order throughout the universe. The word cosmos itself is derived from the Greek word, *kósmos*, meaning "order." Scientists today recognize an amazing amount of order in our universe.

Most scientists believe that our universe is expanding. (There is a fair amount of evidence for this, but it is not a proven fact.) Logically speaking, if it truly is expanding and getting bigger as time marches on, it must have been progressively smaller as we look back into the past. There must also have been a time where all of the space and matter in the universe was concentrated in a single location—a starting point. They refer to this initial point as a *singularity*. What is a singularity? They believe it is an infinitesimally small, infinitely hot, infinitely dense "something," in which the current laws of physics may not apply. Where did it come from? No clue. Why did it appear? Can't say. Can we observe it? Nope. Can we recreate it? No can do. Can we test it? No. Does it even qualify as observational science? They want us to believe that it does, but this idea is utterly disqualified because of these former responses.

We now have legitimate scientific reasons to believe that the universe had a beginning. This was an appalling thought to many scientists who realized it would be difficult to speak of a "beginning" without a "beginner" (or more scientifically, an effect without a cause).

The Kalām Argument, which is very sound logic and accepted by most scientists today, is described in the following syllogism:

• Everything that has a beginning has a cause.

• The universe had a beginning.

• Therefore, the universe has a cause.

Since this newly proposed "singularity" was outside the reach of true science and most scientists did not want to evoke God as part of the equation (i.e., as the "cause"), the issue of how we get something from nothing is largely ignored within the scientific literature. Occasionally, a few bold individuals will openly share their thoughts on the subject and it usually makes for some interesting pondering. I remember hearing a recorded lecture by a scientist a number of years ago, in which he stated:

> Keep in mind that there's a difference between nothing and absolute nothing.

I guess the intended meaning here is that if there was *just nothing* to begin with, it may be able to create an entire universe, but if there was *absolutely nothing*, then obviously it would be impossible!

Here's another statement by the same professor:

> Remember, even where there's nothing, there's always something going on.

Try to wrap your head around that one!

Even though these statements were made about twenty years ago, similar conjecture is still being propagated today. During a BBC documentary ("What happened before the big bang?" 2010-2011), Dr. Michio Kaku (professor of theoretical physics at City University, New York) stated that the apparent problem of getting "something out of nothing" can be potentially resolved, "it all depends on how you define 'nothing'." He went on to state:

> I think there are two kinds of nothing. First there is something I call absolute nothing: no equations, no space, no time, no anything that the human mind can conceive of, just nothing. Then there is the vacuum which is nothing but the absence of matter.

And just where did the pre-existing vacuum come from? No answer was given and neither was there any actual scientific evidence shared in support of this view or any other views discussed during the entire documentary.

Regarding the reason the universe is here, Nobel Laureate physicist Frank Wilczek (Massachusetts Institute of Technology) stated while speaking at the World Science Festival in 2009:

> The answer to the ancient question "Why is there something rather than nothing?" Because nothing is unstable.

It's tempting when hearing statements such as these to respond by feeling that these scientists are just so much more intelligent than we are, that there's no way we'll ever be able to understand such deep concepts (which is an all-too-common response of many college students). A more reasonable response would be to say, "That makes no sense at all!" However, it is human nature to pretend we have a grasp of the complex and not admit something doesn't actually make any sense. Stephen Hawking (British theoretical physicist) wrote a book a few years ago entitled, *A Brief History of Time* (1996 – Tenth Anniversary Edition) in which he expounded on the origin of the universe. One commentator remarked that it was, "heralded as absolutely brilliant by all those who never read it and not understood by those who had." Scientifically nonsensical quotes are not rare; they're fairly prevalent. Here are two more:

Popular Science magazine:

> In the beginning, there was nothing. Then, with a big bang, an almost infinitely small, hot and dense universe exploded into existence.[3] [Author's note: If

there was nothing to begin with, which is what they stated, what exactly was it that exploded? The article from which this quote was taken never even bothered to address this monumental issue, let alone explain it.]

Discover magazine:

The universe burst into something from absolutely nothing—zero, nada. And as it got bigger, it became filled with even more stuff that came from absolutely nowhere.[4] [Author's note: It's amazing just how powerful this "nothing" must have been! We are not allowed to discuss an all-powerful God in scientific circles, but some scientists apparently have no problem talking about a seemingly all-powerful "nothing."]

David Darling (astronomer and author), writing in *New Scientist* magazine, was refreshingly inquisitive about the whole "something from nothing" dilemma:

What is a big deal—the biggest deal of all—is how you get something out of nothing. Don't let the cosmologists try to kid you on this one. They have not got a clue either. . ."In the beginning," they will say, "there was nothing—no time, space, matter or energy. Then there was a quantum fluctuation from which. . ." Whoa! Stop right there. You see what I mean? First there is nothing, then there is something. And the cosmologists try to bridge the two with a quantum flutter, a tremor of uncertainty that sparks it all off. Then they are away and before you know it, they have pulled a hundred billion galaxies out of their quantum hats. You cannot fudge this by appealing to quantum mechanics. Either there is nothing to begin with, in which case there is no quantum vacuum, no pre-geometric dust, no time in which anything can happen, no physical laws that can effect a change from nothingness into somethingness; or there is something, in which case that needs explaining.[5]

While ignoring the bigger problem of getting something from nothing, the scientific community simply focuses on the grand details of the big bang theory, trusting that the public will assume it answers everything, when in reality, it answers very little, if anything at all, as we shall soon see.

I WAS JUST BEING SARCASTIC

When Sir Fredrick Hoyle (English astronomer and atheist for most of his life) heard about a certain newly formulated theory regarding the origin of the universe, he sarcastically referred to it as the "big bang." Even though he was making fun of it and utterly rejected this theory, the new term stuck. Today, everyone has heard of the "big bang," but many do not know of its origin and most have erroneous ideas regarding what it actually purports.

THAT'S WHERE YOU'D BE WRONG

If you think that the big bang was an explosion of matter out into space that created the universe, you would be in good company, because even a large percentage of scientists believe that as well, but you (and they) would also be wrong.

The average scientist has this all-too-simplistic and erroneous idea about the big bang, mainly because it falls outside their area of expertise. It is not a theory that deals with how we got "something from nothing," but more accurately, how we got "something from something."

The big bang does not even come into the picture until after we already "have something"—the singularity—the initial starting point. As was already mentioned, science really has nothing to say about the origin of this singularity, other than mere metaphysical and philosophical speculation. In reality, the big bang merely attempts to explain how this singularity could have morphed into the universe that we are a part of today.

A singularity is what we call a "thermodynamic dead end." It's not going anywhere. It cannot get itself out of this state. It's stuck. Something else has to occur to get it off of dead center, so to speak. This "something else" is what they call the "big bang." Rather than being an explosion of matter out into space, the big bang theory posits that this event actually expanded the initial speck, creating space as it expanded and was the beginning of time itself, as we know it. At some point before this event occurred, they suggest that energy/matter, space and time did not even exist.

Cosmic background microwave radiation, which appears to be evenly distributed throughout the universe, is supposedly the primary evidence of the big bang. The problem is that it actually appears to be too smooth. Since the temperature of the universe appears to be extremely smooth today, something needed to happen during the big bang to produce this condition. A period of "super inflation" is assumed, at which time the universe expanded at a rate one thousand billion, billion, billion times faster than the original expansion. They believe that this also may have kept the universe from collapsing back in on itself—back into another singularity. No one knows what caused this or even what *could* cause this, but it is needed in order to fit with current observations. This again would be another *ad hoc* assumption of the big bang. During and following this accelerated expansion time, the lighter elements were supposedly created (including hydrogen, helium and trace amounts of lithium and deuterium). The big bang, which at this point is an ever expanding cloud of gas (according to the theory), has done all it can do.

We now need another *ad hoc* assumption to produce virtually everything else we see in the universe. This ever-expanding, smooth cloud of gas needed to stop expanding, at least in some areas, to form galaxies. This is where the door is wide open. They have no sound theories of how this happened. Cosmologists generally speak of "tiny ripples" in the otherwise smooth universe, from which formations could possibly occur. This is entirely speculative, however. Dr. James Trefil (professor of physics at George Mason University) states his shock at the mere existence of galaxies:

> There shouldn't be galaxies out there at all, and even if there are galaxies, they shouldn't be grouped together the way they are. . .The problem of explaining the existence of galaxies has proved to be one of the thorniest in cosmology. By all rights, they just shouldn't be there, yet there they sit. It's hard to convey the depth of the frustration that this simple fact induces among scientists.[6]

Contrary to what most people assume, the big bang is not a well-supported scientific theory, although most scientists operate on the assumption that it is. We need to keep in mind that most scientists do not have backgrounds in astronomy and physics and have never really done any studying in cosmology. They merely assume that those who have know what they are talking about and they do not question their conclusions. John Hartnett (PhD physicist and co-author of *Dismantling the Big Bang*) stated in his book:

> Cosmologists would love to be able to explain the origin of stars and galaxies, of planets and of life. They find themselves thwarted. . .and so they occupy themselves with other matters. These other matters are then reported as being the main issues in cosmology, and the impression is created that the main issues are being addressed and satisfactorily answered, but it is an illusion.[7]

AN OPEN LETTER TO THE SCIENTIFIC COMMUNITY

It is certainly not the case that all scientists believe in the big bang. Even among the secular scientific community there are numerous scientists who reject or express serious doubt about the big bang. The following statement (partially reprinted) was signed by at least 218 scientists and engineers, 187 independent researchers, and 105 others in 2008. (Keep in mind that these signers were just the ones who were willing to go public with their dissension. No doubt, many others concur but did not want to risk being ostracized or possibly even losing their jobs.)

The big bang today relies on a growing number of hypothetical entities, things that we have never observed—inflation, dark matter and dark energy are the most prominent examples. Without them, there would be a fatal contradiction between the observations made by astronomers and the predictions of the big bang theory. In no other field of physics would this continual recourse to new hypothetical objects be accepted as a way of bridging the gap between theory and observation. It would, at the least, raise serious questions about the validity of the underlying theory.

But the big bang theory can't survive without these fudge factors. Without the hypothetical inflation field, the big bang does not predict the smooth, isotropic cosmic background radiation that is observed, because there would be no way for parts of the universe that are now more than a few degrees away in the sky to come to the same temperature and thus emit the same amount of microwave radiation.

Without some kind of dark matter (which is generally unobserved on Earth despite twenty years of experiments) the big bang theory makes contradictory predictions for the density of matter in the universe. Inflation requires a density twenty times larger than that implied by big bang nucleosynthesis, the theory's explanation of the origin of the light elements. And without dark energy, the theory predicts that the universe is only about 8 billion years old, which is billions of years younger than the estimate they calculate for the age of many stars in our galaxy.

What is more, the big bang theory can boast of no quantitative predictions that have subsequently been validated by observation. The successes claimed by the theory's supporters consist of its ability to retrospectively fit observations with a steadily increasing array of adjustable parameters, just as the old Earth-centered cosmology of Ptolemy needed layer upon layer of epicycles. . .An open exchange of ideas is lacking in most mainstream conferences. Whereas Richard Feynman could say that "science is the culture of doubt," in cosmology today doubt and dissent are not tolerated, and young scientists learn to remain silent if they have something negative to say about the standard big bang model. Those who doubt the big bang fear that saying so will cost them their funding.

Even observations are now interpreted through this biased filter, judged right or wrong depending on whether or not they support the big bang. So discordant data on red shifts, lithium and helium abundances, and galaxy distribution, among other topics, are ignored or ridiculed. This reflects a growing dogmatic mindset that is alien to the spirit of free scientific inquiry.

Today, virtually all financial and experimental resources in cosmology are devoted to big bang studies. Funding comes from only a few sources, and all the peer-review committees that control them are dominated by supporters of the big bang. As a result, the dominance of the big bang within the field has become self-sustaining, irrespective of the scientific validity of the theory.[8]

MORE DISSENSION: OTHERS CHIME IN

Geoffrey Burbidge (professor of physics at the University of California, San Diego), writing in *Scientific American,* refers to "faith" in the big bang:

Big Bang cosmology is probably as widely believed as has been any theory of the universe in the history of Western civilization. It rests, however, on many untested, and in some cases untestable, assumptions. Indeed, big bang cosmology has become a bandwagon of thought that reflects faith as much as objective truth. This situation is particularly worrisome because there are good reasons to think the big bang model is seriously flawed. . .Why then has the big bang become so deeply entrenched in modern thought? The big bang ultimately reflects some cosmologists' search for creation and for a beginning. That search properly lies in the realm of metaphysics, not science.[9]

Leon Ledermann (Nobel Prize winning physicist):

When you read or hear anything about the birth of the universe, someone is making it up.[10]

FURTHER CHALLENGES FROM SCIENCE

Missing Monopoles: According to the standard big bang model, the extremely high temperatures of the initial "explosion" would have produced unique types of particles, called monopoles. These are massive-sized magnetic particles that have only one pole (as opposed to having both a north and a south pole). However, we do not see any evidence of such particles,

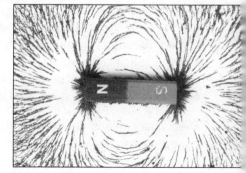

which would indicate that the universe was never that hot, and hence, never underwent the alleged big bang.

Antimatter: Einstein's famous equation $e = mc^2$ shows us the relationship between matter and energy. Matter can be converted into energy and energy can be converted into matter. Our universe, according to the big bang theory, started off with only energy—no matter. The initial energy was later converted into matter. Whenever we see energy converted into matter today, it always produces precisely equal amounts of matter and something we call antimatter. Whereas matter is made up of particles (e.g., electrons and protons), antimatter consists of "antiparticles." The antiparticles are very similar to particles, except they have the opposite charge. For example, an electron has a negative charge and its antiparticle counterpart (called a positron) has a positive charge. A proton has a positive charge and its antiparticle counterpart (simply called an antiproton) has a negative charge.

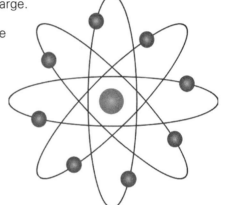

This being the case, when we scan the heavens, we should generally see equal amounts of matter and antimatter. The truth, however, is that our universe appears to consist almost entirely of matter, with only trace amounts of antimatter to have ever been discovered. This is strong evidence that the big bang, as purported by most scientists today, did not occur.

POPULATION III STARS

Most people are unaware that the big bang, even if it did occur, could not produce anything other than the two lightest elements (hydrogen and helium) and trace amounts of lithium. So where did the almost ninety other naturally occurring elements come from? Secular scientists imagine that they were created by supernovas (violent explosions of stars which are extremely luminous and often briefly outshine an entire galaxy). In this view, the initial stars (however they may have formed) contained no "heavy" elements (heavier than hydrogen and helium). The subsequent stars (second and third generation stars) would all contain traces of the heavier elements expelled by earlier supernova explosions. Some of these initial stars, referred to as "Population III" stars, should still be around according to scientists' calculations. However, in the billions of stars that we have observed, we have yet to find even one without any trace of heavier elements.

These are just a few of the scientific problems associated with the big bang model of the origin of our universe.

LIKE OIL AND WATER: THEOLOGICAL CONSIDERATIONS

When we want to emphasize the idea that certain things don't go well together, we often say that they go together "like oil and water." Many people, with good intentions, feel that the best solution to many of the apparent conflicts between science and the Bible is to accept whatever conclusions scientists make and simply put God's "stamp of approval" on them. In other words, we can accept whatever science says—we'll just keep saying "that's the way God did it!" After all, they conclude, "Who cares *how* God did it, as long as we believe *that* God did it?" Let's take a closer look at the essence of the big bang theory and see if it makes sense to use God's rubber stamp.

The theory itself is based on the philosophical assumption of naturalism, meaning that the only aspects to be considered are natural principles which we can see operating today. Nothing outside of science is to be considered. Is this a logical assumption? Do we normally assume that the principles by which something operates are the same principles by which it was created? Not usually. As an example, a refrigerator operates by the forced compression and subsequent expansion of special gases cycling over and over. When the gases are compressed they give off heat (this happens outside the back of your refrigerator. That's why its always kind of warm back there.) When the gases expand (which happens inside the fridge) they absorb heat, cooling the food. This, however, is not how the refrigerator was created in the first place. The design, construction and assembly of many complex parts were necessary to build the refrigerator, which has nothing to do with compression and expansion of refrigerant gases. In the same regard, we can observe and study the principles by which the universe operates today, but to limit ourselves to these principles in explaining its origin would be illogical and unwarranted.

There are many scientists today who will not allow themselves to even consider the possibility of God having had any involvement in our universe, and therefore, they are extremely biased against anything that might even appear to be evidence of design or purpose. The following quote is from Professor Richard Lewontin (geneticist and one of the world's leading evolutionists):

> We take the side of science in spite of the patent absurdity of some of its constructs, in spite of its failure to fulfill many of its extravagant promises of health and life, in spite of the tolerance of the scientific community for unsubstantiated just-so stories, because we have a prior commitment, a commitment to materialism [naturalism]. It is not that the methods and institutions of science somehow compel us to accept a material explanation of the phenomenal world, but on the contrary, that we are forced by our [prior] adherence to material causes. . . no matter how counter-intuitive, no matter

how mystifying to the uninitiated. Moreover, that materialism is an absolute, for we cannot allow a Divine Foot in the door.[11]

In other words: expel God at all costs! The big bang was ultimately an attempt by scientists to explain the existence of the universe apart from God (using completely naturalistic explanations), so why does it make sense to say "That's how God did it!"? If there is a purely natural explanation, there's no need for God to be involved, except for personal religious reasons, which are never allowed to be part of the scientific argument. If naturalistic explanations are inadequate, then there is justifiable reason to at least consider supernatural options. Choosing to exclude God right from the start is not a scientific conclusion, but rather a philosophical decision and should be admitted as being such.

Another theological issue that occurs when trying to marry the big bang and the biblical creation account is found in Romans 1:20 (KJV):

For the invisible things of Him from the creation of the world are clearly seen, being understood by the things that are made, even His eternal power and Godhead; so that they are without excuse.

Paul is telling us that those who deny God are *without excuse*, because the evidence for His existence is all around, throughout the universe. If the big bang is accurate, then the universe does *not* speak of the supernatural, but simply of known principles of science. If we can explain everything by natural processes, we do not need God! It would therefore be unjust of God to judge us in this manner, when the evidence of His existence is not obvious from the mere observation of His creation.

Some will object and say that God guided these processes, but that's actually a contradiction of terms. If He truly guided them, then they are not natural. The big bang will not allow for any unnatural or supernatural influences. For all practical purposes, it is an atheistic theory and the public schools and universities are certainly not teaching a "God-guided" theory of the origin of the universe. On the contrary, they are teaching "naturalism." I believe that the natural physical laws we have discovered are fairly adequate for explaining how the universe operates today, but they are completely inadequate for explaining the origin of the universe itself.

Another problem with inserting the big bang into the biblical creation account is that it introduces contradictions regarding the order of events as listed in Scripture versus what is alleged by naturalistic astronomy and geology. See chapter 10 for a detailed discussion of this particular issue.

CONCLUSION

The question of the origin of our universe is ultimately not a scientific issue, since it is not directly testable. In brief, we can either have faith that "everything came from nothing" or that "everything came from something." Both views require faith, because neither lie within the realm of scientific proof. Believing that everything came from something seems to be much more logical and in line with the current laws of science.

> By faith we understand that the universe was formed at God's command, so that what is seen was not made out of what was visible (Hebrews 11:3, NIV).

Regarding whether or not God used the big bang as His method of creation, the best response clearly seems to be *no* for two reasons. First of all, the Bible does not indicate that God used such a process, but on the contrary, clearly states that He simply spoke things into being, by the power of His word. Inserting the big bang into the Bible also causes many internal contradictions and other theological points of contention. Secondly, the big bang model is far from being a scientifically sound theory worthy of forcing all other concepts to bow to its magnificence and superiority, even though that is exactly what is happening throughout much of modern science today and all too often within the church.

We should always be very cautious when attempting to reinterpret plain teachings of Scripture to "fit" with the latest thinking in modern science. Because modern science changes so often, the meaning of Scripture would continually be subject to change, and therefore also suspect at any given time, losing any real significance or power in our lives. This is not to say that science can never help to bring clarity in any area, but simply that we ought not to change our views when it is in direct violation or contradiction with other clear teachings of God's Word.

> Ah, Sovereign LORD, you have made the heavens and the earth by your great power and outstretched arm. Nothing is too hard for You (Jeremiah 32:17, NIV).

BUT THEN I HAVE ANOTHER QUESTION

Many people at this point (skeptics in particular) would respond with something like, "So you believe God created the universe, because we can't get something out of nothing and the universe is too complex to reasonably have been a result of random forces of nature. Fine! Then who created God?" That is a completely natural and logical question. In fact, if a skeptic is not asking this question, they many not be thinking deeply enough. Because of the significance of this question, I decided to address it separately in some depth (see appendix A).

ENDNOTES

1.   Jastrow, Robert, *God and the Astronomers*, (1992, Norton, New York) p.103.

2.   Wilczek, Frank, www.worldsciencefestival.com.

3.   *Popular Science*, February 2001, p.70.

4.   *Discover*, April 2002, cover text.

5.   Darling, David, "On Creating Something from Nothing," *New Scientist*, vol. 151 (September 14, 1996), p49.

6.   Trefil, James S., *The Dark Side of the Universe*, (New York: Macmillan, 1988, pp. 3,55).

7.   Hartnett, John & Williams, Alex, *Dismantling the Big Bang*, (pp. 70-71).

8.   To view the entire statement, see http://www.cosmologystatement.org .

9.   Burbidge, Geoffrey, "Why Only One Big Bang?" *Scientific American*, (February 1992), p. 120.

10.   As quoted in *The Fire in the Equations: Science, Religion and the Search for God* by Kitty Ferguson, Eerdmans, Grand Rapids, 1995, p. 145.

11.   "Billions and Billions of Demons," *The New York Review*, 9 January 1997, p. 31.

Chapter Four

From Soup to Nuts:
The Origin of Life

American author Fran Lebowitz humorously stated that, "Life is something to do when you can't get to sleep." A more serious definition of life is found on Dictionary.com:

The condition that distinguishes organisms from inorganic objects and dead organisms, being manifested by growth through metabolism, reproduction, and the power of adaptation to environment through changes originating internally.[1]

The latter is just one of numerous attempts to describe and define life. There is no consensus among scientists regarding exactly what life is. Even the Bible doesn't specifically tell us what life is other than Jesus is, "the way and the truth and *the life*" (John 14:6 KJV, emphasis added).

It's interesting to note that there are two topics evolutionists typically don't like to discuss in any detail: (a) the origin of the universe, specifically how you get something out of nothing, and (b) how you get life from non-living chemicals. We've already covered the former topic and in this chapter we'll cover the latter.

To put things into perspective, consider the following progression which is typical of most evolutionary scenarios:

- Universe begins in the big bang (13-15 billion years ago)
- Gases form into the first stars
- Stars cluster into galaxies
- Our sun forms from swirling gases (~5 billion years ago)

- Planets in our solar system form from the same swirling gases (4.6 billion years ago)

- Earth cools over millions of years into a "rock"

- Water forms on the surface of the earth, allegedly from asteroids

- Chemicals leach into the waters and combine to form a single-celled living organism (3.8 billion years ago)

- A single-celled organism reproduces and eventually creates all other known life forms

Each of these steps is certainly very significant and far from being considered simple, but arguably the most complex phase is the one involving inorganic non-living chemicals producing living, reproducing cells.

Have scientists shown how this could have happened? Is there scientific evidence supporting this conjecture? If you read the standard/popular scientific literature, you could easily get the impression that proof for this evolutionary origin of life is old news, something that is not questioned within the scientific community and that they are continually discovering additional evidence to confirm their theories. We'll look a bit deeper at what exactly has been discovered.

The idea of spontaneous generation has been around for a long time. Aristotle (Greek philosopher, 384 BC – 322 BC) developed this idea from the writings of earlier philosophers. It stated that life arose spontaneously from inanimate matter and that it did so on a fairly routine basis. One of the reasons this was a common belief is that the appearance of maggots (flies in their larval stage) was noted on meat or fish that had been left out, and it was thought that they must have been produced spontaneously by the rotting food. This idea was easily refuted by scientists such as Francesco Redi (Italian physician, 1600s) and Louis Pasteur (French chemist and microbiologist, 1800s). All they had to do was to cover the food up and the apparent "spontaneous generation" ceased (existing flies could not land and lay eggs, which hatched into maggots, developing into flies). Because of these and other experiments, the law of biogenesis was formulated by pathologist Rudolf Virchow, stating that "life only comes from life."

Today, those individuals who reject the idea that God created life still need a theory to explain its origin. The modern-day theory is called abiogenesis, a term coined by Thomas Huxley ("Darwin's Bulldog"). It states that life arose from inanimate, inorganic material. This idea, also referred to as chemical evolution, had its origins with Alexander Oparin (Russian chemist) approximately fifty years after Pasteur's work.

You might be thinking that this doesn't sound much different than the thoroughly debunked concept of spontaneous generation. It is and it isn't. It is in the sense that it is still accepted that life came from non-life, but it's different in that it is no longer thought to be a routine occurrence. Evolutionists believe it was a unique event that occurred on the primeval earth (supposedly billions of years ago) when conditions were much different than they are today. Although they would not say that life couldn't arise spontaneously today, they do believe that it is highly unlikely to happen on its own and we should not expect to observe such an event.

So how would you prove that life came about spontaneously from non-living chemicals billions of years ago? In short, you can't. This type of concept is certainly another example of historical science and not operational science (see chapter 2 for an explanation of this critical difference). So, if you can't exactly prove it, is there at least any supportive evidence for abiogenesis?

Back in the 1950s, two scientists (Stanley Miller and Harold Urey—University of Chicago) conducted an experiment to see if they could synthesize amino acids in the laboratory. Amino acids are considered the "building blocks" of life. Although far from constituting life in and of themselves, they are critical foundational pieces of the puzzle. We will briefly take a closer look at the experiment that was performed and discuss its overall significance.

One crucial aspect of the Miller-Urey experiment was recreating the earth's alleged primeval atmosphere. This was more of an attempt to use elements they felt they needed, rather than an objective effort to truly determine what the earth was supposedly like some 4 billion years ago. The main constituents used in the experiment were methane (CH_4), ammonia (NH_3), hydrogen (H_2) and water vapor (H_2O). One element is interestingly absent: oxygen (O_2). Oxygen is certainly crucial for life, but it poses a tremendous problem for experiments of this type. It tends to destroy organic compounds, rather than assisting in their construction. In fact, if even a trace of oxygen was present in this experiment, no amino acids could be formed. It should also be noted that sunlight will break water vapor into its constituent parts; hydrogen and oxygen. Hydrogen can escape the earth's atmosphere, leaving the oxygen behind and creating an oxygen-rich environment. The following quote summarizes the current view on the early earth's atmosphere:

> The accepted picture of the earth's early atmosphere has changed: It was probably O^2-rich with some nitrogen, a less reactive mixture than Miller's, or it might have been composed largely of carbon dioxide, which would greatly deter the development of organic compounds.[2]

Conversely, if oxygen had not been present, the earth would have lacked an ozone layer (O_3) and the elements would not have been protected from ultraviolet radiation. Some see this solar radiation as being useful in the sense that it provides the energy necessary to synthesize the amino acids. However, this type of radiation will actually demolish the amino acids 10,000 to 100,000 times faster than they could form, which is no small problem! Some have attempted to avoid the radiation issue by claiming that life arose around thermal vents deep within the oceans. The ocean depth would provide a natural shielding from such radiation. The problem with this is that water tends to destroy the chemical bonds necessary, so the more water you add, the more of a problem it becomes. Also, the extreme heat would serve to accelerate the breaking down of the acids.

Even if you do produce amino acids in this environment, you need to isolate them once they've formed, because left in those surroundings, they will be destroyed thousands to tens of thousands of times faster than they would form. The actual experiment needed a trap in order to isolate the resultant product from the simulated atmosphere.

So what was actually produced in this experiment? Here's what was formed:

85%—Carcinogenic tar (toxic)

13%—Carboxylic acids (toxic)

2%—Amino acids

The small percentage of amino acids produced in the initial experiment were primarily glycine (1.05% of the total product) and alanine (0.75% of the total product). After literally hundreds of additional attempts (with various modifications) they were only able to fabricate half of the twenty different amino acids that constitute life. Without the entire set, most known proteins cannot be generated. (Proteins are properly folded chains of amino acids and are required for constructing functioning, living cells, but are far from constituting "life" in and of themselves.)

An additional problem with the results of this experiment is that half of the amino acids produced were "left-handed" and half were "right-handed." This phenomenon is technically referred to as chirality and simply means that these acids occur in two major spatial forms which are mirror images of each other. The dilemma is that virtually all amino acids that can potentially be used to construct proteins must be

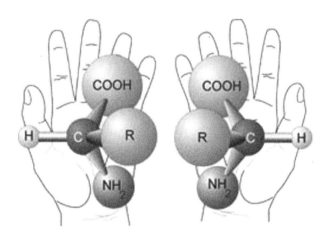

left-handed. Right-handed forms are not only useless, but often toxic and can even be lethal.[3]

We can use a simple analogy to illustrate this dilemma. Let's say you had a huge bag filled with billions of red and blue blocks, half red and half blue. You are blindfolded and given the task of building a chain consisting of just red blocks. Each time you reach into the bag you have a 50-50 chance of getting a red block. You reach in the first time and get a red block—great! You put it on the table and reach for another block. You happen to select another red block! That's great, but not too surprising. After all, you have a 50% chance of getting a red one each time. You set it on the table next to the first red block and now have two red blocks in your "chain." You reach in a third time and get another red block, and a fourth time and get a red block. Now you're getting a bit lucky—four in a row! The fifth time, you get a blue one. You don't simply throw it back in and grab another; you must take the four red blocks you initially got and throw them back in to start all over. Do you think you will ever get a chain of eight? Maybe, if you try a very, very long time. How about twenty-five? Mathematically, the probability of getting twenty-five red blocks in a row is one chance in five thousand million billion! (For those who are inclined: we arrive at that figure by multiplying a 50% probability [0.5] times itself 25 times = 0.5^{25}) Even if you lived to be 1,000 years old and tried selecting a block every second, 24 hours a day, 365 days per year, you wouldn't really even be putting a dent in these odds. Now imagine trying to get 300 red blocks in a row![4] That's what you would have to do in order to produce an average size protein, which contains a few hundred amino acids.[5] Keep in mind that a protein isn't even close to being a living organism.

BUT MAYBE, JUST MAYBE...

Some, while acknowledging a few of the known difficulties, will resort to stating "Just *maybe*, somehow, life truly did start this way." (Some even claim, while being entirely serious, that it *must* have happened, otherwise we wouldn't be here talking about it! This is typically due to the fact that they won't even begin to consider that perhaps God did indeed create life.) Let's take a bit further look at the origin of life from the perspective of probability.

When you flip a coin, there's a 50-50 chance that it will land heads up. That means that for every hundred flips you try it will land heads up about fifty times. It could be a little more or a little less, but probability states that you can expect it to be around fifty. If it were three or ninety-two, that would be very alarming and cause for questioning if there was something fishy going on.

If you were asked to blindly select a specific card from a deck that was thoroughly shuffled, you would have one chance in fifty-two of getting the correct card (assuming the jokers were removed). If someone was able to do this feat successfully, you might be surprised and impressed, but it is not outside the realm of rational probability. In fact, it *should* happen about once for every fifty-two attempts. However, if someone were to do this successfully ten times in a row, you would be justified in your suspicion.

The chance of chemicals naturally combining and producing life is not just one chance in two (a 50-50 chance, like flipping a coin) or even one chance in fifty-two (like the deck of cards example). It's much, much more unlikely than that. Many attempts have been made to calculate the probability of life forming by natural processes from inorganic material and they all yield figures that are so incredibly unlikely, they are considered virtually impossible. One such example comes from Sir Fred Hoyle (famous British astronomer) whom we also reference a few other times in throughout this book. Here's what this former atheist had to say regarding the chance assemblage of life:

> Now imagine 10^{50} blind persons* each with a scrambled Rubik cube and try to conceive of the chance of them all simultaneously arriving at the solved form. You then have the chance of arriving by random shuffling at just one of the many biopolymers on which life depends. The notion that not only the biopolymers but the operating program of a living cell could be arrived at by chance in a primordial soup here on Earth is evidently nonsense of a high order.[6]

[* = 100 billion billion billion billion trillion people]

His example gives you just a glimpse at the incredible unlikelihood of life arising in this manner. It's interesting to note that there are over 10^{19} possible combinations to a Rubik's Cube,[7] meaning that if you were blindfolded, spinning randomly, you would have less than 1 chance in 10 million trillion of getting it solved! That puts things into perspective even further.

Beyond the probability aspect lies the old "chicken and the egg" predicament. Proteins, which we've been discussing, are required to construct DNA. However, DNA is needed to produce proteins! Karl Popper (1902-1994) was considered to be the leading philosopher of science. Very early on he was quoted as saying:

> What makes the origin of life and of the genetic code a disturbing riddle is this: the genetic code is without any biological function unless it is translated; that is, unless it leads to the synthesis of the proteins whose structure is laid down by the code. But. . .the machinery by which the cell

(at least the non-primitive cell, which is the only one we know) translates the code consists of at least fifty macromolecular components which are themselves coded in the DNA. Thus the code can not be translated except by using certain products of its translation. This constitutes a baffling circle; a really vicious circle, it seems, for any attempt to form a model or theory of the genesis of the genetic code. . .

Thus we may be faced with the possibility that the origin of life (like the origin of physics) becomes an impenetrable barrier to science, and a residue to all attempts to reduce biology to chemistry and physics.[8]

Are there any scientists who admit that the Miller-Urey experiment was not successful in vindicating evolutionary speculation regarding the origin of life? Yes! Noam Lahav, author of, *Biogenesis: Theories of Life's Origin* (Oxford University), is just one example.

Soon after the Miller–Urey experiment, many scientists entertained the belief that the main obstacles in the problem of the origin of life would be overcome within the foreseeable future. But as the search in this young scientific field went on and diversified, it became more and more evident that the problem of the origin of life is far from trivial. Various fundamental problems facing workers in this search gradually emerged, and new questions came into focus. . .Despite intensive research, most of these problems have remained unsolved.[9]

Indeed, during the long history of the search into the origin of life, controversy is probably the most characteristic attribute of this interdisciplinary field. There is hardly a model or scenario or fashion in this discipline that is not controversial.[10]

People have every right to believe that life arose spontaneously from non-living chemicals, but they must do so as a statement of faith and it would be the kind of faith that is *in spite* of the evidence and not *in light* of the evidence. It certainly should not be taught as actual science in the classroom.

Will scientists ever be able to create life in the laboratory? My honest answer is. . .I don't know. Why wouldn't I confidently say "no?" If they did create life, wouldn't that prove they were right all along? Let's take a look at this a little further. Let's pretend, for argument's sake, that one day they do actually create a living cell in the laboratory. What do you think would happen? Probably something like the following:

All of the major news networks interrupt their normally scheduled programs to air this absolutely amazing achievement. One of the world's leading biochemists steps up to the microphone, arrayed in his stereotypical full-length white lab coat and says: "Ladies and gentlemen, it gives me great pleasure to announce to you today, that for the first time in the history of mankind, after decades of highly advanced experiments conducted by the most brilliant minds on the planet, using the most sophisticated equipment known to man, we have finally been able to create life in the laboratory, proving beyond the shadow of doubt, that no intelligence was necessary!"

I'm sure you see the irony, but just in case you missed it: What they would actually be proving is that it took a lot of intelligence! Another way of looking at it would be to ask a follow-up question. "Excuse me professor, but did you put any intelligence into your experiments?" How would he respond? If he said "no" he would obviously be lying. If he said "yes" he would be admitting that it did take intelligence to create life, which is the main point of the argument. The argument isn't whether or not man can create life, but rather, does life simply appear on its own, as a natural, inevitable result of time, matter and chance or is intelligence necessary? This would simply serve to support the idea that directed, purposeful intelligence is necessary, which is further confirmation of the biblical narrative.

Scientists may very well hope to one day create life in the laboratory, but if our scientific proclamations are to be based upon what we actually observe today in the real world, it is purely a matter of faith that this will ever happen. The best evidence we currently have indicates that the origin of life requires an outside causal intelligent agent. It is only someone's ingrained worldview that would allow them to conclude otherwise, as George Wald did.

> When it comes to the origin of life there are only two possibilities: creation or spontaneous generation. There is no third way. Spontaneous generation was disproved one hundred years ago, but that leads us to only one other conclusion, that of supernatural creation. We cannot accept that on philosophical grounds; therefore, we choose to believe the impossible: that life arose spontaneously by chance![11]

Wald is certainly not the only person to choose an evolutionary scenario in spite of the fact that science continues to confirm that life does not arise spontaneously from non-living chemicals.

Francis Crick, Nobel Prize winning co-discoverer of the DNA molecule and avowed atheist, stated in 1982:

> An honest man, armed with all the knowledge available to us now, could only state that in some sense, the origin of life appears at the moment to be almost a miracle, so many are the conditions which would have had to have been satisfied to get it going.[12]

Why "almost" a miracle? Well, Crick has already decided that God does not exist, so therefore, it could not possibly be a miracle. This isn't too much different than this satirical scenario. You come home one evening to find a person crawling out your kitchen window and you make the following observations:

- He is dressed in all black.

- He has a ski mask over his face.

- He is wearing black gloves, even though it's mid-summer.

- The kitchen window has been smashed in.

- He has a crowbar in one hand and all your jewelry in the other.

You stop him in his tracks and say to him, "If I didn't know better, I would say you are a robber. But since I don't believe in robbers, I will have to let you go!"

So what is Dr. Crick saying? Is he saying he now believes that God created life? Not at all! His worldview will not allow for that option. He prefers to believe that alien life forms somewhere in outer space (beyond our detection and verification) created life in seed form and sent it to this planet billions of years ago. Crick elaborates on this theory, which he calls "directed panspermia" in his book, *Life Itself: Its Origin and Nature* (1981, Simon and Schuster). One of the more interesting statements found in this book (page 153) is,

> Every time I write a paper on the origin of life, I determine I will never write another one, because there is too much speculation running after too few facts.[13]

What is the current state regarding the view on the origin of life? Those who are truly informed realize that we are possibly farther away from finding a natural solution than we were when Miller and Urey began experimenting back in the 1950s. Even Richard Dawkins admits we just don't know. In the documentary, *Expelled: No Intelligence Allowed*,[14] producer Ben Stein asks Richard Dawkins how life started:

Stein: "How did it start?"

Dawkins: "Nobody knows how it started. We know the kind of event it must have been. We know the sort of event that must have happened for the origin of life."

Stein: "And what was that?"

Dawkins: "It was the origin of the first self-replicating molecule."

Stein: "Right, and how did that happen?"

Dawkins: "I told you we don't know."

Stein: "So you have no idea how it started?"

Dawkins: "No, no. Nor has anybody."

So the theory of organic evolution (life from non-life) takes us "from soup to nuts," meaning from the alleged primordial soup from which life sprang, to beings who are crazy enough to believe that it all happened by accident! (This is only intended as light-hearted humor and to explain the rationalization for the chapter title. I do not wish to convey any disrespect for those individuals who hold views that differ from my own.)

We'll wrap things-up with a few quotes from scientists who are willing to be fairly transparent regarding the lack of evolutionary explanations for the origin of life.

Ken Nealson (professor of earth sciences and biological sciences, University of Southern California):

> Nobody understands the origin of life. If they say they do, they are probably trying to fool you.[15]

Freeman Dyson (British-American theoretical physicist and mathematician):

> Concerning the origin of life itself, the watershed between chemistry and biology, the transition between lifeless chemical activity and organized biological metabolism, there is no direct evidence at all. The crucial transition from disorder to order left behind no observable traces.[16]

Dr. Per Bak (theoretical physicist, Niels Bohr Institute, Copenhagen):

> We are nowhere near understanding the origin of life. But let us try to avoid invoking miracles.[17]

Paul Davies (professor of physics, Arizona State University):

> We now know that the secret of life lies not with the chemical ingredients as such, but with the logical structure and organizational arrangement of the molecules. . .Like a supercomputer, life is an information processing system. . .It is the software of the living cell that is the real mystery, not

the hardware. . .How did stupid atoms spontaneously write their own software?. . .Nobody knows. . .[18]

Alright, just one more quote (from a writer who was inspired by someone who just happens to know a little something about the origin of life):

You give life to everything, and the multitudes of heaven worship you (Nehemiah 9:6b, NIV).

ENDNOTES

1. http://dictionary.reference.com/browse/life.

2. Flowers, C., *A Science Odyssey: 100 Years of Discovery*, William Morrow and Company, New York, p. 173, 1998.

3. Jamali, F., Lovlin, R., Corrigan, B.W., Davies, N.M., and Aberg, G., "Stereospecific pharmacokinetics and toxicodynamics of ketorolac after oral administration of the racemate and optically pure enantiomers to the rat," *Chirality* 11(3):201-205, 1999. > Coppedge, J.F., Probability of left-handed molecules, *CRSQ* 8:163-174, 1971.

4. Possibly even 400—see http://creation.com/why-the-miller-urey-research-argues-against-abiogenesis—*last accessed 9/18/10.*

5. Spetner, Lee M., *Not by Chance: Shattering the Modern Theory of Evolution*, The Judaica Press 1997, p. 31.

6. Hoyle, Fred, "The Big Bang in Astronomy," *New Scientist,* 92(1280):527, 19 Nov 198.1

7. http://en.wikipedia.org/wiki/Rubic%27s_Cube—Last accessed 9/18/10.

8. Popper, K.R., "Scientific reduction and the essential incompleteness of all science," in: Ayala, F. and Dobzhansky, T. (Eds.), *Studies in the Philosophy of Biology*, University of California Press, Berkeley, p. 270, 1974.

9. Lahav, N., *Biogenesis: Theories of Life's Origin*, Oxford University, New York, 1999, p.50.

10. Ibid.

11. Wald, George, "The Origin of Life," *Scientific American*, 191:48, May 1954.

12. Crick, Francis, *Life Itself—Its Origin and Nature*, Futura, 1982, p.88.

13. Ibid.. p. 153

14. "Expelled: No Intelligence Allowed" (2008) Produced by Ben Stein. http://www.amazon.com/Expelled-Intelligence-Allowed-Ben-Stein/dp/B001BYLFFS.

15. Nealson, Ken, "The search for the scum of the universe," www.space. com/scienceastronomy/astronomy/odds_of_et_ 020521-1.html.

16. Dyson, Freeman, *Origins of Life*, New York, NY, Cambridge University Press, 1999, p.36.

17. *New Scientist,* 160(2155):47, October 10, 1998.

18. Davies, P., "Life force," *New Scientist,* 163(2204):27-30, September 18, 1999.

The Fossil Record: A View to the Past

So far, we've discussed the origin of the universe and the origin of life, but to be honest, these topics are not what most people envision when they think about evolution. They aren't necessarily thinking about getting "something out of nothing" or non-living chemicals coming together to form the first single-celled living organism. What they do have in mind is one type of creature slowly turning into something slightly different, starting with less complex life forms and progressing upward through amphibians, reptiles, mammals, primates and human beings (over vast, vast periods of time).

In this chapter we will turn our attention to the great variety of life we see on this planet and specifically which worldview (biblical creation or evolution) best explains what we observe.

When we look at the great variety of life around us, we certainly see some amazing creatures, many of which look nothing like each other. Two examples are

the octopus and the toucan. No one supposes that the octopus turned into the toucan by making a few, slight modifications. However, there are many creatures that do look quite similar and it is much easier to envision one slowly turning into the other, with only a few variations here and there. Take, for example, the horse and the zebra. We can easily envision them having a common ancestor (or even one changing into the other). So is it plausible that molecules-to-man evolution has occurred? Some would say, "There's just no way!" while others would respond by saying, "You know, I can kind of picture it happening, given small changes over a long period of time." We'll have to examine all of this more closely to see which of these responses is truly more appropriate (or maybe the solution lies somewhere in the middle). . .we'll just have to wait and see.

MODELS AND PREDICTIONS

Before we delve any further into this subject, we should take a look at what each of the two major worldviews (models) teach regarding the variety of life and origin of species.

Evolution teaches that approximately 3.8 billion years ago, a single-celled organism came into being that was able to reproduce itself and did so over and over for millions and millions of years. Along the way, occasional changes occurred (some good, some bad), allowing the organism to be slightly improved. This continued for a few billion years and led to the variety of life we see today. In other words, all living creatures have descended from a common ancestor over multiplied millions and billions of years. If this view is true, we should be able to discover supportive evidence of this not only in the fossil record but also in the laboratory.

Biblical creation posits that God created different "kinds" of creatures, fully formed right from the beginning and although they could produce a variety of offspring, they always reproduce '"after their kind" (cf. Genesis 1:11-12, 1:21, 1:24-25), meaning there are limits to how far they can vary. As with the evolutionary model, if this view is correct, we should be able to see supportive evidence of this in the fossil record, as well as in the laboratory.

We can get a better feel for these two origins models from the following illustrations:

Tree of life according to modern evolutionary theory: (Figure A)

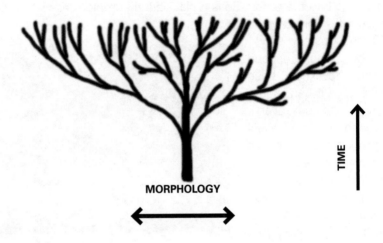

MORPHOLOGY

TIME

Tree of life according to the biblical account of creation: (Figure B)

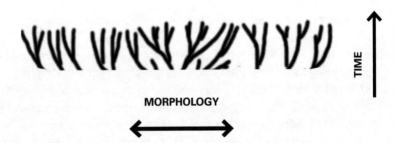

MORPHOLOGY

TIME

Figure A represents all life coming from a single common ancestor that branched off into all other life forms over a few billion years, with some forms becoming extinct along the way. Figure B represents many kinds of life forms being created right from the beginning, many of which produced an interesting but limited variety of the same type (kind) of creature. In this second representation, we also have the phenomenon of extinction.

In the remainder of this chapter we will take a look at specific predictions that each model makes and also what science reveals regarding these two diametrically opposed views. One of the best validations for a theory or model is how well actual discoveries line up with what was predicted. We'll elucidate predictions in a number of categories for both our models and then put them to the test. (In reality, the testing has already been complete for quite some time. We are simply reviewing the results.)

THE IMPORTANCE OF THE FOSSIL RECORD

It is easily discerned from the following quotes that the fossil record is invaluable when considering the case for evolution:

> Although the comparative study of living animals and plants may give very convincing circumstantial evidence, fossils provide the only historical, documentary evidence that life has evolved from simpler to more and more complex forms.[1]

> The most direct evidence that evolution has occurred is presented in the study of the fossils.[2]

> Naturalists must remember that the process of evolution is revealed only through fossil forms; only paleontology can provide them with the evidence of evolution and reveal its course or mechanisms.[3]

> It is doubtful whether, in the absence of fossils, the idea of evolution would represent anything more than an outrageous hypothesis. . .The fossil record and only the fossil record provides direct evidence of major sequential changes in the earth's biota [regional life forms].[4]

So according to Steven Stanley, PhD (professor of geology at Johns Hopkins University, 1969-2005), without the fossil record, evolution would likely be just "an outrageous hypothesis," to use his own words. Keep that intriguing thought in mind as we continue.

FIRST APPEARANCE OF LIFE: PREDICTION

Let's start with considering the first appearance of life in the fossil record. Both creationists and evolutionists agree that the fossil record contains a record of life forms that lived and died in the past. They may argue greatly as to how long ago that was (which we cover in the chapters on the age of the earth), but they are in total agreement regarding it being a record of the history of life.

What does the fossil record tell us? We must again keep in mind that facts don't really tell us anything directly. They must all be interpreted by our worldview to have any significant meaning. Not surprisingly, evolutionists and creationists interpret the fossil record quite differently. (At least when comparing the standard evolutionary model to a literal six-day creation account. We also cover the different views of Genesis within Christianity in the chapters on the age of the earth.) It is necessary, however, to make an important distinction here. Since we will be discussing the fossil record, we need to understand something about where it is found. You have undoubtedly heard of the geologic column and that it is purported to be an accurate representation of the layers in the earth. Evolutionists believe these layers were laid down over millions of years, thus representing a great deal of time—well over 500 millions years according to secular geologists. As an aside, for more information on the alleged existence and meaning of the geologic column, please see "The Geologic Column: Does it Exist?" (Woodmorappe, John, *Technical Journal* 13(2):77–82, November 1999). Creationists who view Genesis as representing a literal six-day creation account believe that most of these layers were deposited rapidly and catastrophically during the Noahic flood (Genesis 6-8). These diametrically opposed views greatly affect the interpretation of the fossils themselves.

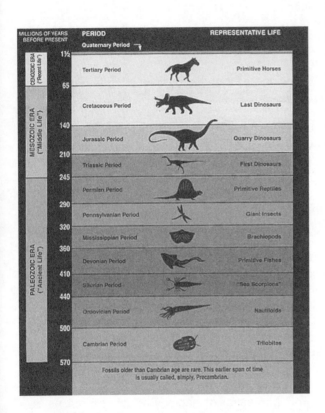

The evolutionary model predicts that the fossil record should show "simple" life forms appearing towards the bottom of the geologic column, because they came into being first and were here long before any multi-cellular life evolved. (In reality, there are no "simple" forms of life, but we are using this term in a relative sense for discussion purposes.)

The creationist model would predict that the progression from bottom to top (of the fossil record) would not represent less complex life forms becoming more complex over millions of years, but rather, the catastrophic burial of creatures in their ecological zones at the time of the flood. Let's take a look at the actual evidence.

FIRST APPEARANCE OF LIFE: OBSERVED DATA

The Cambrian and Pre-Cambrian layers in the geologic column are at the bottom, where evolutionists would expect to find the first signs of the alleged initial "simple" single-celled organisms. However, what we actually see is an incredible explosion of highly complex life coming out of virtually nowhere! The term used to describe this phenomenon is called the "Cambrian explosion." This event (allegedly occurring 530 million years ago) was described by *Scientific American*

as, "Evolutionary biology's deepest paradox."[5] *Time* magazine (December 4, 1995), featured a cover story about this event, entitling it, "Evolution's Big Bang." However, they were not referring to the cosmological big bang that they vociferously believe gave birth to our entire universe. The Cambrian explosion in contrast, was an event in which virtually every major phyla (body plan) appeared suddenly, out of nowhere, fully formed!

> It is considered likely that all the animal phyla became distinct before or during the Cambrian, for they all appear fully formed, without intermediates connecting one form to another.[6]

Referring to the discovery of fossils of highly complex life in the Cambrian rocks, Richard Dawkins stated:

> It is as though they were just planted there, without any evolutionary history. Needless to say, this appearance of sudden planting has delighted creationists.[7]

As an example, we have fossils of trilobites, which posses the most complex eye known to man. This hardly qualifies as an example of "simple, single-celled life" and there are no examples of trilobites with simpler eyes earlier in the fossil record (or even simpler trilobites). This is certainly not what the evolutionists

0.5 cm

were hoping to find. On the other hand, it fits very nicely with the creation model—that God created creatures fully formed and fully functional, all within the six-day creation week, having truly come "out of nowhere."

GENERAL ORDER OF THE FOSSIL RECORD: PREDICTION

Regarding the general order of the entire fossil record, the evolutionary model would predict that "simple" life forms would appear toward the bottom of the geologic column, progressing slowly into more and more complex life forms as you travel up through the layers, and hence, up through allegedly millions and millions of years of evolutionary history.

The creationist model would predict that the appearance of fossils would represent, not *when* a particular life form came into being and *when* they lived, but rather *where* they lived, in general, being subsequently buried at the time of the flood. There is one other aspect associated with the flood model. Obviously, some creatures are much more mobile than others (compare a star fish and a cheetah). The more mobile an animal is, the better suited it would be to avoid the rising flood waters. Generally speaking, the more mobile animals not only would be the last to be buried, but most of them would probably just drown and decompose without leaving any traces.

GENERAL ORDER OF THE FOSSIL RECORD: OBSERVED DATA

What we actually observe fits very well with the Genesis creation account, or more specifically, the catastrophic flood model.

In layers believed to have formed *before* the flood (i.e., those within the Chuar Group) we find fossils of single-celled creatures such as algae and mound formations formed by algae called stromatolites. The fossilization of these creatures does not require catastrophic conditions in order to form, but rather it requires calm environmental conditions, which is what we would expect prior to the flood itself.

In layers believed to have been laid down in the earliest stages of the flood, we find shallow seafloor marine invertebrates (e.g., trilobites and brachiopods). Invertebrates are creatures that do not have backbone. It is also interesting to note that marine invertebrates are found in almost every level of the fossil record. This is completely consistent with the fact that the ocean waters rose and subsequently washed over the continents, carrying with them these creatures. This is also consistent with a catastrophic flood, but not with evolution and deposition over hundreds of millions of years.

In later (higher-up) layers we find fish fossils, but we do not begin to see them until we reach the Temple Butte Limestone level. (See any standard textbook or the internet for a listing of the various layers in the geologic column, but be prepared to read all of the associated evolutionary verbiage that is almost always present.)

We do not find fossil plants or amphibian and reptile footprints until we reach the "Supai Group." Regarding fossils of the land vertebrates, even though we found their footprints lower in the rock record, we don't find their bodies until much later (higher) in the record (e.g., the Moenkopi Formation). Dinosaurs are not seen until even higher (Moenave Formation) and mammals are not seen until you reach the top!

Why would this pattern seem to fit flood geology so well? It's fairly simple. Those living in the lower elevations, specifically seafloor level, would be buried first. Others might be able to attempt to escape the rising flood waters, hence leaving their tracks in one set of layers, but eventually, not being able to keep up with the rising waters, be buried in later, higher up layers. Those that were the most mobile would typically be the last to be buried. As mentioned earlier, there would have been many that were never buried at all, because they simply drowned, which then led to the decomposition of their bodies, not leaving anything to fossilize.

As long as we're on the subject, we could ask why we don't find more fossils of people. You may not be asking that question because you are under the impression that we have a lot of human fossils skeletons and are constantly finding more. In reality, (a) we don't have very many human specimens and (b) it is very rare that one is unearthed. So why don't we find them? We have unearthed literally billions of fossils; where are all the human skeletons?

It's pretty easy to understand once you get a better grasp of the fossil record in general. Here's a breakdown of fossils on a percentage basis:

• 95%—shallow marine invertebrates (e.g., corals and shellfish)

• 5%—all other fossil types

Let's look further into the 5% ("all other types"). Hang in there while we look at a bunch of numbers. A full 95% of this 5% (which is 4.75%) are algae and plant/

tree fossils. The remaining 5% of this 5% category consists of vertebrates (fish, amphibians, reptiles, birds and mammals). This amounts to only 0.25% of the entire fossil record! But it gets even more interesting. Only 1% of this miniscule 0.25% (which equates to 0.0025%) are vertebrate fossils that consist of more than just one bone![8]

Another way of looking at this is to run through the following scenario. Let's assume that there were about 10 million people living at the time of the flood (a reasonable estimate given that it had been over 1,600 years since the creation of Adam and Eve). Let's also assume that every single body had been preserved evenly distributed throughout the estimated 167,939,000 cubic miles of sedimentary (fossil-bearing) layers in the earth. Even with the extremely unreasonable assumption of every human being buried and fossilized, you would still find only one person in every 17 cubic miles of sediment! It truly would be very rare that you would ever come across an example of a human fossil (even given these highly unlikely favorable conditions.[9]

TRANSITIONS WITHIN THE FOSSIL RECORD: PREDICTION

Our two models also make predictions regarding what might be called "transitional forms" within the fossil record. The evolutionary model would predict that between two supposedly directly related life forms, there would be a series of "intermediates," representing the slow, gradual change of one creature into another.

Using a very simplified example, consider the two main objects in Figure 1. If the circular object on the left were to slowly transform into the starred object on the right over a period of time, it might do so through a series of transitions as pictured in Figure 2.

Figure 1

Figure 2

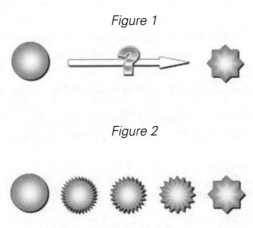

One would expect that there would be numerous transitional stages, as depicted in our simple example.

The creation model would predict that although you might see a variety of a certain type of creature, there would be definite limits and that each specimen would be fully formed, not simply "on its way" to becoming something else. In other words, you would see creatures with feathers and creatures without feathers, but none that are "on their way" to developing feathers (e.g., something with features that were half scale/half feather).

TRANSITIONS WITHIN THE FOSSIL RECORD: OBSERVED DATA

What we have observed through our scientific inquiry is that there exist large gaps between groups of creatures, such as in between invertebrates and vertebrates, amphibians and reptiles, reptiles and birds, etc. Evolutionists are always on the hunt for the proverbial "missing link" which would fill the gap (or more accurately, fit in the gap). The trouble is that there's not just one gap to fill and none of the gaps could be filled with a single or even a few missing links.

I recently happened to notice a book sitting on a teacher's desk entitled, *Why Evolution is True* (Coyne, Jerry, Penguin Press, 2009). The picture on the cover caught my attention. It depicts the evolution of modern birds from a dinosaur, which is widely accepted among evolutionists today. There are four creatures pictured in the transition. Keep that in mind: four. Why is this significant? In and of itself, it's not, but when I opened the book to read the inside flap of the jacket cover, it became somewhat humorous:

> The jacket depicts a chronological sequence of fossils showing the evolution of birds. We do not know whether the actual line of descent included the first three…"

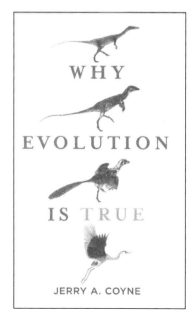

What? You're not sure about the first three? That only leaves one, which is a picture of a great blue heron (a modern bird)! How ironic! I couldn't help but read and re-read that statement with a puzzled look on my face. It somewhat reminded me of something funny I heard many years ago from Steve Martin. (I am not endorsing him as a comedian, however. He is very gifted, but some of his humor is certainly not appropriate.) In one of his performances, he conveyed the following:

You can be a millionaire and never pay taxes! Yes, you can be a millionaire and never pay taxes. People come to me and say "Steve, how can I be a millionaire and never pay taxes?" First, get a million dollars. Next. . ."

The humor was mainly in the fact that he left out all the details of how to get that much money to begin with! Not a minor detail!

Evolutionists would like us to think that many transitional examples have been discovered, but each one of these is very controversial at best and generally turns out to be disqualified after further investigation. Here's how it generally works, and how the public is duped into believing that the "missing links" have been discovered. A fossil discovery will be announced with great fanfare and given much publicity (e.g., being published on the cover of *National Geographic* or *Time* magazine, as well as discussed on all the network nightly news channels). The unveiling will include some very impressive photos or video of the find, adding to the excitement and alleged authenticity of the discovery. The world is informed that "proof" of evolution is once more confirmed and that no truly educated person would even consider doubting it. Many Christians will embrace the findings, feeling that God is all-powerful and could "create" things any way He wishes, and if He chose to use evolution, who are we to question it. (We address this view further in chapter 9.) Others, who believe in the literal six-day creation account, often nervously choose to not think about what is being presented and feel compelled to make sure their "faith" is strong enough to withstand the latest attack on their beliefs. Unfortunately for many of these people, their faith becomes weaker and weaker, often to the point where they walk away altogether, because there's too much of a struggle going on in their mind and they can no longer justify taking the Bible so seriously versus "living in the real world" and not having to "constantly reject science" (or so they feel). This is a very real dilemma for many people, but it is a false dichotomy. They do not have to make that choice, because true science always lines up with what Scripture teaches. The problem is that the church today not only doesn't have a good general understanding of how science works, but there is also way too much Biblical illiteracy! We take bad science and compare it to our weak view of Scripture and end up making erroneous conclusions, which is not at all surprising.

Continuing on with our "missing link" discovery story, what almost always happens is that some time after the announcement, whether days, weeks or months, additional opinions are rendered on the find that disqualify it from being evidence for evolution. However, this is not given the same exaggerated fanfare as was the initial announcement. You won't see the retraction on the cover of any magazine or in any television news stories. It will generally only appear buried deep within the original publication or in some obscure technical journal to which almost no one subscribes. So the public is left with the impression that once again, proof of evolution has been discovered, with the implied message being you cannot trust the Bible. *"When will you Christians ever get a clue! How much longer are you going to blindly cling to your Bibles? When are you going to join the rest of us who live in the 'real world'?"*

EXAMPLES OF OVER-HYPED DISCOVERIES

Archaeopteryx

One example of an over-hyped discovery was *Archaeopteryx*—a supposed missing link between dinosaurs and birds. (As we previously mentioned, according to (modern evolutionary thinking, birds are alleged to have evolved from dinosaurs.) The first specimen was discovered in Bavaria (Germany) in 1861. It was heralded loudly and claimed to be a "feathered dinosaur" (hence, transitional between dinosaurs and birds). Some (including evolutionists)

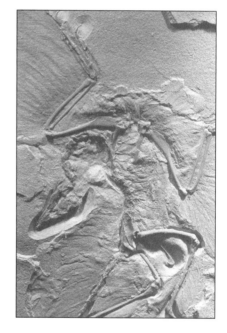

however, alleged that *Archaeopteryx* was a fraud. Further examination revealed that it truly was a legitimate fossil, but had nothing to do with the transition of dinosaurs into birds. Two major features that were initially of particular interest (and which led to it being considered a transition) were its long, drooping tail and teeth in its beak. Modern birds do not have teeth, but a number of extinct birds do. In short, *Archaeopteryx* was a fully-formed bird, not just on its way to becoming one. Alan Feduccia, world-renowned expert on birds stated:

> Paleontologists have tried to turn *Archaeopteryx* into an earth-bound, feathered dinosaur. But it's not. It is a bird, a perching bird. And no amount of 'paleobabble' is going to change that.[10]

One significant factor in dethroning *Archaeopteryx* as a true missing link is the fact that fossils of fully formed birds have been found lower in the geologic record, which, according to evolutionists, would represent a time period significantly earlier than when *Archaeopteryx* supposedly lived.[11] *Archaeopteryx* certainly could not be an ancestor to modern birds if birds had already existed for some time.

Sadly, *Archaeopteryx* still appears in many school textbooks and museums as an example of a "missing link" and as a testimony to Darwinian evolution.

Archaeoraptor

Another example of an over-hyped discovery was that of Archaeoraptor. In 1999 *National Geographic* published a find that was illegally imported from China. The article was entitled, "Feathers for T-Rex?"[12] It was alleged to have been the missing transition from dinosaurs to birds. Many bold claims were made. The article stated, ". . .we can now say that birds are theropods just as confidently as we say that humans are mammals. Everything from lunch boxes to museum exhibits will change to reflect this revelation."[13]

It turned out that the Archaeoraptor fossil was a fraud! A Chinese farmer unearthed fossils from two different locations and glued them together, then illegally sold it on the black market. It was a combination of the head and body of a bird-like creature and the tail of a dinosaur. The composite fossil eventually found its way to Utah where it was displayed in a small dinosaur museum.

Storrs Olson (curator of birds, National Museum of Natural History at the Smithsonian Institution, Washington DC) chimed-in with the following comments:[14]

> National Geographic has reached an all-time low for engaging in sensationalistic, unsubstantiated, tabloid journalism.

> Sloan's article takes the prejudice to an entirely new level and consists in large part of unverifiable or undocumented information that 'makes' the news rather than reporting it.

> The feathered dinosaur pictures are] simply imaginary and have no place outside of science fiction.

Shortly after this hoax, another fraud was discovered in China involving a faked tail attached to a flying pterosaur. This one even fooled editors of the prestigious journal, *Nature*.

Tiktaalik

In 2006, the secular media grandiosely announced the discovery of *Tiktaalik*, which they claimed lived 375 million years ago and was a transition between fish and tetrapods (four-limbed vertebrates, such as amphibians, reptiles and mammals). One specific claim was that *Tiktaalik's* fins evolved into legs and were used for walking. However, these fins were not connected to the main skeleton and therefore, could not have supported its own weight on land. Even if

Tiktaalik was a legitimate transition, it wouldn't solve the huge gap issue related to the origin of tetrapods:

> Of course, there are still major gaps in the fossil record. In particular we have almost no information about the step between *Tiktaalik* and the earliest tetrapods. . .[15]

Much more could be said regarding this alleged missing link, but a fairly recent discovery is probably the most significant. In January 2010, tetrapod footprints were discovered, in Poland, in rock layers that are considered by evolutionists to

Drawing by Nobu Tamura

be *18 million years older than Tiktaalik!* According to this discovery, tetrapods had already been around for millions of years, which would instantly dethrone *Tiktaalik* as their ancestor. (Note: I do not accept these conventional dates of millions of years, but am simply pointing out that even according to the evolutionists own naturalistic system, *Tiktaalik* is disqualified.) ScienceDaily.com reported:

> These results force us to reconsider our whole picture of the transition from fish to land animals.[16]

Ida

A fourth over-hyped example is that of *Darwinius masillae* or "Ida," as she is commonly known. The fossil was discovered in 1983 just outside of Frankfurt, Germany, and was nicknamed after the daughter of the owner of the museum where it has been housed since 2007. Its announcement was purposely timed to coincide with a scientific paper, a new documentary and a book on the fossil. Its unveiling was conveniently in 2009, which just happened to be Charles Darwin's 200th birthday and the 150th anniversary of the publication of *The Origin of Species*. For further detail on this particular "discovery," along with its dethroning and numerous interesting quotes, see chapter 7 on the origin of man.

With Ida, the public has once again had etched forever on their minds more "visual proof" of evolution, never realizing that this was just one more example of "much ado about nothing."

When discoveries such as this fall out of favor, as this one already has, evolutionists typically only admit to problems when something new comes along which apparently solves the dilemma or allows them to go off in a new direction. There have been countless times when headlines read something like: "New Find Baffles Scientists" or "Just About Everything We Believed is Wrong." Instead of being able to get excited, thinking that maybe, just maybe, they are willing to rethink things and admit that evolution really is not a valid scientific viewpoint, they just tell us how the amazing new discovery is still highly supportive of evolution, it's just that it didn't happen the way they used to think. My question has always been: If you've been wrong time and time again about your hypotheses and have constantly replaced them with something significantly different (and often contradictory), why should we believe that you are actually correct this time?

The History Channel used the phrase: "The most important find in 47 million years."[17] When Hurum (co-author of the original article) was asked if he thought the sensationalism surrounding the find was overdone, he didn't think so, stating, "That's part of getting science out to the public to get attention. I don't think that's so wrong."[18]

THE FOSSIL RECORD: CONCLUSION

Darwin himself was very aware of the lack of evidence from the fossil record and referred to is as potentially being the "greatest objection" to his theory:

> . . .numerable transitional forms must have existed but why do we not find them embedded in countless numbers in the crust of the earth?. . .why is not every geological formation and every stratum full of such intermediate links? Geology assuredly does not reveal any such finely graduated organic chain, and this perhaps is the greatest objection which can be urged against my theory.[19]

He chose to shrug off this apparent enigma, however, by assuming that it was only due to the lack of exploration. We just had not unearthed enough fossils yet. Stephen J. Gould (1941–2002) who was one of the world's leading evolutionists, commented on the lack of transitional forms referring to the phenomenon of "stasis," or staying the same and abrupt appearance, meaning fully-formed creatures coming out of nowhere:

> We have long known about stasis and abrupt appearance, but have chosen to fob it off upon an imperfect fossil record.[20]

> Everybody knows the fossil record doesn't provide much evidence for gradualism; it is full of gaps and discontinuities. . .most species don't change.

They may get a little bigger or bumpier, but they remain the same species. This remarkable stasis has generally been ignored. It if doesn't agree with your ideas, you don't talk about it. . .the fossil record doesn't show gradual change, and every paleontologist has known that ever since Cuvier.[21]

Today, one cannot skirt the issue by claiming the fossil record is too incomplete, because it has become extremely rich. Most credible scientists don't try to use the imperfection of the fossil record as an excuse. However, they also are not fazed by the lack of evidence either. Some have cleverly adjusted their model to better match what is actually observed (or in this case, what is not observed).

PUNCTUATED EQUILIBRIUM TO THE RESCUE (OR NOT)

Punctuated what? As I just mentioned, some have concocted theories that attempt to better coincide with the lack of transitional fossils in the rock record. We will touch on this very briefly, although much could be said regarding this topic. The most prevalent view among a relatively small percentage of evolutionists is a concept called "punctuated equilibrium." "Punctuated" refers to something being emphasized or accentuated and "equilibrium" alludes to stability or "staying the same":

> Did life on Earth change steadily and gradually through time? The fossil record emphatically says no. For millions of years, life goes along uneventfully; then suddenly, a series of natural disasters disrupts the status quo. Episodes of rapid evolutionary change punctuate long intervals of stasis, during which little or no change takes place.[22]

This view was popularized by the late Stephen J. Gould in the early 1970s. Gould refers to the main reason a new theory is needed:

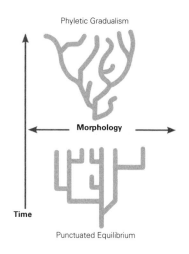

> The absence of fossil evidence for intermediary stages between major transitions in organic design, indeed our inability, even in our imagination, to construct functional intermediates in many cases, has been a persistent and nagging problem for gradualist accounts of evolution.[23]

Compared to Darwinian evolution, Gould's hypothesis represents a vastly different view than what Charles Darwin had in mind. The traditional evolutionary view is that life forms changed gradually and very slowly over multiplied millions of years. The theory of punctuated equilibrium proposes that instead of slow, gradual change, evolution proceeded by large and relatively quick changes, followed by very long periods of little or no change at all. In this view, the changes happened so quickly that they generally were not recorded in the fossil record.

The idea of slow, gradual evolution has numerous insurmountable barriers in and of itself (genetic and otherwise) and the idea of "rapid evolution" only serves to confound them even further. For the evolutionist, the theory of punctuated equilibrium sets up a "head's we win, tails you lose" scenario. If they ever truly do discover legitimate transitional forms (and many of them) they will claim it is proof of the traditional slow, gradual Darwinian evolution. If these transitions are not found, they will claim that it is evidence for "punctuated equilibrium" (it happened so fast, you couldn't see it). In reality, it is a theory based on a lack of evidence. This is evidenced by a statement from Dr. Colin Patterson (1933-1998, British Museum of Natural History in London; was one of the leaders of the philosophy of biological systematics):

> Well, it seems to me that they have accepted that the fossil record doesn't give them the support they would value so they searched around to find another model and found one. . .When you haven't got the evidence, you make up a story that will fit the lack of evidence.[24]

This obviously is not any more credible than saying you have a theory that there are millions of invisible, imperceptible green aliens all around us and that the fact that you have never seen them is proof they are there!

The fossil record has failed to provide support for Darwinian evolutionary theory and even a few evolutionists will admit to this:

> Niles Eldredge (American paleontologist) and Ian Tattersall (paleoanthropologist and curator at the American Museum of Natural History): "He [Darwin] prophesied that future generations of paleontologists would fill in these gaps by diligent search. . .One hundred and twenty years of paleontological research later, it has become abundantly clear that the fossil record will not confirm this part of Darwin's predictions. Nor is the problem a miserably poor record. The fossil record simply shows that this prediction was wrong."[25]

> Mark Ridley (British zoologist): ". . .a lot of people just do not know what evidence the theory of evolution stands upon. They think that the main evidence is the gradual descent of one species from another in the fossil record. . .In any case, no real evolutionist, whether gradualist or punctuationist, uses the fossil record as evidence in favour of the theory of evolution as opposed to special creation."[26]

So how is it that most people, including scientists, believe the fossil record actually supports Darwinian evolution? Professor David Raup (paleontologist, University of Chicago) sheds some light on this question:

> A large number of well-trained scientists outside of evolutionary biology and paleontology have unfortunately gotten the idea that the fossil record is far more Darwinian than it is. This probably comes from the oversimplification inevitable in secondary sources: low-level textbooks, semipopular [sic] articles, and so on. Also, there is probably some wishful thinking involved. In the years after Darwin, his advocates hoped to find predictable progressions. In general these have not been found, yet the optimism has died hard and some pure fantasy has crept into textbooks.[27]

CLOSING POINTS

The story of evolution is one of small changes acting over unimaginably long periods of time, starting with a single-celled organism and continuing on up through modern man. If true, the fossil record should confirm this, but as we have seen, it simply does not. Furthermore, a fossil in and of itself can never be used as evidence for evolution, because it is nothing more than the remains of a dead creature that does not contain a record of any change, only of what it was. Fossils will only "show" evolution within the context of first believing that evolution has occurred and then proceeding to construct a story of how one fossil was the ancestor of another. The science textbook, *Biology* (McGraw-Hill, 1994), stated:

> Many people suppose that phylogeny can be discovered directly from the fossil record by studying a graded series of old to young fossils and by discovering ancestors, but this is not true. The fossil record supplies evidence of the geological ages of the forms of life, but not of their direct ancestor-descendant relationships. There is no way of knowing whether a fossil is a direct ancestor of a more recent species or represents a related line of descent (lineage) that simply became extinct.[28]

Francis Hitching (British author, journalist and filmmaker) made this profound statement:

> It takes a while to realize that the "thousands" of intermediates being referred to have no obvious relevance to the origin of lions and jellyfish and things. Most of them are simply varieties of a particular kind of creature, artificially arranged in a certain order to demonstrate Darwinism at work, and then rearranged every time a new discovery casts doubt upon the arrangement.[29]

"Missing links" have come and gone and will continue to do so because of the unwillingness to let go of the evolutionary paradigm, which must be maintained at all cost, even at the expense of reputable science. The fossil record truly gives us great insight into the history of life on Earth. However, far from constituting one of the strongest lines of evidence for evolution, it stands as a great testament to the catastrophic event of the Genesis flood.

ENDNOTES

1.   Dunbar, Carl, *Historical Geology*, John Wiley & Sons Inc. (1970), p. 47.

2.   Stephenson, W., *Zoology*, McGraw-Hill Companies (2006), p. 249.

3.   Grassé, Pierre, *Evolution of Living Organisms*, Academic Press, New York, 1977, p. 82.

4.   Stanley, S.M., *New Evolutionary Timetable*, Basic Books, p.72, 1981

5.   Levinton, J., "The Big Bang of Animal Evolution," *Scientific American*, November 1992, pp.52-59.

6.   Futuyma, Douglas, *Evolutionary Biology*, Sinauer Associates, 1985, p.325.

7.   Dawkins, Richard, *The Blind Watchmaker*, [1986], Penguin: London, 1991, reprint, p.229.

8.   *Creation*, 14(1):28-33, December 1991.

9.   Catchpoole, Sarfati, Wieland and Batten, *The Creation Answers Book*,, Creation Book Publishers, LLC, 2007, p. 198

10. Feduccia, A.; cited in: V. Morell, "Archaeopteryx: Early Bird Catches a Can of Worms," *Science* 259(5096):764-65, 5 February 1993.

11. *Nature*, 322; 8-21-1986; *Science* 253; 7-5-1991.

12. Sloan, Christopher P., *National Geographic*, Vol. 196, No. 5, November, 1999, pp.98-107.

13. Ibid., p.102.

14. Olson, S.L., open letter to: Dr Peter Raven, Secretary, Committee for Research and Exploration, National Geographic Society

15. Ahlberg, P.E. and Clack, J.A., "Palaeontology: A firm step from water to land," *Nature*, 440(7085):747-749, 6 April 2006.

16. Ahlberg, Per, "Fossil Footprints Give Land Vertebrates a Much Longer History," *ScienceDaily*, 8 January 2010, http://www.sciencedaily.com/releases/2010/01/100107114420.htm—last accessed 9/19/10.

17. http://www.history.com/content/the-link—Note: This webpage (containing the claim "The most important find in 47 million years.") was created in conjunction with the announcement, but has since been removed.

18. MSNBC.com, "'Missing link' primate likely to stir debate," 5/19/2009, http://www.msnbc.msn.com/id/30826552/—*last accessed 9/19/10.*

19. Darwin, Charles, *The Origin of Species by Means of Natural Selection*, The Modern Library, New York, p. 124-125.

20. Gould, Stephen J., "The Paradox of the First Tier: An Agenda for Paleobiology," *Paleobiology*, 1985, p. 7.

21. Gould, Stephen Jay, lecture at Hobart & William Smith College, 14/2/1980.

22. Brett, Carlton E., "Stasis: Life in the Balance." *Geotimes*, vol. 40, Mar. 1995, p. 18.

23. Gould, Stephen J., "Is a new and general theory of evolution emerging?" *Paleobiology*, Vol. 6(1), January 1980, p. 127.

24. Patterson, Colin, as quoted in Sunderland, Luther, *Darwin's Enigma*, Master Books (1998) p.100.

25. Eldredge, Niles, and Tattersall, Ian, *The Myths of Human Evolution*, New York: Columbia University Press, 1982, p.45-46.

26. Ridley, Mark, *New Scientist*, June, 1981, p.831.

27. Raup, David M., "Evolution and the Fossil Record," *Science*, Vol. 213, No. 4505, 17 July 1981, p.289

28. Knox, B., Ladiges, P., & Evans, B., eds., *Biology*, [1994], McGraw-Hill: Sydney, Australia, 1995, reprint, p.663.

29. Hitching, Francis, *The Neck of the Giraffe: Or Where Darwin Went Wrong*, Pan: London, 1982, p27.

Chapter Six

The Genetic Record: What's Going on Inside?

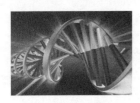

Having just completed a brief look at the fossil record, which is a record of life in the past, we will now turn our focus to examining a record of life in the present. In doing so, we'll largely be transitioning from a world of historical/forensic science into the world of operational science. (Refer back to chapter 2 for an explanation of these two types of science.) When discussing what is believed to be our "evolutionary history," there is a lot of story telling that occurs. With operational science, there is (at least theoretically) less tolerance for "just-so stories" and more room (and need) for repeatable experimentation.

As mentioned in the previous chapter, it doesn't actually take that much imagination to envision one creature slowly changing into something slightly different over time, especially when simply considering their external appearances.

For example, *Tiktaalik* is allegedly thought to be a transitional form ("missing link") between fish and tetrapods (four-legged creatures, such as amphibians, reptiles and mammals). We could envision the front fins maybe slowly becoming stronger, getting longer, developing toes, head getting shorter, etc., and eventually leading to a fully-fledged salamander. One of the major problems with this exercise is that it solely focuses on the external similarities while ignoring the internal

Drawing by Nobu Tamura

Tiktaalik

Salamander

differences, which are what drives the external appearance. This was also an issue for Darwin, who had no idea of the immense complexity and inner workings of the cell (which he considered to be nothing more than a blob of gel-like substance). Consider a simple example of two very similar looking pills. In this case, from the outside they look identical. But let's introduce some additional information about these

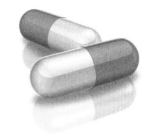

capsules: one is just an aspirin and the other contains hydrogen cyanide—an extremely deadly poison. While being similar on the outside, they are worlds apart internally.

You could also consider comparing an Etch-A-Sketch with an Apple iPad. There are obvious similarities between the two, but there are enormous differences as well, primarily related to the internal contents. You can't just remove the white control knobs on the Etch-A-Sketch, round the corners off, and poof!. . .you have an iPad! While this description of how an iPad arose from an Etch-A-Sketch is inherently ridiculous, it's similar logic to that evolutionists use to describe how *Tiktaalik* evolved into other four-legged creatures (which itself is a process much more complicated than an Etch-A-Sketch evolving into an iPad).

In this chapter we will go "behind the scenes" and explore the internal workings of life in an attempt to determine whether Darwinian concepts are confirmed or discredited.

BAIT AND SWITCH—REVISITED

Back in chapter 1, we discussed the "Bait and Switch" technique. In short, evolution, when stated as being an undeniable fact, is described as molecules naturally turning into every other life form on the planet over a few billion years. However, when they discuss alleged evidence for evolution, a very different definition is generally used—that of "change." We see change (definition 2), so therefore evolution (definition 1) must be true.

The "bait" in this case is telling the general public that evolution is a fact and that you would have to be crazy not to believe in it. Consider the following quotes:

> *Richard Dawkins*: "You cannot be both sane and well educated and disbelieve in evolution. The evidence is so strong that any sane, educated person has got to believe in evolution."[1]

Ernst Mayr. "No educated person any longer questions the validity of the so-called theory of evolution, which we now know to be a simple fact."[2]

The "switch" comes into play when it's time to present the actual evidence. At this point the primary focus is on showing examples of "change" and then equating it to "evolution." In the study of logic and reasoning, this is technically called the fallacy of equivocation, in which two unequal entities are purported to be the same. A simple example would be to say that being "wealthy" is the same thing as being "smart."

The trouble is that most students (and the public in general) do not realize what's happening when the switch occurs. They certainly aren't thinking, "Hey, that's a fallacy of equivocation!" An even more common fallacy of equivocation is that "evolution = science." It is conveyed in the following question: "Evolution is science, and science has created cell phones and computers; do you really want to say you don't believe in science?" In this scenario, if you say you don't believe in evolution, it's the same thing as saying that you don't believe in science. Who would want to say that? No one I know. Consequently, many people are intimidated into accepting evolution out of fear of being viewed as someone who rejects science (thus appearing extremely uneducated and out of touch with reality).

TERMINOLOGY CAUTION

You mostly likely have heard people refer to "micro" and "macro" evolution. Micro evolution is used to refer to small changes within a given type of creature, whereas macro evolution is intended to refer to changes that cause one type of organism to turn into something completely different over time. Some people even say that while they don't believe in macro evolution, they do believe in micro evolution. Others will say that macro evolution is simply the accumulation of micro evolution over long periods of time. While the small changes referred to as being micro evolution certainly do occur, I usually caution people regarding using the term micro evolution. For one reason, it really isn't evolution in the sense that is typically conveyed in the media and in the classroom (which usually refers to the "molecules-to-man" concept). Secondly, it gives people the impression that if there really are small amounts of evolution occurring, given enough time they could theoretically accumulate and produce large-scale change. This however, is not true at all, which we will clearly see in this chapter. I advise people to refer to these small-scale changes simply as variation within a specific kind of organism.

THE ENGINE OF EVOLUTION

Just as an engine is needed for an automobile to function properly, evolution also requires an "engine" of sorts to progress as alleged. "Change" is the undoubted key to evolution, but what actually drives this change? We could also point out that it must be the right kind of change, but we'll get to that later. According to evolutionists, the primary forces driving the evolutionary progress are mutation and natural selection. Let's briefly define each of these and then delve into the roles they play.

Mutation:

> A permanent change in the DNA sequence of a gene. What does that mean? Let's keep it simple for now. When a cell reproduces, it has to make a copy of its DNA, which is the blueprint-like structure that contains the information necessary for its development and functioning. When it makes a random mistake copying some of that information—that's called a mutation. This can occur for a number of reasons, but for now, just think of a mutation as a DNA copying error or misspelling.

Natural Selection:

> Merriam-Webster.com defines "natural selection" as: "a natural process that results in the survival and reproductive success of individuals or groups best adjusted to their environment and that leads to the perpetuation of genetic qualities best suited to that particular environment." This is also often referred to as "survival of the fittest." In simpler terms, it is just a phrase that describes the observation that those creatures best suited to survive in their environment will survive in greater number than those less well-suited (or not fit at all). Therefore, they will pass along their genetic traits in greater number. Over many generations, the organisms in the population consist of these "more beneficial" traits.

One additional essential factor that is not mentioned here is that of a great deal of time—millions and billions of years. We cover this topic in the chapters regarding the age of the earth, so we will not touch on it here, other than to mention that evolution requires these protracted periods of time for the "goo-to-you" process. Now that we've briefly defined these terms, let's explore them in more detail.

MUTATIONS

In a nutshell, evolution purportedly proceeds via random changes and selective reproduction of changes which are in some way "beneficial." The changes arise by mutation (i.e., random copying errors). According to Austin Cline (former regional director for the Council for Secular Humanism, MA – Princeton University) :

> The primary mechanism of significant change in DNA is mutation. . .These facts, that 1) DNA determines the nature of an organism and that 2) there are mechanisms through which DNA can be modified, are the basis of evolution. It is through these facts that evolution happens.[3]

Let's think about these mutations (copying errors) for a minute. We know that our DNA stores a ton of information and it all needs to be copied during reproduction.

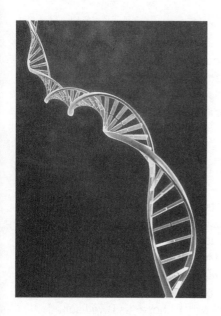

As long as we're talking about DNA, I'll take a moment to give a quick and interesting mini-lesson on cell biology. (Stick with me; you're sure to be fascinated. If nothing else, you can use it as trivia to impress your friends and bore your enemies!)

A typical human adult has about 100 trillion cells in their body. Each of these cells contains within its nucleus thin strands of DNA, which are long chains of molecules built by connecting together smaller molecules called nucleotides. These strands take on the form of a twisted ladder that most people are familiar with (see illustration). Each cell contains virtually the entire set of information needed for the construction and daily functioning our bodies. The sum total of this information is called the "genome." One way of envisioning this is to picture our DNA as being a set of instruction manuals. The nucleotides (rungs on the DNA ladder) serve as individual letters within the pages of the manuals. Small groupings of these nucleotides ("letters") combine to form words. Specific groupings of the words form chapters, which we call "genes." By combining many genes (or "chapters") together, "volumes" are formed within our manuals. We call these volumes "chromosomes." The chromosomes, when taken altogether, form the complete set of manuals (or "genome").

The cells that house all of this within our bodies are microscopic in size. You can fit about 10,000 on the head of a pin! If you were to reach into just one cell and remove all the DNA, strung together end-to-end, it would be about six feet long. To give you a better idea of what that is like in our "macro world," if we magnified the cell so that it was the size of a basketball (which would require magnification of about 110,100 times), the strand of DNA (from this single cell) would be 125 miles long! Now there's a lot of information on this strand, as you can imagine, since it houses all of the information not only to build, but also to operate, our entire body. Here's another mind-bender. If you were to remove all the DNA strands from all the cells in your body and string them together end-to-end (please don't try this at home) it would reach from the earth to the moon over 473,000 times![4] (By the way, it's about 240,000 miles from Earth to the moon.) Another way of looking at it, your DNA would stretch around the equator of the earth 14 million times![5] It's hard to imagine just how long of a distance that truly is, so here's another analogy. Let's say you wanted to take a trip equal in distance to the length of your own DNA. (Strange idea, but maybe you are running out of vacation ideas.) Furthermore, since this is our story and we can make it whatever we want it to be, let's say you just happen to own a rocket that can travel the speed of light—186,000 miles per second (physically impossible, but hey, this is our story)! It would still take you seven days[6] just to reach the end of your own DNA! Simply amazing! Here's another interesting fact about the compact nature of our DNA. Even though it is incredibly long, it's so thin you could fit all the DNA in your body into something the size of two aspirin tablets![7] Now that's compact!

Let's get back to considering the information in the DNA of just one cell. All of the information is in an encoded form determined by the arrangement of nucleotides, similar to how the specific arrangement of letters on a page convey information and meaning. If you were to write out this information (from just one cell) into English, it would fill about one thousand, five hundred page books![8] This information is highly compacted in order to be in such a small space (the nucleus of the cell). You often hear talk about the importance of backing up the data on your computer's hard drive. To give you an idea of the amazing storage capacity of our DNA, let's say you had just a teaspoon amount of DNA and wanted to back it up onto CDs. How many CDs would you need? For reference sake, your need to know that a typical CD (700M) can hold over 16,000, five-page Word documents (~42K each). Would it take 100? That would be a lot of CDs. Would it take 1,000? That would really be a lot! What if I told you it would actually take one million CDs! That would be very stunning, but it would also be a lie. In reality, you would have to be given one million CDs every second. . .for 9.5 years! Then you would finally have enough CDs to complete the backup. Now that is almost unbelievable, but it's true.

One last analogy and then we'll move on. According to Dr. Werner Gitt (former director and professor at the German Federal Institute of Physics and Technology—Braunschweig, Germany):

> The knowledge currently stored in the libraries of the world is estimated at 10^{18} bits. If it were possible for this information to be stored in DNA molecules, 1 per cent of the volume of a pinhead would be sufficient for this purpose.[9]

This just blows away any storage capacity within our high-tech computer world, in which I spent eighteen years as a programmer, prior to transitioning into full time ministry.

Realizing that the DNA in each cell contains virtually all the information necessary to construct our entire bodies (every single part and sub-part), it's very intriguing how cells function on an individual basis. A cell in your toe has all the information for your entire body and could make a liver, an eyeball (wouldn't that be weird), a lung, an eardrum, etc., but it somehow knows to only make a toenail cell right there. The point here is that since each cell contains the entire genome (info for the entire body) when they need to be copied, there's a lot of room for error. Imagine if you had to copy one thousand, five hundred page books; could you do it without making any errors?

When animals reproduce, both the male and female make special copies of their DNA into distinctive kinds of cells and combine them together, which then develops into the offspring. During this process, copying errors can occur. Since there are about 3 billion individual "letters" in each cell's DNA, there are 3 billion chances for point mutations to occur. (A point mutation is when just one "letter" or nucleotide is changed, added or deleted.) Like the process in which regular body cells are copied, this copying process has great potential for error.

Studies have shown that a typical error rate is about 1 error for every 1-10 billion nucleotides copied! That's actually a very high accuracy rate. In human terms, it would be like someone copying up to 3,333,333 pages from various books and only incorrectly transcribing one letter in one word! (Assuming there's an average of six letters per word, and five hundred words per page.) That truly is amazing accuracy!

Mutation rates would be orders of magnitude higher, but the cell has amazing systems for repairing DNA errors "while the paint is still wet." There are three systems involved—one that provides error avoidance, another that makes corrections during replication and a third, more advanced system that works to catch mistakes not caught by the first two.[10] The presence of this tertiary repair system is, in and of itself, impossible to explain on evolutionary grounds.

Although we've established that copying errors are rare, they certainly do occur. We need to take a detailed look at these mistakes to see if any of them could be of benefit to Darwinian evolution. Details often make all the difference in the world, so it's critical that we look into this further to see what's actually happening. Dr. Lee Spetner (biophysicist, Johns Hopkins University), in his book, *Not By Chance: Shattering the Modern Theory of Evolution,* conveyed the following humorous story regarding the importance of getting the details right. He said there was a, guest speaker at a dinner of leading industrialists, who was introduced as a successful speculator who, in two weeks, made 370 million dollars in uranium. After the speaker had risen to speak and acknowledged the applause, he said that since he was a stickler for details, he wanted to first correct a few in the introduction. "First of all," he said, "it wasn't uranium, it was uranium oxide. Second, it wasn't two weeks, it was ten days. Third, it wasn't 370 million, it was 730 million. And fourth, I didn't make it, I lost it!"[11]

The point? Details matter!

General Effects of Mutations

Evolutionists will argue that although there certainly are deleterious mutations, most are actually neutral, meaning they do not affect the fitness of the individual in any way. For example, a mutation that would cause one's hair to be reddish in color (yes, red hair is a mutation) would be visibly noticeable, but would not affect the health or reproductive ability of the individual. Of course, if no females were ever attracted to males with red hair that would greatly affect their chances of continuing their genetic legacy! My wife is at least one exception to this, fortunately for me! (You can guess what color hair I have.) Regarding neutral mutations, up until fairly recently, evolutionists were saying that most of our DNA (possibly 95%) is actually "junk" (i.e. not used in coding for the proteins that our bodies need to operate). Mutations in "junk DNA" might indeed be considered neutral—if such DNA truly had no biological function.

Today, we know it's not a matter of "junk DNA"—it has been more a matter of "junk science." The junk DNA paradigm wasn't simply helpful to the evolutionary story—it was indispensable. This is a powerful example of how evolutionary presuppositions have actually hindered good science. They assumed that these areas with unknown functions had no purpose at all and were the direct result of evolution. This assumption was made because it aided the evolutionary story and eliminated major evolutionary problems (such as very high rates of information-destroying mutations which should cause catastrophic degeneration). For most mainstream scientists there was every reason to accept the junk DNA concept uncritically—with their eyes closed! John Mattick (professor of molecular biology at the University of Queensland) stated that,

> the failure to recognize the implications of the non-coding DNA will go down as the biggest mistake in the history of molecular biology.[12]

What we know now is that most, if not all, of the genome is functional, serving some type of role. The public research consortium entitled ENCODE determined back in 2007 that nearly 100% of the genome is transcribed into RNA—and is therefore functional. Furthermore, they discovered that most of the genome is transcribed in both directions making most DNA sequences not just functional, but dually functional. *New Scientist* (March 2010) stated,

> The blueprint for life is not all about genes. Now we are finally pinning down how much differences in non-coding DNA—stretches of the molecule that don't produce proteins and used to be considered "junk"—shape who we are.

> In recent years, researchers have recognized that non-coding DNA, which makes up about 98 per cent [*sic*] of the human genome, plays a critical role in determining whether genes are active or not and how much of a particular protein gets churned out.

> Now, two teams have revealed dramatic differences between the non-coding DNA of people whose genes are 99 per cent [*sic*] the same. "We largely have the same sets of genes. It's just how they're regulated that makes them different," says Michael Snyder, a geneticist at Stanford University in California.[13]

Clearly, we can safely conclude that the majority of our DNA (if not all) is not "junk," but is functional. Therefore, randomly changing its code will consistently be deleterious and we'll look further into this as well. Side note: Even if there truly are stretches of the DNA that do not serve any current function, it could just as easily, and actually more logically, be due to natural degeneration over time. More about that shortly.

Beneficial Mutations

The term "beneficial mutation" comes up quite often in discussions regarding evolution. It is commonly believed that although most mutations seem to be harmful (or at least nearly neutral), there are occasional "good" mutations and those are the ones that allow evolution to progress. So is it true that while most mutations are deleterious there are at least some of that are positive or beneficial? That's a great question and there's a lot of misinformation regarding this specific issue.

Evolutionary scientists tout beneficial mutations as the key to evolution's grand success over the past few billion years. Very often you will hear well-meaning creationists, whether scientists or not, state that, "There are no such things as 'beneficial mutations;' they're all harmful, if not lethal." We need to be careful, however, because occasionally we observe mutations that can, at least in some sense, be deemed "beneficial." The key point here (as we will shortly see) is that they cannot account for "molecules-to-man" evolution.

Defining a "benefit" is a subjective exercise because it completely depends upon your perspective. If it pours outside all day today, is that a benefit or not? If you were hoping to spend the day at the beach, it certainly wouldn't seem like a benefit. If you had grudgingly promised the next door neighbor you would mow his lawn while he was gone, it probably would be considered a benefit.

One of the main mutational benefits that would be required as far as evolution is concerned is increased survivability. It must aid the individual in being able to pass on its genes. If it can't do this, it's an evolutionary dead-end. A second necessary benefit would be the addition of new genetic information—proteins that will code for new traits or functions. We'll take a look at some alleged "beneficial mutations" and see whether or not they truly qualify as being beneficial in the context of molecules-to-man evolution.

Proof of Evolution—Right Before Your Eyes!

Professor Richard Dawkins once stated that:

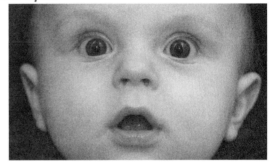

> Evolution has been observed. It's just that it hasn't been observed while it's happening.[14]

Somewhat of a strange statement, but the main point is that we don't necessarily get the chance to observe evolutionary changes, because they happen too slowly. Evolutionists assert the following logic:

• Evolution is change.

• We observe changes in living organisms.

• Therefore, evolution is true!

Once again, this smacks of equivocation, claiming that "evolution" is synonymous with "change." But what about these changes? Are there any that actually offer evidence of "molecules-to-man" evolution?

Evolutionists are often accused of not having any evidence that would qualify as being more along the lines of "operational science," which typically deals with experiments that can be conducted and observed in the laboratory, as well as being repeatable over and over. (Again, please refer back to chapter 2 for further discussion of operational and historical science). However, imagine yourself being in a high school or college classroom where the teacher/professor conveys the following:

Today students, we are going to take a look at one of the strongest proofs of evolution. In this situation, it's actually a case of seeing evolution right before our eyes.

You are all familiar with bacteria, some of which are good and some bad. When we want to get rid of the bad bacteria, we often create antibiotics in hopes of eradicating them. The way the antibiotic works is that the bacteria absorb them through their cell walls—seeing it as "food." They also create an enzyme that breaks down this "food" which then turns it into a poison, thus killing the host! That's how antibiotics work. However, we've noticed something extremely interesting over the years. From time-to-time, these "bad" bacteria will reappear and start multiplying again. We get out our antibiotics and apply them again, except this time most of them are not dying! We take them into the laboratory and find out that they have literally "evolved resistance" to our antibiotics in a fairly short period of time. We can see evidence of evolution in the laboratory right before our eyes! If this much evolution can happen in a short period of time, just imagine what can happen over millions and millions of years! And the creationists say we have no proof! I guess they just don't know anything about science, which is not surprising, because they reject science anyway, believing only in the Bible.

So how are these students supposed to respond? I can certainly tell you how they generally do respond. The non-Christian students sitting in the class say, "That makes a lot of sense to me." The Christian students in the class typically also respond by saying, "That makes a lot of sense to me." At this level, what is being presented admittedly seems very logical. So how do we respond to what the professor shared? It sounds watertight.

Those of you who have been around a while (probably those who are at least in their thirties) may remember the well-known radio broadcaster, Paul Harvey (1918-2009). He was famous for his broadcasts entitled, "The Rest of the Story," in which he would convey an interesting true-life account that in most cases was already somewhat familiar to most people. However, he would then go on to share some fascinating background information that few had ever known. He would end each segment by stating, "And now you know. . .the rest of the story." So what's the fascinating background information in our narrative? Let's take a look.

When discussing bacteria, we are usually talking about millions and millions. Within these large populations, there can exist some "mutant" bacteria—ones which have undergone a random change in their DNA when they were created via cell division from their "parent." In our specific example, the mutant bacteria are those who have lost the ability to create the enzyme that breaks down the antibiotic into a poison. No enzyme, no poison. No poison, no death. So while all the other normal bacteria are absorbing the antibiotic, breaking it down and dying, the mutant bacteria survive. They then reproduce themselves (including passing along the mutation) leading to a new population of bacteria that are largely all resistant. (I say "largely" because in the initial population of millions of bacteria, there may be some normal bacteria that survived because the antibiotic did not actually reach them, or for some other fortuitous reason.)

Now, is this mutation a benefit to the bacteria? Let's see. Before they mutated they were killed by the antibiotic. After mutating, they were able to survive the affects of the antibiotic. Seems like a benefit to me! (Unless of course, these bacteria were asked to mow their neighbor's lawns, in which case, maybe they would preferred to have perished. Just a little more bad humor.) These mutants are able to continue passing along their genes, which is critical to evolutionary scenarios. I would say that this truly is a "beneficial mutation," at least when discussing survivability. We need to make one very important additional note, here. In their normal environment, where there is no antibiotic, these mutant bacteria are at a distinct disadvantage, because they have a harder time breaking down their food (because of the missing enzyme) and cannot compete well with their normal, healthy counterparts. Natural selection will often weed out these weaker specimens. So the apparent advantage is only applicable to this special situation. . .with the introduction of an antibiotic.

Also, keep in mind that survivability is only one of the necessary evolutionary key elements. The other is the ability to increase the total information content of the genome and this is where the story changes. In our example, the bacteria actually lost the ability to produce an enzyme that normally assists the bacteria in breaking down its food. These mutated bacteria can survive in the presence of the antibiotic, but are actually not as healthy as the non-mutated bacteria because of the mutation. They actually have less information in their genome. They are going down-hill. Yes, there was a change. Yes, they became resistant. Yes, it was a benefit to them because they survived. But all of this happened at the expense of the loss of information. Evolution requires the addition of new information, continually, through alleged millions and millions of years. So these bacteria have actually adapted to a special circumstance, not by adding additional information, but by the process of "de-evolution" (i.e., loss of information). Therefore, the example of antibiotic resistance cannot be used as evidence for "molecules-to-man" evolution. In honor of Paul Harvey, now you know. . .the rest of the story!

As an aside, there are a few other ways that bacteria can become resistant, but none of them involve an increase in information. For example, antibiotic resistance can be transferred from bacteria "A" to bacteria "B." Bacteria "B" does become resistant, but the resistance information already existed. Information was simply transferred, which can be a benefit, but no new information was generated.

Blind Cave Fish

Let's look at another example of a beneficial mutation that is alleged to be evidence of molecules-to-man evolution: blind cave fish. On occasion, we observe fish living in caves that have no eyes. What generally happens to produce this phenomenon is that normal fish sometimes find their way into underwater caves and end up getting trapped there. Over time, the fish will undergo mutations, some of which may affect (and prevent) the development of their eyes. In a normal environment, losing their eyes would be very detrimental and generally fatal to their survival. Finding food would be very difficult and they would not be able to avoid predators. However, in the unique environment of the caves where there is no light, eyes would serve no purpose. In fact, they would actually be a detriment. As the fish bump into rocks and cave walls, they can damage their eyes, which could easily lead to them becoming infected, which could even lead to their death. This real-life scenario leads to the survival of the eyeless fish and the extinction of the normal ones in that particular setting. Once again, I would have to say that the mutant fish certainly had an advantage (albeit minor) and we would therefore consider this mutation to be beneficial when it comes to survival. However, as with antibiotic resistance, this example involves the *loss* of function, not the addition of new genetic information.

You may come across some interesting research related to blind fish that has been used as evidence for evolution. Scientists have bred these blind cave fish with their normal counter-parts and in some cases been able to restore some level of vision. This was heralded as being a great success and further evidence of how evolution works. In reality, all that happened was that when the DNA from both fish combined (to form the offspring) the mutated portions that code for sight-related functions were over-ridden by the unaltered segments from the healthy fish. This unremarkable experiment was used to further the case for evolution, even though it had nothing to do with evolution, because the information needed for sight already existed. It was not created via random mutations as evolutionary theory purports.

Wingless Beetles

A third example of a "beneficial" mutation is that of the wingless beetle. As with the previous examples, mutations in beetles cause varying effects and in this case it's the loss of wings. In a normal situation, not having wings poses a great detriment, particularly not being able to escape your predators as well as all of the other beetles. This would lead to the demise of the wingless beetle in their normal habitat, seeing that they did not survive to pass on their mutated genes. However, there is a situation in which these wingless mutants may actually have a distinct advantage over their winged counterparts. Let's envision the beetles living on an island where the climate changes significantly, specifically, it gets much windier. The winged beetles would be much more apt to be blown out to sea, while the wingless beetles would remain largely unaffected. As with the previous examples, however, the benefit comes at the expense of a loss of function/information (e.g., that which coded for the development of wings).

So the verdict regarding beneficial mutations is that they certainly do exist, in rare instances, but in none of these cases is there an increase in information, which is the key point. There are definitely changes occurring, but they are headed in the wrong direction!

There's one other note that really needs to be pointed out. Stories about evolution often talk about creatures adapting to their environments. They do it in a way that gives the public the impression that these creatures see a need for a certain change and then subsequently make efforts to produce the needed change. For example, consider the following clip about dinosaurs from a *Discovery News* article:

> Presumably, the sauropods evolved large body size as a strategy to deter predators.[15]

Looking at this with just a bit of humor, here's what they want us to think. Apparently, there was a time in the past when dinosaurs were not as large as they eventually came to be. So they were sitting around a campfire one night discussing the threat from all their predators and this is how it went:

Dino #1: "Hey guys, things are not going very well for us. We have to figure out a better way to deter our predators. You have any ideas of what we could do?"

Dino #2: "No, our brains are too small."

Dino #3: "Maybe we could hop on our motorcycles and escape."

Dino #1: "No, motorcycles haven't even been invented yet!"

Dino #3: "Good point."

Dino #4: "Maybe we could get some machine guns to deter them."

Dino #1: "No, they haven't even been invented yet either!"

Dino #4: "Oh yeah. . .I hadn't thought of that."

Dino #5:   "I know, what if we evolve really large body sizes? That should scare them away!"

Dino #1:   "Great idea! So are we all in agreement on this? Alright then, let's do it!"

The point here is that adaptation does not mean seeing a need and then purposely setting out to make appropriate changes to meet that need. It is more a matter of random changes occurring and some of them happening (by chance) to be a benefit in a given setting or environment. Summarizing: adaptation = random changes + luck.

Information

As long as we are taking about the challenge of adding information, let's take some time to think further about information itself. On a more technical level, information has been defined as "An encoded, symbolically represented message conveying expected action and intended purpose." For our purposes, we're going to keep our discussion fairly light. Entire books have been written on this subject, including *In the Beginning Was Information* by Dr. Werner Gitt, whom we quoted earlier— (Master Books, 1997).

In 1860, Oxford, England, the "Great Debate" took place, which pitted Samuel Wilberforce (archbishop and professor of theology and mathematics at Oxford University) against Thomas Huxley (evolutionist and agnostic). Folklore has it that during the debate, Huxley claimed that six monkeys randomly typing on six typewriters, given enough time, could eventually type the works of Shakespeare. It is further alleged that Wilberforce conceded the argument to Huxley. It is true that if you start typing randomly, occasionally you will type something meaningful. The idea would be that you keep the meaningful segments, toss the rest and keep going. Theoretically, if you did this long enough, you could produce some significant content. Others since that time have used similar arguments in effort to demonstrate that random events can produce information. In reality, this is not true at all. Space does not permit, but our genetic information does not work this way because randomly inserting and deleting nucleotides ("letters") within our genes does not create new information. Another very important factor is that even though you can imagine short segments of meaningful information randomly forming, they would actually be destroyed much faster than they accumulate. Perhaps a simpler way of visualizing this is by using a puzzle analogy. You might imagine that if you have a box of 1000 puzzle pieces, if you shake it long enough eventually the puzzle would come together as a whole, one piece at a time. Theoretically, this is true if once two pieces were correctly joined they never came apart again. In real life, a few pieces might actually "fall together," but the continued shaking of the box would most likely disengage these two pieces before the next appropriate piece found its way into position. The shaking action of the box serves much better as a destroyer than a builder.

Johnjoe McFadden (writing in *Quantum Evolution*) stated:

> A billion universes each populated by billions of typing monkeys could not type out a single gene of this genome.[16]

When you think about it, matter does a great job of storing information. This book, for instance, consists primarily of paper and ink and contains a fair amount of information (or if you're a skeptic, you might say "misinformation!"). A compact disc (CD) is made primarily of plastic and aluminum and can hold a lot more information than paper of the same size. Computer hard drive disks are made from magnetic and non-magnetic metals and do an even better job of storing data. Currently, a typical desktop computer hard drive will store anywhere from about 500GB to 1TB.

For any "non-techie" readers, a "GB" is a gigabyte and represents 1 billions bytes. A "TB" is a terabyte and represents 1 trillion bytes. A byte (for the most part) consists of 8 "bits", and a "bit" (short for "binary digit") is the most basic unit of computing, such as a 1 or a 0, an "on" or an "off." For comparison, a 16 GB flash drive (which is a portable hard drive about the size of your thumb) could hold about 500,000 one-page Microsoft Word documents. That's a lot of documents in a very small space!

So what's the main point with all of this? The point is that although matter (e.g., paper, ink, metal, plastic, etc.) does a great job of storing information, in none of these cases did the matter actually create the information being stored! You can trace the source of the information in each case back to an intelligent, volitional cause (i.e., a human being). Matter is completely incapable of creating information.

Now let's turn the focus back to our DNA. What do we see? We see matter (amino acids, nitrogen bases and phosphates) storing a lot of information, much more than what was previously discussed regarding computer hard drives. (Consider the DNA storage capacity details we shared earlier in this chapter.) If everything that we experience on a day-to-day basis regarding information points to an intelligent source, why, when we look at our own DNA that contains the equivalent of hundreds of thousands of pages of information, would we conclude that it is simply the result of random actions of particles interacting with each other over billions of years? I was recently on a large state university campus, interviewing students regarding their beliefs about the world in which we live. I asked one particular student (who was graduating in a few days with an advanced degree in engineering) if he could give me some examples of places where we find information. He said, "Libraries, books, computers, magazines, etc." We then discussed the materials used in each of these mediums along with their inherent ability to store the information. I then asked him if he thought the information itself was actually created by those materials. He said, "No." I then asked, "Where then did it originate?" He said, "From people." I agreed and said, "Yes, from intelligent men and women who purposefully recorded their thoughts, ideas and instructions." I then asked if he knew anything about DNA. He knew a few basic details, but was completely unaware of the immense amount of information it stores. I then asked him where he thought this information came from. He responded by saying he believed that it was created randomly by matter. I asked if he could he could give me a few examples from the real world wherein matter creates information. He told me there were lots of them. I asked for just one. He paused for quite a while and then admitted he could not think of any. I asked him again about the source of the information on our DNA and he said he still believes in came about by random actions of matter, because he did not want to consider the God had anything to do with it.

I believe the most logical conclusion, consistent with our own everyday experience, is that genetic information, like all information, comes from an intelligent source and that all biological information has as its source the same God who created and sustains the universe (Genesis 1:1).

GENETIC ENTROPY

Another incredible barrier to evolution is the phenomenon of "genetic entropy." Entropy itself can most simply be defined as the measure of the amount of disorder in a system. The general rule is that when left to themselves, systems always move from a state of order to disorder, from organization to disorganization, from usefulness to uselessness. Consider your car. Over time, it will break down and start to rust, becoming less organized and less useful. With the proper outside assistance (e.g., work from an auto mechanic) this general tendency can be slowed down, but not stopped.

The term "genetic entropy" reflects the fact that genetic systems are also subject to entropy. Genetic systems degenerate over time due to harmful mutations, internal frictional forces and other factors. Therefore, all genetic systems eventually break down over time. If you've ever received a fax that was sent from a copy of another fax, you know how it can lose clarity very quickly. Fairly often, much of it may even be completely illegible. Similarly, the genetic information in your own DNA is a copy from both of your parents, and their genetic information is a copy from both of their parents, and so on. According to evolution, your DNA can theoretically be traced back to some single-celled organism that lived almost 4 billion years ago! Imagine the unbelievable number of copies that would entail, and the associated systematic loss of information!

Evolution is purported to progress through successive beneficial mutations. Let's say, for argument's sake, that somehow mutations can truly create new information now and then. We still have a major problem due to genetic entropy, because for every good mutation there are many more harmful mutations. Estimates are that for every alleged beneficial mutation, there may be one million that are deleterious! Because of the nature of mutations, you can't just keep the "good" ones and weed out the bad. When individuals reproduce, it's an all or nothing situation. They either reproduce their genome, including all their good and bad mutations together, or they don't. They can't just transmit their good mutations and leave all the bad ones behind. In fact, natural selection has no way to differentiate between most good and bad mutations, as they are normally very subtle in their effect. It does not act on the level of the nucleotide (where the mutations are occurring), but rather, on the resultant effect that the mutation has on the individual as a whole.

Regarding this being an "all-or-nothing" process, it's not like natural selection is an intelligent agent making well thought out decisions. For example, it doesn't say, "Hey, I know this individual looks very healthy and could easily reproduce, but I happen to know that one of his genes has a nasty mutation and even though it won't really hurt him, I don't want that sticking around, so let's get rid of him." Conversely, it doesn't say, "This guy over here seems pretty sickly, but he happens to have a minor mutation that might be of some use some day, so let's keep him around."

Dr. John Sanford (inventor of the "Gene Gun" and author of *Genetic Entropy & the Mystery of the Genome* – 2007) also comments on the "all-or-nothing" scenario. He compares it to trying to choose the best television by checking the quality of each individual screen pixel on all of the various TV sets. He further explains that the problem is much worse, because in real-life, there are "pixels, within pixels, within pixels, within pixels!" (p. 49)

Sanford adds another analogy to illustrate another point:

> Let's imagine a new method for improving textbooks. Start with a high school biochemistry textbook and say it is equivalent to a simple bacterial genome. Let's now begin introducing random misspellings, duplications, and deletions. Each student, across the whole country, will get a slightly different textbook,

each containing its own set of random errors (approximately 100 new errors per text). At the end of the year, we will test all the students, and we will only save the textbooks from the students with the best 100 scores. Those texts will be used for the next round of copying, which will introduce new "errors," etc. Can we expect to see a steady improvement of textbooks? Why not? Will we expect to see a steady improvement of average student grades? Why not?[17]

He goes on to answer his own questions. He states that virtually none of the errors introduced into the textbooks will be an improvement and that each textbook across the country will be, generally speaking, equally flawed. Furthermore, the changes will be too subtle to have any real affect on the student's grades, because there are too many other factors that drown-out the minor affects of the misspellings or errors. These other factors include the individual student's aptitude, the amount of sleep they get, their general health, personal motivation on any given day,

African Wild Dog

tensions in personal relationships at home or with friends, and even "bad luck." Any particular student doing exceptionally well on a test will have done so largely because of these "other factors" as opposed to any potential affect caused by the misspellings within the textbook itself. The main point here is that survivability often has a lot more to do with extraneous factors than it does with the affects of mutations, especially considering that most mutations are "nearly neutral" (too small of an effect to be noticed by natural selection).

Let's take a look at an example where the mutation does produce something that is clearly related to survivability. Say there is a wild dog that happens to add 100 point mutations (single "letter" changes) to its offspring's genes when it reproduces. (This is a reasonable estimate of how many individual nucleotides/letters are accidentally changed from parent to offspring for any large mammal.) Let's say that 99 of those 100 mutations are "neutral" or bad, but one happens to produce longer, thicker fur. Further, let's imagine that the environment in which the wild dogs live becomes progressively more challenging related to finding food. Subsequently, the dogs begin to migrate further north in search of sustenance. The climate in this new location just happens to be much, much colder. In this situation, any dog with the mutation that produces longer, thicker fur now has a distinct survival advantage. We can retrospectively look back at the point mutation that led to the longer, thicker fur and say that it was actually "beneficial," at least in this given environment. Had they migrated further south and it was much warmer, it could easily be considered detrimental. The main point, however, is that along with the one "beneficial" mutation, the same dog also has 99 other mutations, most or all of which are deleterious, and all 100 will get passed along to its progeny. During the time that the one beneficial mutation is spreading through the population, many thousands of deleterious mutations will continue to accumulate in each one of the allegedly "superior" dogs.

As far back as 1950, it was believed that if deleterious mutations ever reached a rate of one per person per generation, long-term genetic deterioration would be unavoidable. This rate would equate to each person taking their DNA, along with its existing mutations (mistakes), and adding one more additional mutation when passing it along to their children. Believe it or not, it is now estimated that there are actually approximately 100 mutations per person per generation. Since most mutations are deleterious to some extent, this presents a tremendous problem for the idea of evolution over millions of years and should lead to serious genetic degeneration in just a few hundred generations. Considering the rate at which mutations are accumulating and the alleged passage of deep time, one scientist (A.S. Krondashov, evolutionary professor at the University of Michigan) has asked, "Why have we not died 100 times over?"[18]

Let's look at another analogy to keep all of this understandable. Many people use Microsoft Office for producing spreadsheets, letters, email, databases and many other types of computer documents. It obviously consists of a ton of programming code. Now imagine introducing 100 random errors to this code and giving it to someone else. We don't expect that the random changes will improve the performance of the software, but it's possible that some changes are small enough or unique enough to not be noticeable to the user. As an example, maybe one of the numerous fonts normally listed in a drop-down menu in a seldom used Office program appears to be missing. This will certainly not cause the entire Office Suite not to function. You can still create your spreadsheets, letters, etc., without any adverse effect whatsoever. Now, let's take that copy of that software and introduce an additional 100 random changes to the code and give it to another friend. What if we continued this process over and over? Would this gradually improve the software or would it eventually render it useless? I think the answer is obvious.

A very interesting sidebar to this discussion on genetic entropy is that of the lifespan of biblical characters who lived after the flood. Sanford states that genetic degeneration should result in

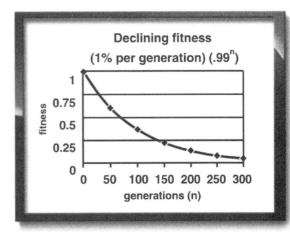

Declining fitness
(1% per generation) $(.99^n)$

fitness — generations (n)

fitness loss which follows a classical decay curve.   Interestingly, when you plot the life spans of the people mentioned in the Bible who were born subsequent to Noah, their life spans follow just such a curve. (For those of you who are mathematically minded, the correlation coefficient is 0.90—which means that the biblical data fits the decay curve very closely).

What's the significance of this? Well, we have one of two choices regarding the reality of these patriarch ages. Either the biblical writers faked the ages in an attempt to try to simulate and convey an exponential decay curve for anyone who might later analyze the data (an extremely unreasonable option), or they simply recorded the actual ages, which we now see is exactly what we would expect from genetic degeneration caused by the accumulative affect of mutations. This is just one more way that the Bible is shown to be historically reliable.

Before we move on, I want to interject an important tangential point. While genetic entropy is a serious concern for all humanity, I believe there is another trend occurring within the body of Christ that is alarming. I call this trend "christian entropy." Just as genetic information will degenerate significantly over time when there's no external, intelligent agent working to slow or reverse the trend, our biblical literacy and strength of our faith will deteriorate from generation to generation if we do not proactively ensure that we are mentoring our children and ensuring that they are equipped to defend their faith and live a life that is honoring to God. We can only pass on what we already posses ourselves. To help stem "christian entropy" we need to make sure that we ourselves are mature in our faith, which is directly related to our understanding of God's Word. We need to be very intentional in mentoring our own children and those whom God has placed in our lives.

NATURAL SELECTION

We've already defined "natural selection" and mentioned that it is also referred to as "survival of the fittest." Natural selection is often considered to be a "tautology," which is a statement that is true, but circular in its logic. Say I told you that my friend Ralph is one year older than me and you asked, "How old are you?" If I respond by telling you that I am one year younger than Ralph, those statements are "tautological" in nature. They may be true, but they don't really say much of anything. (Not only that, but you still don't know either one of our ages!) In a similar sense, when considering "survival of the fittest," you may ask, "Who are the fittest?" "The ones who survive," comes the reply. "Who are the ones that survive?" you further enquire. "The fittest!" This is true, but not really very helpful. Who are the fittest? The ones who survive. Who are the ones that survive? The fittest! And round and round you go. Some have recognized this long ago:

> To speak of an animal as 'fittest' does not necessarily imply that it is strongest or most healthy, or would win a beauty competition. Essentially it denotes nothing more than leaving the most offspring. The general principle of natural selection, in fact, merely amounts to the statement that the individuals which leave most offspring are those which leave most offspring. It is a tautology.[19]

Natural selection is often ascribed a great amount of power as the driving force behind evolution. In reality, it really doesn't *do* anything. It is simply a description of what is observed in nature. It would be like someone who attended a college football game (e.g., the Wisconsin Badgers vs. the Iowa Hawkeyes) later describing the game by simply stating "the team with the most points won the game." For analogy's sake, let's officially call this description, "The Game Description." Would anyone say, "Wow, it's amazing how 'The Game Description' caused the Badgers to win the game!"? Obviously, "The Game Description" didn't cause anything. It's just a description of what always happens—the team with the most points wins. Which team won? The team with the most points. Which team had the most points? The team that won. No meaningful information regarding cause or explanation is provided by "The Game Description."

In the same sense, natural selection is not a force capable of doing anything, it is just a description of reality. Nevertheless, this term is continually used in statements such as, "Natural selection caused the reptile's scales to turn into feathers over millions of years, so it could adapt to a new environment." Richard Lewontin (professor of biology emeritus – Harvard University, Alexander Agassiz Professor of Zoology in the Museum of Comparative Zoology, Emeritus) had the following to say regarding natural selection:

> Evolution cannot be described as an adaptive process, because all organisms are already adapted. Natural selection is functioning essentially to make it possible for organisms to maintain their status of adaptation instead of improving it. Natural selection does not seem to improve the chance of the species to survive in the long run, but simply makes it possible to trace or keep up with the surroundings, that constantly change.[20]

Even in the above quote in which natural selection is described as being much less powerful than what is usually taught, it is still portrayed as "doing something," when in reality it is not a force, but simply a description.

Aside from the fact that there are those who use this phrase inappropriately, natural selection does accurately represent what is actually observed in nature. Those that are fit, survive. Those that aren't, don't. It truly does describe the "survival of the fittest." What it does not do, however, is explain the *arrival* of the fittest! (i.e., How did we get those "fit" creatures to begin with?)

The modern evolutionary synthesis is a remarkable achievement. However, starting in the 1970s, many biologists began questioning its adequacy in explaining evolution. Genetics might be adequate for explaining microevolution, but microevolutionary changes in gene frequency were not seen as able to turn a reptile into a mammal or to convert a fish into an amphibian. Microevolution looks at adaptations that concern only the survival of the fittest, not the arrival of the fittest. As Goodwin (1995) points out, "the origin of species—Darwin's problem—remains unsolved."[21]

(Reminder. See the section entitled "Terminology Caution" earlier in this chapter regarding the use of "micro" and "macro" evolution.)

To revisit our wild dog analogy: the ones with the longer, thicker fur could be considered the "fit ones." Natural selection describes why the dogs with the longer, thicker fur survive, but it does not tell us how we got dogs to begin with! It cannot and does not ever create anything new. It only works with what already exists. It's great at weeding things out and getting rid of things, but cannot create them to begin with:

> Contrary to popular public belief about how evolution is supposed to occur, it doesn't matter what the environment is like. If the genetic information for a certain trait or characteristic is not already in the DNA (or genetic code) of a species then there is nothing in the environment that is capable of putting that information there so that the species would develop that particular trait or characteristic. In other words, it doesn't matter how much a lizard may need to fly in order to be able to survive. If the genetic information for feathers and wings are not in the DNA of a lizard then that lizard will never develop feathers and wings.[22]

One further refinement regarding natural selection. We call it "survival of the fittest," but it could also be called survival of the luckiest, because often those who survive aren't necessarily the fittest, but the luckiest! There can be isolated populations that may actual represent individuals who are more fit than others, but they may get wiped out by a local catastrophe. Their "fit" genes are gone. In this case the others that survived were not the fittest, just the luckiest! Even in the case of dogs with longer fur, as mentioned earlier, if the environment had become warmer rather than colder, the other dogs would be deemed the fittest. So even in that case, the dogs with long fur were truly the "luckiest."

Sadly, most people are under the impression that natural selection was discovered by Charles Darwin and that it somehow provides undeniable proof of evolution. (Some even say it is synonymous with evolution.) The truth is that it was recognized twenty-four years earlier by Edwin Blyth, a scientist/creationist, and comports perfectly with the Genesis account of creation. God created everything perfect, but Adam's sin brought a curse upon the entire creation (Romans 8:22), and even though we observe variations within each kind, overall, things have been going down hill ever since.

VESTIGIAL ORGANS

Having concluded that natural selection cannot create anything new, but does a fairly good job of eliminating things, we might ask the following question: "Does it get rid of everything that it should?" Evolutionists don't think so and believe that this is further evidence for their theory.

We will now look further into the line of purported evidence for evolution known as "vestigial organs." From the evolutionist's standpoint, "vestigial" refers to things that are "leftovers" from earlier stages of evolution. Their belief is that as life progressed through a long, long line of simpler types of creatures progressively becoming more complex, not all of the "simpler" structures were completely eliminated by natural selection. As a result, we possess a few useless vestiges of these previous life forms—structures that were once useful in an earlier stage, but no longer serve a purpose (and for whatever reason have not yet been "weeded-out" by natural selection). If evolution were true, we should not be at all surprised to find such useless organs in our bodies.

According to one popular life-science textbook:

> Evolution is not a perfect process. As environmental changes select against certain structures, others are retained, sometimes persisting even if they are not used. A structure that seems to have no function in one species, yet is homologous to a functional organ in another species, is termed vestigial. Darwin compared vestigial organs to silent letters in a word—they are not pronounced, but they offer clues to the word's origin.[23]

By 1890, evolutionists had compiled a list of approximately 180 vestigial organs in the human body, which they claimed was strong evidence of our evolutionary history. Today, however, this list has been dwindled down to zero, because we have discovered that each "vestigial" organ actually does have a useful function. This fact has caused evolutionists to all but abandon the concept of vestigial organs as proof of evolution. A few still use this concept, though, to sway unsuspecting students into believing evolution.

The Appendix

One very common alleged "vestigial organ" is the appendix. Scientists used to claim that it served no purpose, but was simply "left-over" from earlier stages of evolution. According to the 1997 *Encyclopedia Britannica:*

The appendix does not serve any useful purpose as a digestive organ in humans, and it is believed to be gradually disappearing in the human species over evolutionary time.[24]

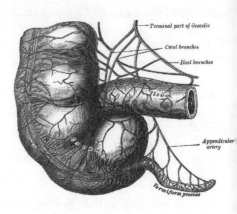

The "useless appendix" argument was even used as far back as the infamous Scopes Trial in 1925:

There are, according to Wiedersheim, no less than 180 vestigal [sic] structures in the human body, sufficient to make of a man a veritable walking museum of antiquities. Among these [is] the vermiform appendix. These and numerous other structures of the same sort can be reasonably interpreted as evidence that man has descended from ancestors in which these organs were functional. Man has never completely lost these characters; he continues to inherit them though he no longer has any use for them.[25]

Today, we know that the appendix does serve a purpose. It plays an important role in the immune system, primarily in early stages of growth. Sadly, it is often still presented as evidence for evolution.

Tonsils

Tonsils are another popular example of a vestigial organ. In reality, as was the case with the appendix, tonsils play an important role in our immune system. They are composed of lymphoid tissue, which forms white blood cells called lymphocytes—cells that attack germs in the body. Doctors today are aware that their unnecessary removal can easily lead to significant health risks, which has caused a significant decline in tonsillectomy rates over the past fifty years.

The Coccyx

The coccyx is another commonly touted alleged vestigial organ which is purported to be a leftover remnant of a tail (from when we were in an ape-like stage of evolution). It is well known today that the coccyx is not a tail, but simply a set of bones at the end of our spinal column and serves a very important purpose, including being an anchor point for muscle attachments. On a related note, some biology textbooks include drawings of human embryos, pointing out the vestigial tail and also what they believe are vestigial "gill slits" leftover from when we were fish! Doctors today know these are not gill slits and that they have nothing to do with breathing. They are simply folds in the skin and are responsible for developing into some very important organs such as the thymus and the parathyroid glands, which aid in immunity and calcium control.

Haeckel's Embryos

Historically, a concept called "ontogeny recapitulates phylogeny" helped bolster the belief in vestigial organs. This very impressive sounding phrase stated more simply, conveys the idea that the development of the individual (ontogeny) recaps, reviews, summarizes, etc., the development of the entire group of creatures (phylogeny). In layman's terms, as an individual creature develops from an embryo it goes through stages that mimic each of the stages represented in its evolutionary history. For example, since evolution teaches that humans evolved through a fish stage, when the human embryo develops, it, too, goes through a fish-like stage, hence the reason for the alleged "gill slits." This concept, also known at the "biogenetic law," was proposed in 1866 by German biologist Ernst Haeckel—a huge proponent of Darwin.

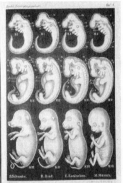

Haeckel produced a series of drawings to illustrate the similarities in embryonic development of various animals as proposed by his "biogenetic law" (see graphic). What many today are not aware of is that Haeckel forged his drawings to better exemplify his theory. The following quotes illuminate Haeckel's work:

> This is one of the worst cases of scientific fraud. It's shocking to find that somebody one thought was a great scientist was deliberately misleading. It makes me angry. . .What he [Haeckel] did was to take a human embryo and copy it, pretending that the salamander and the pig and all the others looked the same at the same stage of development. They don't. . .These are fakes.[26]

> . . .he also fudged the scale to exaggerate similarities among species, even when there were 10-fold differences in size. Haeckel further blurred differences by neglecting to name the species in most cases, as if one representative was accurate for an entire group of animals.[27]

Sadly, these drawings still appear in some textbooks today, directly or indirectly stating that they provide legitimate confirmation of Haeckel's theory and Darwinian evolution in general, even though evolutionists now admit the "biogenetic law" has no place in science.

Seeing that the list of 180 vestigial organs has dwindled all the way down to zero, the evolutionists have had to regroup and come up with a "rescuing device" (see chapter 14 for a definition) in order to "save face," so to speak. They have redefined "vestigial organ" as:

> any organ that during the course of evolution has become reduced in function and usually in size.[20]

This new definition presupposes evolution to begin with—assuming evolution is a fact and also presuming to know how important something was in the past. It is also very subjective in that "reduced in size" could be just about any amount (½%, 3%, 28%, etc.). Since there are numerous examples of such organs (not just within humans), this new definition becomes virtually meaningless.

Creationists can easily and consistently attribute these changes in functional efficiencies and usefulness to the overall effects of the curse on creation, due to Adam's sin. While we would expect to see phenomenon such as this, we would not expect the opposite—things getting better and better, more and more useful, more and more complex.

ICONS OF EVOLUTIONS

Haeckel's embryos are part of a larger group of evidences that are considered to be classic "icons of evolution." Dr. Jonathan Wells has written a book (*Icons of Evolution*, Regnery Publishing, Inc., 2000) in which he evaluates a list of ten icons commonly found in the scientific literature and classroom textbooks. We'll take a brief look at a few of these icons.

Homology

We began this chapter by mentioning that for many people it is not very difficult to imagine one creature slowly changing into another (assuming you don't consider the tremendous increases in information required for the transformations and simply focus on the outward similarities). Various animals will often have similar structures and evolutionists claim that this is due to the fact that one is a descendant of the other or they share a common ancestor. This line of alleged evidence is called "homology." Dictionary.com defines homology as: "a

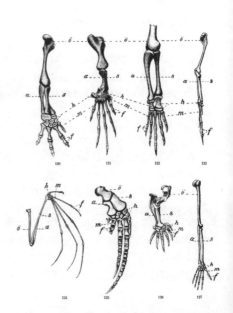

fundamental similarity based on common descent." Again, this definition states that the reason certain animals or structures within various animals are similar is because they descended from a common ancestor. Apparently, the evidence is so strong that it "cannot be denied by reasonable people."

> If you look at a 1953 Corvette and compare it to the latest model, only the most general resemblances are evident, but if you compare a 1953 and a 1954 Corvette, side by side, then a 1954 and a 1955 model, and so on, the descent with modification is overwhelmingly obvious. This is what paleontologists do with fossils, and the evidence is so solid and comprehensive that it cannot be denied by reasonable people.[29]

Stephen Barr (professor at the Bartol Research Institute, University of Delaware) further explains:

> Why is it that bats and whales have so much in common anatomically with mice and men? Why do virtually all vertebrate forelimbs have the same basic 'pentadactyl' (five fingered) design? (This is one of numerous examples of 'homologous' structures exhibited by related species.)[30]

For an evolutionist, the reason a pterosaur, a bat and a bird have similar bone structures in their wings is due to their evolutionary relationship. However, if they were honest, they would admit to their circular argument regarding homology:

"Why do they have similar wing structures?"

"Because they share the same evolutionary heritage."

"But how do you know they share the same evolutionary heritage?"

"It's simple. Because they have similar wing structures."

What seems interesting is many times we find creatures that have similar structures, but are not believed by evolutionists to be directly related to one another. In these cases they are conveniently called "analogous" structures, meaning that although they are very similar and share the same function, they evolved separately from one another (and only happen to look similar because they needed to have that form in order to function).

This is a typical "heads, I win; tails, you lose" scenario. If the similar structures are supportive of traditional evolutionary models, they call it homology and claim it as support for evolution. If they find similar structures in creatures not assumed to have a shared common ancestry, they label that as analogy and refer to it as evidence of how evolution can produce similar functional structures out of necessity, even in unrelated creatures. Either way, it allegedly supports the evolutionary model. How convenient!

There is a very significant problem with using similarity as evidence for evolutionary relationship and it has to do with the development of the structures themselves. As we know, genes are responsible for developing all of the features and functions of life. What has been discovered is that in many instances, these similar structures are controlled by completely different genes. However, if one creature evolved into the other (or at least from a common ancestor), the structures should have developed at the direction of the same gene, but they don't! This is completely at odds with what would be predicted by the evolutionary model.

> Because homology implies community of descent from. . .a common ancestor it might be thought that genetics would provide the key to the problem of homology. This is where the worst shock of all is encountered. . .[because] characters controlled by identical genes are not necessarily homologous. . .[and] homologous structures need not be controlled by identical genes.[31]

Furthermore, similarity in structures can just as easily be used as evidence for a common designer! If all life truly was created by the same creator, we should expect to see some elements of common design and that's exactly what we see. Since the general idea of similar structures is (at least on the surface) consistent with models of evolution (common descent) and creation (common designer), in reality, it cannot be used as "proof" for either side. However, when we look deeper than just on the surface, we see that the detail behind the similarities often does not match up with what would be expected by the evolutionary theory.

Peppered Moths

According to Britain's newspaper, *The Independent* (August 25, 2007), the peppered moth is, "the quintessential example of Darwinism in action." *Nature* magazine stated, "the prize horse in our stable of examples has been the evolution of 'industrial melanism' in the peppered moth. . ."[32]

Here's how the story goes. These moths (*Biston betularia*) appear in two different shades: light and dark. It was observed prior to the Industrial Revolution in England that there were more of the lighter colored moths than the dark variety. This was allegedly due to the fact that lighter colored moths were better camouflaged against the tree trunks, which were often covered with fungus-like organisms called lichens. The birds were said to have been flying by and seeing the dark-colored moths against the light-colored tree trunks, would swoop down and pick them off, leaving most of the light-colored moths to live for another day. However, after the Industrial Revolution, when large amounts of pollution darkened the tree trunks (killing the light-colored lichen), the dark-colored moths were now better camouflaged and were much less likely to be eaten. This shifted the population from largely light-colored to predominantly dark-colored moths.

Henry Bernard Davis Kettlewell is the British geneticist who conducted various experiments regarding the predation of these moths and there is much controversy surrounding his work. One of his own colleagues referred to him as "the best naturalist I have ever met, and almost the worst professional scientist I have ever known."[33]

Picture by Olaf Leillinger

The pictures used in many textbooks associated with this "evidence for evolution" are typically ones of dead moths glued to tree trunks, which is not even where these moths perch. They only fly at night time and rest high in the trees on the underside of branches, much less exposed to their predators, not the trunks as depicted in the textbooks.

Although much of the research behind the peppered moth story is very questionable, there have been some experiments verifying that shifts in light and dark moth populations did occur (but not necessarily the way Kettlewell described). The important question would be: "Is the change in colors of the peppered moth population evolution in action?" The answer is a resounding, "No!" In reality, this is actually a good example of natural selection occurring in the real world. However, it has nothing to do with molecules-to-man evolution because the changes that occurred did so in a population in which there were already two different colors of moths, as even evidenced in the foreword to the 1971 edition of Darwin's *Origin of Species*:

> The experiments beautifully demonstrate natural selection—or survival of the fittest—in action, but they do not show evolution in progress, for however the populations may alter in their content of light, intermediate or dark forms, all the moths remain from beginning to end *Biston betularia*.[34]

Summarizing the whole story, before the Industrial Revolution we had light and dark colored moths of the same species. During and after the Industrial Revolution we had light and dark colored moths of the exact same species. It was not a case of light colored moths turning into dark colored moths and even if they did, they are all still just moths. There was no change in the genetic information present in the *Biston betularia* (peppered moth) species.

I mentioned that evolutionists felt that the peppered moth was "the prize horse in our stable of examples." It is fitting to end this segment with the expanded context of that quote:

> Until now. . .the prize horse in our stable of examples has been the evolution of 'industrial melanism' in the peppered moth, *Biston betularia*, presented by most teachers and textbooks as the paradigm of natural selection and evolution occurring within a human lifetime. . . My own reaction [to the true story] resembles the dismay attending my discovery, at the age of six, that it was my father and not Santa who brought the presents on Christmas Eve. . .for the time being we must discard *Biston* as a well-understood example of natural selection in action, although it is clearly a case of [micro]evolution. . . It is also worth pondering why there has been general and unquestioned acceptance of Kettlewell's work. Perhaps such powerful stories discourage close scrutiny. . .our field [of evolutionary biology] is not self-correcting because few studies depend on the accuracy of earlier ones.[35]

Horse Series

Another classic line of evidence for evolution is the infamous "horse series," starting with *Hyracotherium* (also known as "Dawn Horse") and moving all the way up to *Equus* (modern-day horses). According to *World Book Encyclopedia*,

> Horses are among the best-documented examples of evolutionary development.[36]

Horses living today come in all sorts and sizes. Just consider the range between the world's smallest and largest living horses. The largest living horse stands 6' 7 1/2" from hoof to shoulder and weighs 2,400 pounds, while the smallest is only 17 inches![37] Of all the horse species that are recognized today, most are capable of breeding with each other, evidencing the fact that they are essentially the same kind of animal. This is exactly what we would expect, considering the Genesis creation account repeatedly mentions that each animal would reproduce *after its kind*.

There are a number of problems with the alleged evolutionary horse series. First, it is alleged that the four-toed "horses" evolved into the modern single-toed horse. However, there are fossils of three-toed and single-toed species appearing in the same rock formation (in Nebraska), proving that both lived at the same time. This is strong evidence that one did not evolve into the other.

There is also an inconsistency regarding the number of ribs each proposed species had. It goes from fifteen to nineteen, back to eighteen. Moreover, the number of lumbar vertebrae changes from six to eight and back to six again, which is very inconsistent with what would be expected if evolution were true.

The first in the series, *Hyracotherium*, was named so because of its resemblance to the hyrax or rock badger. You can visit many zoos today and see these creatures, which apparently have not changed in fifty million years, while their alleged decedents evolved all the way into modern horses!

There are over a dozen proposed family trees regarding the evolution of the horse, making it obvious that it's all a matter of guess work and "story-telling." If horse evolution was so well documented, as suggested by *World Book Encyclopedia*, then there would be general agreement between evolutionists.

Even though the evolutionary horse series has been discredited, it still persists in various textbooks, magazines and museums as further evidence for evolution.

Dr. Niles Eldredge (evolutionist curator of the American Museum of Natural History):

> I admit that an awful lot of that [imaginary stories] has gotten into the textbooks as though it were true. For instance, the most famous example still on exhibit downstairs [in the American Museum] is the exhibit on horse evolution prepared perhaps 50 years ago. That has been presented as literal truth in textbook after textbook. Now I think that that is lamentable. . .[38]

The previous quote is even more interesting in light of the following (also taken from Sunderland's book *Darwin's Enigma*). While being interviewed on a network television program, the host,

> asked him to comment on the creationist claim that there were no examples of transitional forms to be found in the fossil record. Dr. Eldredge turned to the horse series display at the American Museum and stated that it was the best available example of a transitional sequence.[39]

The previous quote speaks volumes as to the obvious agenda that exists within the scientific community in furthering belief in evolution, even at the expense of using fraudulent and/or outdated "evidence."

Human and Ape DNA Similarities

Much has been made of the alleged unusually high degree of similarity between human and chimp DNA. The truth is, the more we study, the more we find that the stories being presented are inaccurate and highly deceptive. We will cover this in more detail in the next chapter, which concerns the origin of mankind.

Sexual Reproduction

Let's take a moment to talk about the birds and the bees. There are a number of life forms that reproduce through a process called "asexual reproduction." This simply means there is no sexual male-female interaction occurring, just the dividing of the organism into two separate entities. (A few examples are yeast budding, all bacterial reproduction and vegetative reproduction in plants.) A huge problem for evolutionists has been trying to figure out how asexual reproduction evolved into sexual reproduction. A great deal could be said about this, but we are just mentioning this in passing (and risking giving the impression that it isn't all that significant of a dilemma when in reality, it's HUGE). We aren't going to get into the nitty-gritty here or even discuss the genetics, but you really only have to ponder this on a simple level to see the magnitude of the problem.

Think of it this way. At some point in our alleged evolutionary past, there were only organisms that reproduced asexually (no males, no females, just duplicating DNA and dividing in two). What if somehow (and it would be a *huge* "somehow") an asexual organism mutated into a "female"—whatever that might mean? What would it do? How would it survive and produce further offspring just like itself? Who would invite it to the high school dance? It couldn't be a male, because they haven't been "invented" yet. Well, maybe our asexual organism mutated into a male first instead. (Males seem more like mutants, anyway; right? Be careful how you answer that!) How would this male procreate and pass on its genes? And how would it spend its time when it's not watching football? Also, there wouldn't be any females around to let him know that those pants don't go with the shirt he has on. Looks like they'd have to appear on the scene at the same time, in the same place, and find each other so they could reproduce, which is not at all likely in an evolutionary scenario. If you think about the mechanics for a minute, they obviously have to have the right "plumbing" so to speak, somewhat like a lock and key (only much more complex). One part has to be well designed to fit with the other and that's just thinking about configurations, not to mention all that has to be properly developed internally for anything to happen. These first two lucky contestants must also "like" each other and it's also imperative that he doesn't forget their anniversary or there will be no "Johnny, Jr." Evolutionists may attempt to wax eloquent regarding their musings of how it might have happened, but it's simply another case of fanciful "just-so" stories.

One theory, among many, would have us believe that, "It must have been something I ate":

> One primitive organism ate another one, but rather than completely digesting it, some of the "eaten" organism's DNA was incorporated into the "eater" organism.[40]

David C. Page (MD) conceded,

> Why sex chromosomes evolved is still a mystery.[41]

Even Richard Dawkins admits:

> There are many theories of why sex exists, and none of them is knock-down convincing. . .Maybe one day I'll summon up the courage to tackle it in full and write a whole book on the origin of sex.[42]

THE DEVIL'S IN THE DETAILS

It is commonly stated that "the Devil's in the details," meaning that it is usually the details that present the most formidable challenges to whatever is under consideration. In the case of examining the world around us, we could say that it is both God and the devil that are in the details. I say God in the positive sense that He is the one who has masterfully designed life to such an extent that only those who chose to reject Him a priori would deny His handiwork. This is a great challenge—for evolutionists to discover 100% naturalistic explanations in every area, not requiring any supernatural action. I say the devil in the negative sense that he is indirectly responsible (via the fall of mankind) for all of the death and deterioration we observe.

The following quote sums things up very nicely (by Professor Maciej Giertych, PhD, head of the Genetics Department, Polish Academy of Science, Institute of Dendrology, Poland.):

Genetics has no proofs for evolution. It has trouble explaining it. The closer one looks at the evidence for evolution the less one finds of substance. In fact the theory keeps on postulating evidence, and failing to find it, moves on to other postulates (fossil missing links, natural selection of improved forms, positive mutations, molecular phylogenetic sequences, etc.). This is not science.[43]

It has also been stated that "the more things change, the more they stay the same." Although this was originally meant as a humorous expression, there is some truth to it in the context of biology. While we certainly see change, there are definite boundaries. In a sense, the more change we see (simple variation), the more evidence we have that things stay the same (i.e., that one type of creature does not change into something completely different). This is once again, confirmation of the biblical creation account in which we are told that creatures would reproduce *after their kind* (Genesis 1: 11-12, 21, 24-25).

BONUS SECTION (AKA: The Grand Finale)

Subsequent to the publication of the first edition of this book, I was invited to attend a BioInformatics Symposium at Cornell University (Ithaca, New York). There were about twenty-seven lectures given in three days! It was very intense, but also very fascinating. The conference focused mainly on information theory and information within our DNA. I would like to share just a few things I gleaned from these phenomenal presentations; some of which scientists have known for a few years and some of which would be considered more "cutting edge." An entire book is currently in the works by some of those who spoke at the conference.[44] In closing this chapter, I would like to convey (in a simplistic manner) some of the fascinating discoveries discussed by the elite group of speakers.

One of my favorite times of year is the Fourth of July. Our family has a long-standing routine for that day and it always ends with going to see the fireworks in the city where we live. The display is spectacular and I never get tired of

watching. The grand finale is always superb and just when you think it must be over, another barrage ensues. In a way, I would consider the information I am about to share to be the "grand finale" of this chapter. As interesting as much of what I already shared might be, I think this last section will blow you away and leave you in awe! When watching fireworks, we usually aren't too amazed by those who are lighting them off, we are more amazed by those who designed and created them. In the same sense, I don't want you to be amazed at the scientists who discovered these things (and certainly not the one who is telling you about them–me) but rather, the one who created it all—the God of the Bible! He is the only one truly worthy of glory and honor.

Earlier in this chapter we discussed mutations and how they affect the information content of our DNA. I want to take this one step further and consider how likely or unlikely these mutations would be to improving the information over time, given what we now know about the complexity of our DNA.

Imagine the following challenge. Let's say a friend of yours wanted help decorating their home. Your task was to assist with the placement of a new coffee table in their living room. For simplicity's sake, let's say they have no sense of style and don't care were it ends up. We certainly are not talking about my wife at this point, who happens to be a wonderful interior design consultant. (I'm trying to get Brownie points here, so indulge me for the moment. For the younger readers who don't know what "Brownie points" are, go ask your parents.) Would your task be difficult? Not, not at all. You can put it anywhere and it won't be problem. However, what it your friend said, "By the way, it has to be at least two feet away from any of the walls"? That should not be a problem—still plenty of options available. Let's say, however, that not only does it have to be two feet away from any wall, it also can't be in the path of where people would want to walk. Now it's a bit more challenging, but still not really a problem. You ask if there are any other stipulations and they say, "Actually, here's the entire list":

- It has to be at least two feet away from any of the walls.

- It can't be in the path of where people would want to walk.

- It can't be next to anything that has blue in it.

- It must be near a chair or sofa.

- It can't be near the window.

- It can't be next to the television.

- It must be within five feet of something else of the same color.

- It can't be directly under the track lighting.

- It can't be where any of the old coffee tables used to be.

It quickly becomes much harder to find a solution that meets each of these criteria. You think you have found a good spot, but then you realize it's by the television. You move it away from the television to solve that issue, but then notice that it's under the track lighting. You move it out from directly under the track lighting, but now it's no longer within five feet of something the same color. You would probably end up pulling your hair out and giving up. There are just too many criteria.

We see something similar to this when we look at the construction of the information on our DNA. Virtually every random change to the code, even if it could once in a great while make a slight improvement somewhere, somehow, would actually be messing up some other level of information. The DNA's information is said to be "poly-constrained," meaning there are many different constraints. We will take some time to look at a few examples.

Consider the following sentence: "Was it a car or a cat I saw?" The most interesting thing about this simplistic phrase is that it can be read forwards and backwards! Let's re-write it in all capitols without punctuation to make it even clearer: WAS IT A CAR OR A CAT I SAW

We call these types of phrases "palindromes." Imagine if this is what we saw on our DNA. If we introduce a random change to this sentence (via mutations) we would not only be affecting the reading going from left-to-right, but also from right-to-left. In reality, scientists have discovered that much of our DNA can actually be read forwards and backwards![45] This example, however, is too simplistic, because it's the same message going both ways. Our DNA is more complex than this.

Let's look at a more realistic example. This one is shorter, because it is much harder to find significantly larger examples in the world of literature. Consider the phrase "star desserts." Left-to-right it refers to something like high quality chocolate. (Technically, for something to be considered "dessert" it must contain chocolate. I don't have a reference on this, so you'll have to trust me. Yes, this is an example of how one's bias taints their conclusions!) When you read this phrase backwards (right-to-left), it spells "stressed rats," which is something completely different altogether. Perhaps somewhere in the world stressed rats would be considered a superb confectionary item, but I'm not sure I would be interested in making that a priority vacation destination.

In this previous example, we have two separate messages; one forwards and one backwards. If we introduce a random change, how would that affect everything?

Let's say we randomly remove the letter "d." It no longer spells "star desserts" and backwards it no longer spells "stressed rats." Even if you introduced a random change that somehow seemed to slightly improve one word or message, you would in virtually every case be destroying the secondary backwards message. In reality, we don't just see short, fairly insignificant phrases like the on in our example, we see up to entire chapters with messages (instructions) going forwards and backwards!

Let's interject an analogy at this point in order to help clarify the incredibly complexity of DNA and how virtually insurmountable the challenge is for evolutionary scenarios. Imagine for a moment that you work for a smart phone factory. It's your job to help write the instruction manual that will be used by the manufacturing plant to assemble these high-tech phones. Your boss comes to you one day and says, "I have a project for you. I need you to write a chapter in the manual that details how these phones will download apps from the web." You reply by saying, "Sure, that's my area of expertise. I can do it. No problem." As your boss walks away, he suddenly stops, turns around and says, "Oh, I forgot to mention one little detail. When you write your chapter on how to download apps, you have to write it in such a way that if you read it backwards, it gives instructions on how to get the phone to play videos and music files!" You would look at him in disbelief. You may even laugh and say, "You're kidding, right? That's humanly impossible!" You'd be right. That is humanly impossible. I've done computer programming for over eighteen years and this is even impossible to do using a computer! Stop and let that sink in for a bit. That's mind boggling! So you have to ask yourself, how did this complex information get there to begin with? Did it accumulate slowly by random processes over millions and millions of years or did it originate from a pre-existing intelligence? Once again, imagine making a random change (duplicating a letter, deleting one, transposing two, etc.). Would this improve the left-to-right chapter? The vast majority of changes will destroy existing information. Even in those very rare cases where there might be a slight improvement in one word in one sentence, you are destroying information in the corresponding right-to-left (backwards) set of instructions.

In addition to the complexity of information traversing in both directions, there are further challenges to the "molecules-to-man" evolutionary story. Consider the following nonsensical phrase:

I like chocolater that evening.

The reason this sentence is fairly strange is that it is actually two separate phrases that overlap: "I like chocolate" and "later that evening." They overlap in the middle, sharing the letters "late." Therefore, introducing a random change to this segment (e.g., changing the "e" to an "h") destroys both messages. In the world of DNA, these overlapping segments are not just a few letters, but can be up to entire chapters! [46]

We're not done yet, however. Let's take the previous phrase again, but this time we will look at just specific segments:

I *like* chocola*ter that* evening.

If we take the italicized segments and splice them together, it spells "I like her hat." Once again, if we introduce a random copying error (delete the first "h"), it now spells "I like er hat." This particular phenomenon is called alternative splicing.[47,48] In our DNA, there are long sentences and short paragraphs that get spliced together to form additional sets of instructions! There are even splice segments that come from completely different genes. It is like taking various sentences and paragraphs from separate chapters in a biochemistry textbook, splicing them together and creating new, useful information. Once again, this not only demonstrates the incredible complexity of the code, but also the immeasurable barrier it poses to improvement via random mutations.

There are yet other layers that we will not take the time to go into, such as equidistant spaced codes, encryption and cell membrane/nucleus communication that further compound the evolutionary story of random, purposeless mutations increasing the complexity and functionality of the genome.

Life is truly amazing, and science continues to discover layer upon layer of complexity—in my mind, the fingerprints of God, our Master Designer!

ENDNOTES

1. Richard Dawkins, in Lanny Swerdlow's, "My Short Interview with Richard Dawkins," Richard Dawkins Foundation for Reason and Science, http://richarddawkins.net/articles/94-my-short-interview-with-richard-dawkins —last accessed 8/21/12.

2. Mayr, Ernst, "Darwin's Influence of Modern Thought," *Scientific American,* 28, no 1, 2000, 78-83).

3. Cline, Austin, *Genetics & Mutations*—"How Genetic Mutations Drive Evolution: Mutations in our Genes Produce Evolutionary Changes Over Time," http://atheism.about.com/od/evolutionexplained/a/GeneticsMutationsDNA.htm —last accessed 7/12/12.

4. Figure based on 100 trillion cells, 6 ft of DNA in each cell & 240,000 miles from the earth to the moon.

5. Figure based on 100 trillion cells, 6 ft of DNA in each cell, Earth diameter = 7,926.41 miles.

6. Figure based on 100 trillion cells, 6 ft of DNA in each cell, speed of light = 186,000 miles per second.

7. http://creation.com/the-marvellous-message-molecule—*last accessed 9/21/10*, Jérôme Lejeune, *Anthropotes* (Revista di studi sulfa persona e la famiglia), Istituto Giovanni Paolo 11, Rome, 1989, pp. 269-270.

8. Sarfati, Jonathan, *The Greatest Hoax on Earth? Refuting Dawkins on Evolution,* Creation Book Publishers (2011) p. 44.

9. Gitt, Werner, *Creation Ex Nihilo Technical Journal,* 1996, vol. 10, no. 2, p. 184, online: http://creation.com/images/pdfs/tj/j10_2/j10_2_181-187.pdf—*last accessed 9/21/10.*

10. Bergman, J., *Creation Research Society Quarterly,* 41:265-273, (2004).

11. Spetner, Lee, *Not by chance!*, The Judaica Press, Brooklyn, N.Y. 1997, p. 132.

12. Mattick, John, From a transcript of the ABC TV science program *Catalyst*, episode titled 'Genius of Junk (DNA)', broadcast 10 July 2003, www.abc.net.au/catalyst/stories/s898887. htm—*last accessed 9/21/10.*

13. "'Junk' DNA gets credit for making us who we are," 16:11, 19 March 2010, by Ewen Callaway, http://www.newscientist.com/article/dn18680-junk-dna-gets-credit-for-making-us-who-we-are. html.

14. Dawkins, Richard, in an interview with Bill Moyers, *Now*, 3 December 2004, PBS network.

15. *DiscoveryNews*, Jennifer Viegas, Tue Mar 23, 2010.

16. McFadden, Johnjoe, *Quantum Evolution*, New York: W.W. Norton & Company, 2002, p. 84.

17. Sanford, John, *Genetic Entropy & the Mystery of the Genome*, Ivan Press, 2005, p. 50.

18. Krondashov, A.S., "Contamination of the genome by very slightly deleterious mutations: Why have we not died 100 times over?" *Journal of Theoretical Biology*, 175::583-594, 1995.

19. Waddington, C.H., *The Strategy of the Genes*, Allen & Unwin, London, (1957), p.64-65.

20. Lewontin, Richard, "Adaptation," *Scientific American*, 239, Sept,, 1978: p.213.

21. Gilbert, Scott, Optiz, John, and Raff, Rudolf, "Resynthesizing Evolutionary and Developmental Biology," *Developmental Biology*, 173, 1996, pg. 361.

22. Ranganathan, Babu G., "DNA: the God particle (part 1)," *Pravda*, March 30, 2009.

23. Lewis, R., *Life*, 3rd ed., WCB/McGraw Hill, New York, p. 395, 1998.

24. *New Encyclopædia Britannica*, 1:491, 1997.

25. Darrow, Clarence and Bryan, William J., *The World's Most Famous Court Trial: The Tennessee Evolution Case,* (Clark, NJ: The Lawbook Exchange, Ltd., 1997) p. 268.

26. Hawkes, Nigel, *The Times*, London, 11 August 1997, p. 14.

27. Pennisi, Elizabeth, "Haeckel's Embryos: Fraud Rediscovered," *Science,* 277(5331):1435, 5 September 1997.

28. Hale, W.G. and Margham, J.P., *The Harper Collins Dictionary of Biology*, Harper Perennial, New York, p. 555, 1991.

29. Berra, T., *Evolution and the Myth of Creationism*, Stanford Univ. Press, p. 117, 1990.

30. Barr, S.M., "Untangling evolution," *First Things,* 78:15, 1997.

31. deBeer, Gavin, *Homology: An Unsolved Problem* (London: Oxford University Press, 1971), pp. 15-16.

32. Coyne, Jerry, *Nature*, 396, 35-36, 1998.

33. Coyne, J.A., "Evolution Under Pressure," *Nature* 418 (2002): 19.

34. Matthews, L. Harrison, foreword to the 1971 edition of Darwin's *Origin of Species*, (London, J.M. Dent and Sons)

35. Coyne, J.A., "Evolution Under Pressure," *Nature* 418 (2002): 35f

36. *World Book Encyclopedia*, 1982 ed., p. 333.

37. "The world's tallest horse meets the world's smallest," *MailOnline*, http://www.dailymail.co.uk, 27 July 2007—*last accessed 9/21/10.*

38. Eldredge, Niles, *Harper's Magazine*, February, 1985, page 60.

39. as quoted in: Luther D. Sunderland, *Darwin's Enigma: Fossils and Other Problems*, 4th ed., Master Book Publishers, Santee, California, 1988, p. 82.

40. Judson, Olivia, *Dr. Tatiana's Sex Advice to All Creation*, New York: Metropolitan Books, (2002). pp. 233–4.

41. http://media.hhmi.org/hl/01Lect4.html —last accessed 8/21/12.

42. Dawkins, Richard, *Climbing Mount Improbable*, New York: Norton, 1996, p.75.

43. Keane, G.J., *Creation Rediscovered*, in the Foreward, Melbourne (Australia), 1991.

44. *Biological Information: New Perspectives,* Marks, R.J., II, et al. (eds.) ISRL 38, ("In Press" at the time of the publication of this book (September 2012).

45. Sanford, John, *Genetic Entropy & the Mystery of the Genome*, Ivan Press, 2005, p. 41.

46. *Biological Information: New Perspectives*, Marks, R.J., II, et al. (eds.) ISRL 38, ("In Press" at the time of the publication of this book (September 2012).

47. Pan, Q., Shai, O., Lee, L.J., Frey, B.J., and Blencowe, B.J., "Deep surveying of alternative splicing complexity in the human transcriptome by high-throughput sequencing," *Nature Genetics,* 40 (12): 1413–1415, (Dec 2008).

48. Matlin, AJ, and Clark F, Smith, "Understanding alternative splicing: towards a cellular code," *Nature Reviews,* 6 (5): 386–398, CWJ (May 2005).

Chapter Seven

Monkey Business:
The Origin of Mankind

> "*Descended from the apes! My dear, let us hope that it is not true, but if it is, let us pray that it will not become generally known.*"
>
> - Wife of the Bishop of Worcester
>
> (Her response just after having had Darwin's theory of evolution explained to her. 1859)

"Evolution can't be true! If we evolved from apes, why are there still apes around?"

I've heard this comment countless times from very sincere, well-meaning people. Unfortunately, it misrepresents what evolutionists believe and also misunderstands evolution in general. When people ask me "If we evolved from apes, why are there still apes around?" I usually respond by humorously saying, "Because some of the apes were given a choice!" After they roll their eyes and give me a sympathy laugh, I continue by giving a more serious response. Technically, evolutionists do not believe we evolved directly from an ape, but merely that apes and humans share a common ancestor. Interestingly though, when asked what this common ancestor looked like, the typical response is: "kind of like an ape." It would be better (and certainly safer) to say that evolutionists believe humans evolved from an ape-like creature, even though it arguably is a matter of semantics. Interestingly, *Time* magazine

continued this belief with the cover story of its July 23, 2001 issue.

Secondly, even if we did evolve from apes, it wouldn't necessarily mean that apes couldn't still be around. Let's say we have two populations of creatures: population A and population B. When evolutionists claim that A evolved into B, they do not mean that every single creature in population A changed into a creature in population B. It could easily be that when some from A changed into B, others did not, thus resulting in there being both A and B at the same time. Over time, it would be possible that all creatures within population A die out or become extinct, leaving just B. On the other hand, some within A might be fit enough to survive, but do not evolve, thus giving us both A and B simultaneously over a longer period of time.

This graphic is probably the most easily recognizable icon of evolution. However, it actually disturbs many modern evolutionists, because it continues to convey the impression that they believe we evolved directly from apes. While it is true that this is what they used to teach, most have changed their views on human evolution. They now believe that at some point in the distant past, perhaps six to ten millions years ago, there existed a creature that gave rise to two major lineages: apes and humans.

This chapter is a bit tricky to write, because there isn't a very clear-cut human evolutionary scenario. Ask three different evolutionists how we evolved and you're likely to get five different answers! Museums, magazines and textbooks are littered with numerous pictures, fossils and skeletons of "ape-men," so what are we to make of all of this? Many people feel that it is very difficult to argue about human evolution because of the sheer volume of "evidence" that exists. Countless skulls, bones and skeletons; how could we *not* agree? Are we foolish and anti-scientific for not simply going along with their story? This chapter will shed some much needed light on human evolution—what we actually know and what we don't know.

THE BIBLICAL RECORD

Some will attempt to say that "evolution is just God's way of creating everything." However, there is nothing in the Bible that even hint's at such an evolutionary tale for the origin of man (or life and the universe, for that matter). The Bible clearly states:

> So God created man in his own image, in the image of God he created him; male and female he created them (Genesis 1:27, NIV).

> Then the LORD God formed the man from the dust of the ground and breathed into his nostrils the breath of life, and the man became a living being (Genesis 2:7, NIV).

> So it is written: "The first man Adam became a living being"; the last Adam, a life-giving spirit (I Corinthians 15:45, NIV).

There is no direct or indirect discussion of imparting a soul into an ape-like creature and calling this new hybrid, "Adam" (or doing something similar for the creation of Eve). Even so, there are many other reasons to reject evolution as God's means of creation, many of which we cover in other portions of this book.

NOT A UNIFIED FRONT

The popular public school textbook, *Biology*, states:

> But all researchers agree on certain basic facts. We know, for example, that humans evolved from ancestors we share with other living primates such as chimpanzees and apes.[1]

Statements such as this give students (and the public in general) the impression that there is a united front amongst scientists regarding human evolution. This is actually far from reality. Not only do evolutionists continually argue with each other, but as a group, their story keeps changing and their prize evidences routinely become dethroned (albeit without the public hearing much about it).

Evolutionists are split regarding their view of human evolution. One major view is that *Australopithecines* evolved into *Homo erectus* in several areas, who in turn evolved into *Homo sapiens* (modern man). The other contending view, referred to as the "Out of Africa" scenario, is that various hominoid and human types existed in different places around the world, but the humans who migrated out of Africa became dominant, eliminating the others directly and indirectly (via natural selection). Modern humans arose singularly from this group allegedly anywhere from 100,000 to 300,000 years ago. This second scenario is considered by most evolutionists to be the correct view.

A LITTLE CREATIVITY

There's plenty of room for artistic license when working with fossils. It basically entails finding a bone (or bones) and then creatively coming up with a story to explain to the public why this particular discovery exhibits further evidence for human evolution. For instance, *Discover* magazine reported:

> Everybody knows fossils are fickle; bones will sing any song you want to hear.[2]

What this refers to is the fact that there exists a lot of pressure within the evolutionary community, including paleontologists (scientists who study fossils) to have their personal discoveries yield highly significant results. For example, if a paleontologist discovers a toe bone of an anatomically modern human being, no one is going to get very excited. However, if it were to be concluded that this toe bone might actually belonged to the oldest hominoid ever discovered, well that's a different story altogether. Now they will get published. They may even get their picture on the cover of *National Geographic* or *Smithsonian* magazines. They are likely to receive a large amount of grant money for further research, as well. You can start to see the intrinsic pressure to potentially conclude something otherwise not warranted by the evidence. It is sometimes known as "publish or perish." If you have nothing significant to report, you may well perish from lack of funding or peer support. Donald Johanson (discoverer of the famous "Lucy" skeleton) candidly admitted:

> There is no such thing as a total lack of bias. I have it; everybody has it. The fossil hunter in the field has it. . .In everybody who is looking for hominids, there is a strong urge to learn more about where the human line started. If you are working back at around three million, as I was, that is very seductive, because you begin to get an idea that that is where Homo did start. You begin straining your eyes to find Homo traits in fossils of that age. . .Logical, maybe, but also biased. I was trying to jam evidence of dates into a pattern

that would support conclusions about fossils which, on closer inspection, the fossils themselves would not sustain.[3]

Along these same lines, the *Weekend Australian* reported:

> The discoverers of skulls are consequently greatly attached to, and jealous of the reputation of, their charges. It is not only that it makes the owner a top dog in the discipline of paleoanthropology, and an avoider of the fate of perishing through not publishing; finding the oldest member of the Hominidae—the family of Man—is like winning gold at the Olympics. You can go on lecture tours, appear on television and attract corporate dollars. . . Having your remains pushed on to a simian side-branch is like being a gold medalist found harboring anabolic steroids.[4]

Walking with Cavemen (a television documentary series about human evolution co-produced by the BBC and Discovery Channel) included a comment on interpretations and the scarcity of evidence:

> The thing about science is that there isn't just one truth. Everything is interpretation, and in this case, if you were to gather every piece of fossil evidence on which interpretations about early humans are based, it would fit quite easily into one small car.[5]

APE-MEN ON PARADE

So then, exactly what is it that we are seeing in the museums and school textbooks? Good question. Every "ape-man" you've ever seen or ever will see, falls into one of four categories:

1. An ape that they tried to make look more human-like.

2. A human that they tried to make look more ape-like.

3. A fraud or mistake in which human and ape bones were claimed to have been from the same specimen.

4. Evidence from something that was neither ape nor human.

Let's take a look at a few of the more well-known examples that have been part of the arsenal of alleged evidence for human evolution.

Nebraska Man: This was the name given to an alleged human ancestor after the discovery of a single bone by Harold Cook (an occasional paleontologist) back in 1917, in northwestern Nebraska. The scientific name assigned to this new ape-man was *Hesperopithecus haroldcookii*, in honor its discoverer, Harold Cook. (As an aside, these scientific-sounding, often hard to pronounce names serve to give the public the impression that the discoveries are scientifically incontrovertible. In this case, the name simply means "western ape.")

This particular find was eventually used in connection with the famous Scopes "monkey" trial in 1925. Regarding this evidence, Henry Fairfield Osborn (then president of the American Museum of Natural History, New York) stated:

> What shall we do with the Nebraska tooth? Shall we destroy it because it jars our long preconceived notion that the family of manlike apes never reached the western world. . .Or shall we continue our excavations, difficult and baffling as they are, in the confident hope, inspired by the admonition of Job, that if we keep speaking to the earth we shall in time hear a more audible and distinct reply? Certainly we shall not banish this bit of Truth because it does not fit in with our preconceived notions and because at present it constitutes infinitesimal but irrefutable evidence that the man-apes wandered over from Asia into North America.[6]

You can see from the artist's depiction (*Illustrated London News*, June 24, 1922) that they were able to determine quite a bit about Nebraska Man. He's pretty much everything you'd expect an ape-man to be. He is standing almost fully upright, unlike an ape, and had a club in his hand (so he presumably knew about "stone-age" tools). Pictured behind him is his "spouse/partner" who is making a fire. We also see domesticated animals in the background, such as horses and camels. So what was this amazing evidence that afforded them so much information? A single bone: a tooth! Imagine someone walking up to you, handing you a tooth and asking you to figure out what this guy looked like. How would you know what his hair looked like, or if he used "stone-age" tools, or if he knew about fire, stood upright or had domesticated animals? You wouldn't. But it sure makes for an interesting story if you throw all those things in there, knowing that much of the public will assume that all of these features were garnered from the evidence. To make matters worse, it was later discovered that the tooth was from a pig! How's that for artistic license? There are many indications that a huge motivation behind the development of Nebraska Man was the impending Scopes trial. (See chapter 1 for further detail on this trial.) The timing was not coincidental.

This is an example of alleged evidence that falls into category 4, previously listed (evidence from something neither ape nor human.) Thankfully, Nebraska Man has been removed from the textbooks, but there were many others that followed to take its place.

Piltdown Man: This alleged ape-man was "discovered" in Piltdown, England, in 1912 and given the name *Eoanthropus dawsoni* or "Dawn Man." It consisted of a human skull and the lower jaw of an orangutan. The "discoverer," Charles Dawson (medical doctor and amateur paleontologist), claimed they were from the same specimen. Piltdown Man (appearing in numerous textbooks) remained a hoax for over fifty years! The teeth had been filed to look more human and the bones had been discolored to make them appear much older. Imagine all of the worlds "experts" examining this and writing papers, completely oblivious to the fraud, or at least choosing to ignore the evidence.[7] This is an example of alleged evidence falling into category 3.

Lucy: Classified as *Australopithecus afarensis* (meaning "southern ape from the Afar region of Africa"), Lucy is one of our more commonly known alleged ancestors. Discovered by Dr. Donald Johanson in 1974, it was claimed that she lived about 3.5 million years ago and walked upright. Only about forty percent of her skeleton was found. Just as a bit of free trivia, in the camp where they were working, they were playing the famous Beatles song entitled, *Lucy in the Sky with Diamonds*. That's how she got her name!

Speaking of taking advantage of "artistic license," National Geographic artist, John Gurche, stated:

> I wanted to get a human soul into this ape-like face, to indicate something about where [s]he was headed.[8]

There's a definite agenda behind the scenes.

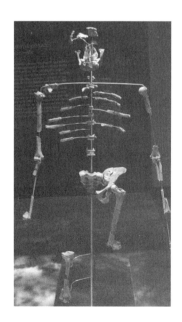

One of the more interesting facts about Lucy is that when they initially found this specimen, they did not find any foot or hand bones. So why did they put human-like hands and feet on Lucy in the museums? They discovered human-like footprints in the same rock layer and did not believe that humans had even evolved yet, so Lucy must have left those tracks! Therefore, Lucy must have had human-like feet! And what goes better with human feet than human hands? It's all part of the complete package to give more credence to the idea of human evolution. You see, if humans had left those tracks, Lucy obviously could not be on her way to evolving into the first human; they would have already been around! Since discovering Lucy (a single specimen of *Australopithecus afarensis*), they have unearthed other similar fossils, which did include foot and hand bones. According to paleoanthropologists Jack Stern and Randall Sussman, the *Australopithecines* have hands that are "surprisingly similar to hands found in the small end of the pygmy chimpanzee-common chimpanzee range" and that the feet are "long, curved and heavily muscled" like those of living primates that engage in tree climbing as well as bipedality (walking on two legs). They go on to say that no living primates have such hands and feet "for any purpose other than to meet the demands of full or part-time arboreal (tree dwelling) life."[9] Lamentably, many museums still display Lucy as having human-like feet and hands, otherwise people might actually think that she is nothing more than an extinct chimpanzee—which is actually is was she is! This is an example of alleged evidence that falls into category 1 (an ape that was made to look more human).

Neanderthal Man: It was in 1856 that Neanderthal Man was discovered in Neandertal Valley near Düsseldorf, Germany. He was originally given the name *Homo neanderthalensis* which indicated that he was considered to be a different species than modern man (which is classified as *Homo sapiens*). You can see what they originally believed he looked like from the drawing created in 1909 (Figure 1). Because of overwhelming evidence, Neanderthals have been upgraded by evolutionists to *Homo sapiens neanderthalensis*, making them fully human, but still viewed as potentially being our more brutish ancestors. Due to evolutionary bias, along with the fact that a few of the early specimens were from individuals now known to have suffered from rickets and arthritis (which can curve the bones), original depictions of Neanderthals were given a stooped posture and drawn to look much more primitive than modern man. However, the differences exhibited in subsequent specimens are nothing outside the range of attributes found in modern humans. Figure 2 depicts a more recent rendition of a Neanderthal.

Figure 1

The Neanderthals were simply an isolated group of people living in a post-flood

Figure 2

environment, specifically during the Ice Age, who subsequently suffered from vitamin D deficiency due to a lack of sunlight. This would explain the existence of rickets and arthritis found in some of the individuals.

Even Donald Johanson admits that Neanderthals should be placed in the same category as modern humans:

From a collection of modern human skulls Huxley was able to select a series with features leading "by insensible gradations" from an average modern specimen to the Neandertal skull. In other words, it wasn't qualitatively different from present-day Homo Sapiens.[10]

We also have further evidence that Neanderthals were fully human and not much different from modern man. They lived in communities, made bone tools, created various works of art (jewelry and paintings), made musical instruments and buried their dead. We even find Neanderthals buried with modern humans!

Much has been made out of comparing Neanderthal DNA to that of modern man, but it is not within the scope of this book to cover this on-going, heated debate. For further detail, the reader is encouraged to review the web article "Neandertal Genome Like Ours."[11] This is an example of alleged evidence that falls into category 2 (trying to make something fully human look more ape-like).

We will summarize a few other alleged ape-men from the past and then cover a couple that are of a more recent vintage.

Homo habilis: Also known as "handy-man," this ape-man was introduced by famed paleoanthropologist Richard Leakey, after having discovered a skull and legs bones in Kenya, Africa, in 1972. Experts today, however, regard *Homo habilis* as simply being a mixture of *Australopithecus* and *Homo erectus*, meaning it is not even a legitimate category (it never even actually existed). As an interesting aside, there is poignant story behind the dating of the famous *Homo habilis* skull (KNM-ER 1470), as outlined in the following Creation Ministries International web article:[12]

A layer of volcanic ash in East Africa, called the KBS tuff, became famous through the human fossils found nearby.

Using the potassium-argon method, Fitch and Miller were the first to measure the age of the tuff. Their result of 212–230 million years did not agree with the age of the fossils (elephant, pig, ape and tools) so they rejected the date. They said the sample was contaminated with excess argon.

Using new samples of feldspar and pumice they 'reliably dated' the tuff at 2.61 million years, which agreed nicely.

Later, this date was confirmed by two other dating methods (paleomagnetism and fission tracks), and was widely accepted.

Then Richard Leakey found a skull (called KNM-ER 1470) below the KBS tuff, a skull that looked far too modern to be 3 million years old.

So Curtis and others re-dated the KBS tuff using selected pumice and feldspar samples, and obtained an age of 1.82 million years. This new date agreed with the appearance of the new skull.

Tests by other scientists using paleomagnetism and fission tracks confirmed the lower date.

So by 1980 there was a new, remarkably concordant date for the KBS tuff, and this became the one that was widely accepted.

Which illustrates that, contrary to popular belief, the dating methods are not the primary way that ages are decided. The dating methods do not lead, but follow. Their results are always 'interpreted' to agree with other factors, such as the evolutionary interpretation of geology and fossils.

Homo erectus: This alleged ancestor is also called "'upright man." However, *Homo erectus* is fully human having shown evidence of tool usage, fire, artwork, burying their dead and having a brain size within the normal range of modern man. The controversial Indonesian fossil find called "Flores Man" would fall into this category and evidence has been discovered that indicated the knowledge of seafaring skills.[13]

Cro-Magnon: Discovered in France in 1868, Cro-Magnon man has always been depicted as being a very brutish recent ancestor of modern humans. However, all evidence now shows him to be fully human, exhibiting a number of racial characteristics that made him somewhat distinctive. Best known for the beautiful paintings and cave drawings, it is undeniable that he was fully human (and of much more recent heritage than alleged—because of the marvelous preservation of the stunning artwork).

Johnny-Come-Lately

Each of the ape-men we have discussed has been in the literature for quite a few years. We'll now take a brief look at two of more recent origin.

Ida: In May of 2009, there was an orchestrated media blitz over the announcement of *Darwinius masillae* (nick-named "Ida" in honor of one of the scientist's daughters). This discovery would allegedly remove any doubt about the validity of human evolution. The actual fossil was unearthed by amateur fossil hunters in 1983, but it took a number of years for it to find its way to a research team.

Numerous grand claims were heralded in accompaniment with the announcement, including, "This changes everything,"[14] "The closest thing we can get to a direct ancestor,"[15] and "The most important find in 47 million years."[16]

Here are a few quotes giving testimony to the grandiose nature of the claims.

Science News: "This is the first link to all humans. . .truly a fossil that links world heritage."[17]

New York Daily News: "It is the scientific equivalent of the Holy Grail. This fossil will probably be the one that will be pictured in all textbooks for the next 100 years."[18]

Sky News Online: "The search for a direct connection between humans and the rest of the animal kingdom has taken 200 years—but it was presented to the world today at a special news conference in New York."[19]

If the subliminal (and I am quite sure unintended) message reflected in the *Sky News* quote means that we finally now have a "direct connection between humans and the rest of the animal kingdom," then that would mean that up until now, it has been missing! It makes you wonder how they have been able to be so dogmatic when making authoritative statements such as, "Evolution is a fact, like apples falling out of trees."[20]

It further implies that if it were to turn out that Ida is not a legitimate "missing link," we're right back to square one—not having any direct evidence. Sadly for them, Ida has already fallen out of favor as evidence for human evolution. Within hours of the unveiling of Ida, even many evolutionists were skeptical and critical of the over-hyped announcement.

Live Science: "The PR campaign on this fossil is I think more of a story than the fossil itself," said anthropologist Matt Cartmill of Duke University in North Carolina. "It's a very beautiful fossil, but I didn't see anything in this paper that told me anything decisive that was new."

"Most experts agree that the find is significant, if only for its impressive degree of completeness, but some were put off by the bells and whistles that went along with the publicity campaign around Ida..."

"It's not a missing link, it's not even a terribly close relative to monkeys, apes and humans, which is the point they're trying to make."[21]

Live Science: "The discovery of the 'Ida' fossil, announced this week as though the 47-million-year-old lemur-like female were a rock star, seemed at first like one to celebrate."

"Today [days later—ed. note] we know better. . . [T]here are doubts about whether [humans are] really descended from Ida. Problem is, most of the coverage is done, and the public could be left with the impression that Ida is a rock-solid missing link in the human evolutionary chain..."

"It's not a missing link, it's not even a terribly close relative to monkeys, apes and humans, which is the point they're trying to make," said Chris Beard, a curator of vertebrate paleontology at the Carnegie Museum of Natural History in Pittsburgh. . ."

"The debacle started to unfold when the finding, cloaked in secrecy while a media engine was being primed, leaked out in *The Wall Street Journal*, and then in London's *Daily Mail*. Then *The New York Times* wrote about the media circus that was to ensue. All this was published before anyone but the research team (and its tightly controlled media team) knew the details of the finding. . ."

"Ida's unveiling was highly scripted (with some 'Barnum and Bailey aspects,' said paleontologist Richard Kay of Duke University). More important, it can now be said the findings may well have been significantly overstated. We won't know for sure until further research is done. But if this event causes the public to distrust science and media, that distrust is well placed."[22]

BBC News: Dr Chris Beard, curator of the Carnegie Museum of Natural History and author of *The Hunt for the Dawn Monkey*, said he was "awestruck" by the publicity machine surrounding the new fossil. . ."I would be absolutely dumbfounded if it turns out to be a potential ancestor to humans."[23]

So another "proof" bites the dust! Let's look at one final candidate:

Ardi: *The Associated Press* headline read, "Before Lucy Came Ardi, New Earliest Human Ancestor Found" and went on to state, "The story of humankind is reaching back another million years with the discovery of 'Ardi,' a hominid who lived 4.4 million years ago in what is now Ethiopia." Such was the introduction to *Ardipithecus ramidus*, or Ardi for short, who is not so much a brand new "ape-man" discovery, but more of a rehashing of a prior claim.[24] Once again, it's interesting that the fossil evidence for this alleged hominoid was discovered way back in 1994! It's also interesting that the bone fragments were found scattered over the distance of about one mile, making it very challenging to reconstruct a representative individual! I guess that's where creativity comes in handy.

According to *Discovery News*, "it is as close as we have ever come to finding the last common ancestor of chimpanzees and humans."[25]

Nothing in this find was really of any kind of ground-breaking nature. This creature was not only significantly different from modern humans, but also very different from modern apes (and certainly not a hybrid of the two). According to Timothy White (paleontologist, University of California-Berkeley's Human Evolution Research Center), "It's not a chimp. It's not a human."[26]

Overall, it doesn't really change the evolutionary picture much one way or the other, and certainly does not pose a challenge to creationists. In fact, even *Nature* magazine concluded from earlier research that it is possible that...

> "[*Ardipithecus*] *ramidus* is neither an ancestor of humanity, nor of chimpanzees. . ."[27]

Nothing new has been discovered that would change this view. So much for the media hype. This is just another example in a long line of over-hyped discoveries by people who are overly eager to find supportive evidence of their theories.

HUMAN AND CHIMP DNA SIMILARITIES

You've probably heard claims made stating that humans and chimpanzees share DNA that are up to 99% identical, giving compelling evidence of their shared evolutionary lineage. *National Geographic News* (back in 2005) posited 96% similarity:

> Darwin wasn't just provocative in saying that we descend from the apes—he didn't go far enough," said Frans de Waal, a primate scientist at Emory University in

Atlanta, Georgia. "We are apes in every way, from our long arms and tailless bodies to our habits and temperament. . ." A comparison of Clint's genetic blueprints with that of the human genome shows that our closest living relatives share 96 percent of our DNA. The number of genetic differences between humans and chimps is ten times smaller than that between mice and rats.[28]

Scientific American (2009) claims that the similarity is as high as 99%:

Six years ago I jumped at an opportunity to join the international team that was identifying the sequence of DNA bases, or "letters," in the genome of the common chimpanzee (*Pan troglodytes*). As a biostatistician with a long-standing interest in human origins, I was eager to line up the human DNA sequence next to that of our closest living relative and take stock. A humbling truth emerged: our DNA blueprints are nearly 99 percent identical to theirs. That is, of the three billion letters that make up the human genome, only 15 million of them—less than 1 percent—have changed in the six million years or so since the human and chimp lineages diverged.[29]

Scientists have known for quite some time that claims of close to 99% similarity are fallacious, as evidenced by the title of the following article: "Relative Differences: The Myth of 1%" (*Science Magazine* 2007).[30] It is truly unfortunate that this information does not readily find its way into the mainstream media.

In the process of comparing human and chimp DNA, an attempt was made to line up the genomes to see how well they match. However, in order to do this (and achieve a high percentage match) scientists had to introduce tens of thousands of chromosomal rearrangements. This is somewhat akin to "looking in the back of the book for the answer" and then retroactively changing your response to match what it was supposed to be. You cannot simply move these genes around in whatever order might suit your needs, because their order may have important effects on gene expression.[31]

Physician William Hurlbut (Stanford professor and member of the President's Council on bioethics):

Even where genes are similar, the timing and degree of gene expression (making proteins) can result in dramatically different adult body structures and functions.[32]

How did they come-up with such high percentages? Let's take a look.[33]

1. First of all, the chimp genome is about 10-12% larger than the human genome (and the gorilla genome).

2. Secondly, when the chimp genome was first sequenced, it largely consisted of un-oriented, random fragments. They actually used the human DNA sequence as "scaffolding" to establish the proper sequence for the chimp, but this assumes that the two are related, which is what they are trying to prove.

3. Thirdly, they only used DNA sequence fragments that initially seemed to display a high level of similarity. Anything that didn't line-up was excluded from comparison.

4. Lastly, they only considered the protein coding portions of the genes in their comparisons. However, this is a very, very small percentage of the entire genome, because most of the genome (what used to be thought of as "junk DNA"—already addressed here) consists of segments that are involved in gene regulation, which provides instructions on how to use the protein coding segments. This is a very significant point, because we know that the same gene can code for completely different functions in different creatures. It's all a matter of what the "regulatory instructions" tell them to do, but they were not comparing these "instruction" segments.

To their credit, there are some evolutionists who realize these figures are greatly inflated. According to one study, it was as low as 86%.[34]

For argument's sake, let's temporarily say that we actually are 96% similar to chimps with respect to our DNA. That leaves a 4% difference. Given that the human genome consists of 3 billion nucleotides (or "letters"), a 4% difference would still represent 120 million nucleotides ("letters") that are different! This equates to the amount of information found in forty 500-page books! So thinking back to the section on mutations for a moment, that would mean in the time since humans supposedly split off from apes (assumed be about six million years ago), these accidental changes to our "instruction manual" (the genome) are responsible for creating 20,000 pages of highly complex, useful information, all the while not significantly effecting the rest of the manual in any truly detrimental way! This stretches the imagination beyond reason. Not only that, but evolutionists themselves recognize the challenge of coming up with the insurmountable amount of necessary "beneficial" changes in such a "short" time. This problem is commonly known as "Haldane's Dilemma," named after evolutionary scientist J. B. S. Haldane (British geneticist and biologist), in 1957.

We should also point out that mere similarity does not necessarily indicate common ancestry. As mentioned previously, similarity can be equally attributed to a common designer. Additionally, differences in certain gene sequences may have extremely insignificant affects, while differences in others may produce profoundly different outcomes. Consider the following sentence and the two that follow which are each about 97% identical to the original sentence.

Original:

"It is unquestionably true that all scientists believe evolution is an absolute fact and do not question it in the least."

Alteration #1:

"It's unquestionably true that all scientists believe **that** evolution is an absolute fact and do not question it in the least."

Alteration #2:

"It is unquestionably **not** true that all scientists believe evolution is an absolute fact and do not question it in the least."

Even though each of these alterations differs from the original by only 3%, the meaning of the first alteration is identical to the original, having only added the extraneous word "that." However, the second alteration conveys the complete opposite meaning, having added the word "not." The point here is that it's not just the amount of change that ultimately matters, it's the significance of the change.

These are just a few challenges to what is currently being promoted as extremely strong evidence for human evolution. It is a shame that these details are almost always notoriously absent from science classroom discussions on evolution and from the media in general. *The Weekly Standard* (in 2008) made a very poignant comment:

Even if the "98 percent" figure is true—and as we shall see, it probably isn't—this is nonsense. We are no more "98 percent chimp" then we are 40 percent salad because we share approximately that percentage of genes with lettuce.[35]

NO MORE MONKEYING AROUND

We will wrap up this chapter by reviewing a few more quotes regarding the fossil record and the origin of man:

The Times (London):

Few sciences produce such abundant returns from so few fragments of fact as paleontology.[36]

Dr. Henry Gee (ardent evolutionist, senior editor—biological sciences for the journal *Nature*):

> Despite decades of patient work we still know rather little about the evolution of humanity. . .the remains we have are very scarce and very meager and that means that there are probably lots of different species that existed, lived for hundreds of thousands of years and then became extinct and we know nothing about them. . . All you need is just one to completely blow apart your well entrenched comfortable idea of the linear progress of evolution.[37]

> Fossil evidence of human evolutionary history is fragmentary and open to various interpretations. Fossil evidence of chimpanzee evolution is absent altogether.[38]

> To take a line of fossils and claim that they represent a lineage is not a scientific hypothesis that can be tested, but an assertion that carries the same validity as a bedtime story—amusing, perhaps even instructive, but not scientific.[39]

ENDNOTES

1.   Miller and Levine, *Biology*, 2000, p. 757.

2.   Shreeve, J., "Argument Over a Woman," *Discover,* 11(8):58 (1990).

3.   Johanson, Donald C., and Edey, Maitland, *Lucy: The Beginnings of Humankind,* (New York: Simon & Schuster, 1981), pp. 257,258.

4.   Woods, Arthur, *The Weekend Australian*, 14-15 January, 1989.

5.   Dickson, E., and Sarler, F., "How far have we really come?" *Radio Times*, 22-28 March 2003.

6.   Osborn, H.F., "The Earth speaks to Bryan," *The Forum,* 73:796-803, 1925.

7.   White, A.J. Monty, "The Piltdown Man Fraud," 24 November 2003, http://creation.com/the-piltdown-man-fraud—*last accessed 9/23/10.*

8.   Gurche, John, *National Geographic*, March 1996, p. 109.

9.   *American Journal of Physical Anthropology*, 1983, vol. 60, pages 279-317.

10.   Johanson, D., and Shreeve, J., *Lucy's Child*, William Morrow and Company, New York, 1989, p.49.

11.   http://creation.com/neandertal-genome-like-ours—*Last accessed 9/18/10.*

12.   http://creation.com/how-dating-methods-work—*Last accessed 7/16/12.*

13.   *Nature*, 392(6672):173-176, 12 March 1998.

14. http://www.revealingthelink.com—Note: This website was created in conjunction with the announcement, but the headline phrase "This changes everything" has since been removed.

15. Franzen, Jens L.; et al., "Complete Primate Skeleton from the Middle Eocene of Messel in Germany: Morphology and Paleobiology," *PLoS ONE*, 4 (5): e5723, (2009).

16. Ibid. ref #14.

17. "Common Ancestor of Humans, Modern Primates? 'Extraordinary' Fossil Is 47 Million Years Old," *ScienceDaily*, May 19, 2009; http://www.sciencedaily.com/releases/2009/05/090519104643.htm—*last accessed 9/23/10*.

18. http://www.nydailynews.com/news/us_world/2009/05/19/2009-05-19_missing_link_found_fossil_of_47_millionyearold_primate_sheds_light_on_.html#ixzz0G934GaPW&B—*last accessed 9/23/10*.

19. Watts, Alex, "Scientists Unveil Missing Link in Evolution," *Sky News Online*, May 19, 2009.

20. Gould, Stephen J., as quoted in Adler, 1980, 96[18]:95.

21. Moskowitz, Clara, "Amid Media Circus, Scientists Doubt 'Ida' Is Your Ancestor," *LiveScience*, May 20, 2009.

22. Britt, Robert Roy, "Ida Fossil Hype Went Too Far," *LiveScience*, May 20, 2009.

23. McGourty, Christine, "Scientists Hail Stunning Fossil," *BBC News*, May 19, 2009.

24. Schmid, Randolph E., *Associated Press*, October 1, 2009.

25. Viegas, Jennifer, interviewing and quoting Tim White , *Discovery News*, Thu Oct 1, 2009, http://news.discovery.com/archaeology/ardi-human-ancestor.html—*last accessed 9/18/10*.

26. Ibid.

27. Gee, H., "Uprooting the human family tree," *Nature* 373(6509):15, 5 January 1995.

28. Lovgren, Stefan, "Chimps, Humans 96 Percent the Same, Gene Study Finds," *National Geographic News*, August 31, 2005.

29. Pollard, Katherine S, "What Makes Us Human?" *Scientific American*, May 2009.

30. Cohen, Jon, "Relative Differences: The Myth of 1%," *Science*, 29 June 2007, Vol. 316. no. 5833, p. 1836.

31. King, M.C., and A.C. Wilson, "Evolution at two levels in humans and chimpanzees," *Science*, 188, 107-116, (1975).

32. Smith, Wesley J., "The U.N. Monkeys Around," *The Weekly Standard*, August 22, 2008, http://www.discovery.org/a/6851—*last accessed 9/23/10*.

33. Anderson, Daniel, "Decoding the dogma of DNA similarity," June 6, 2007, http://creation.com/decoding-the-dogma-of-dna-similarity—last accessed 9/23/10. Also, special thanks to Dr. Robert Carter from Creation Ministries International for information given through personal correspondence (September 2010).

34. Anzai, T., et al., "Comparative sequencing of human and chimpanzee MHC class I regions unveils insertions/deletions as the major path to genomic divergence." Proceedings of the National Academy of Sciences. 100 (13): 7708-13, (1975).

35. Smith, Wesley J., "The U.N. Monkeys Around," *The Weekly Standard*, August 22, 2008.

36. Nigel Hawkes in The Times (London), 23 September, 1995

37. "Alien from Earth," *NOVA* documentary, November 11, 2008.

38. Gee, Henry, "Return to the planet of the apes," *Nature,* 412, 131-132 (12 July 2001).

39. Gee, Henry, *In Search of Deep Time: Beyond the Fossil Record to a New History of Life*, New York, The Free Press, 1999, page 126-127.

The Best Evidence for Creation: It May Come as a Surprise!

Many people are intrigued by all of the fascinating evidence in support of biblical creation, but don't feel they could remember it all or comprehend it deeply enough to confidently defend their faith when engaging with a skeptic. Quite often, they are not even looking to memorize the top five evidences, but would rather be given the one piece of evidence, the one fact—the "silver bullet," if you will—that would stop the skeptic in their tracks. I can relate to this, because there are many times when I've heard a lecture on a particular topic of interest and walked away with two thoughts: (a) that was an awesome and powerful talk, and (b) there's no way that I could convey what I just heard to someone else—I wouldn't know where to begin!

As with many other complex issues, there is no real "silver bullet" argument for creation or Christianity in general that would make every skeptic instantly admit defeat and experience a change of heart. At the same time, it is important to note that the same holds true regarding evolution and atheism, so this is not something unique to Christianity. Ultimately, this is truly a spiritual issue and the facts will often not have the effect we would expect. It's not a matter of having the right facts to change someone's heart; it's more of a changed heart helps people see the facts in a new light. In a sense, the resurrection of Christ should be a "silver bullet" regarding the defense of Christianity, but it obviously has not worked that way for many people. Chapter 14 covers a number of important points in regard to discussing the creation/evolution controversy with others.

With all of that said, I personally believe there is one particular evidence for creation that truly is the very best, far above all the rest. I have had countless people approach me and ask something like "What would you say is the very best evidence?" I usually preface my answer by telling them that although I am extremely confident in the answer I give, they may be a bit disappointed at first, meaning that they will probably expect to hear something different, something more "flashy." I am completely convinced, after over twenty-six years of researching and lecturing, that the very best evidence for creation is—(drum roll, please)—the Bible! You may be able to see why some people are somewhat confused and a bit disappointed with my answer. You may even feel the same way at this point. They aren't exactly sure what they are looking for, but they do know my answer isn't it. They usually want to hear something more along the line of the complexity of DNA or the intricacies of the human brain, but the Bible—they can't give that answer to a skeptic! They'd be laughed off the planet!

Let's explore this a bit deeper for a minute. As mentioned in earlier chapters, "science" in general represents conclusions drawn by men and women who were not there in the beginning, did not observe the origin of the universe or life, are fallible and thus prone to making mistakes (and sometime even lie), and they are studying a fallen, sin-cursed world that is not the way God originally created it. Add to that the realization that facts do not speak for themselves. They must all be interpreted by a filter (such as one's own presuppositions or worldview) in order to have any significant meaning. With this in mind, it is easy to see how scientists can, and often do, come up with erroneous conclusions. So when we are talking about scientific evidence (whether in support of creation or evolution), in a very real sense, it is always tentative, often having contrary interpretations by the opposing side. Also, future discoveries could potentially modify or nullify current interpretations.

Let's contrast that against the Bible. If the Bible truly is the Word of God, then whatever it says is true, whether we like it or not, and whether or not we completely understand it. The Bible is very clear that God created everything in six days; the universe, the solar system and all life in this planet, including mankind. I know what you are probably thinking right now, "Yeah, but that's the Bible and the skeptic doesn't believe the Bible was written by God. In fact they may not even believe that God exists, so you can't use the Bible!" I've heard similar responses from many different people over the years. Let's examine this a bit further.

So you think you can't use the Bible as an argument? For a Christian, it is true that their presupposition is that the Bible is inspired by God and therefore true. All of our beliefs stem from this presupposition. It is our worldview, our starting point. The skeptic would have us believe that we are not allowed to bring our biases or presuppositions into the argument. Too many Christians buy into that demand, feeling that the skeptic has made a valid point. The truth is, they haven't. Just like us, they also have biases and presuppositions. Try this one for a presupposition: they believe that the Bible is *not* inspired by God and therefore not always true. Some of them also have a presupposition that God does *not* exist. These are two biases that they believe to be true, but cannot prove, so they remain simple presuppositions. There's absolutely nothing wrong with having a presupposition or bias. In fact, it's virtually impossible not to have one. The important question isn't whether or not you have a bias, but more specifically, "Does your bias consistently make sense of the world in which we live?" This leads us into a line of thought called "presuppositional apologetics." I know, it sounds daunting, but it's actually fascinating. I decided to add a short overview in appendix B, because I did not want to get too bogged down with something that is more apropos to a discussion with an atheist or agnostic regarding the existence of God, than simply when discussing the creation versus evolution debate. I would highly recommend taking the time to look at this line of reasoning and use it as your main defense of the Christian worldview.

Bringing us back to our main point again: if the Bible is truly the inspired Word of God, then whatever it says it true. Since it tells us that He created everything in six days, then that must be true. The natural question that always follows is, "But how do you know the Bible was actually written by God?"

I was speaking to a class of eighth grade students at a Christian school as part of a series in which I was covering a basic defense for the Christian faith. This particular school only went through junior high, and every student (except for one who was going to be homeschooled) was going to be entering the public school system for their high school years. I was specifically focusing on preparing them to stand strong in their faith during their next four years, when their environment would be significantly different, to say the least.

Approximately ninety percent of the students had attended a Christian school since kindergarten or first grade, in addition to attending church each week with their parents. I asked the class how many of them believed that the Bible is the inspired Word of God. Every hand went up. A great response, but not too surprising. I then asked how many could tell me why they believed it is the inspired Word of God. Four hands were raised and these were the responses I received:

Because it says it is.

Because I believe it is.

Because it was written by God.

Because that's what I've been taught.

It is readily apparent that these responses are not really legitimate answers, certainly none that would appease a skeptic. In essence, none of them really knew why they could trust the Bible and subsequently each one would be more vulnerable to losing their faith, because they lack true conviction.

The existence or non-existence of God cannot be proven scientifically, because of the non-material nature of God (science is powerful, but limited to commenting on the physical universe and its constituents). We discussed that a bit in the chapters 2 and 3. However, observations of the natural world around us (science) only make sense within the context of a Christian worldview. (See appendix B for further discussion.)

In a similar fashion, the inspiration of the Bible cannot technically be "proven" in the strictest sense. Once again, observations of the natural world around us (science) and our own human experiences only make sense within the context of a Christian worldview. Regarding conversations with skeptics, you may very well state something like, "My presupposition is that I believe the Bible is the inspired Word of God and true in all it conveys. Your presupposition is that it is not. Let's discuss our lines of reasoning for our beliefs and how they comport to the world in which we live." Having a grasp of presuppositional apologetics (appendix B) at this point would be extremely helpful, but knowing that it may take you a while to develop this approach to defending your faith, I will share a few things that I believe are tangible and serve as an encouragement.

In the remainder of this chapter, we will briefly look into the nature of the inspiration of Scripture. I share these "evidences" not as ultimate proof, but as things that are hallmarks of what we would expect to see if the Bible truly is the inspired Word of God. They serve as a great encouragement and faith strengthener to the Christian and certainly a formidable challenge to the skeptic. However, for actual "proof," you would have to stick with "presuppositional apologetics" (appendix B).

PASSING THE TEST

There are a number of tests that you can apply to any religious writing to determine whether or not it is consistent with the claim of being authored by

God. These are not special "Bible" tests, they are generic tests that can be equally applied to any text in question. The main tests are as follows:

- Internal Consistency

- Historical Accuracy

- Scientific Accuracy

- Prophetic Accuracy

We will briefly define and explore each one of these areas.

INTERNAL CONSISTENCY

If you were to read a particular religious book and find that it was contradicting itself, you would immediately begin to question the integrity of its author. In short, if we find actual contradictions in whatever source we are examining, that would be strong evidence that God was not the author.

Let's take a minute to go through an interesting exercise. We'll start by taking two university professors who have the following pedigree:

- They are natural born US citizens.

- They lived their entire lives in the US.

- They speak English as their primary language.

- They are both sixty years old.

- They have PhDs in US History.

- They are professors of US History.

- They teach at the same university.

Let's also say that we ask them to each write a fifty page research paper on one controversial topic—the assassination of JFK. Would they be in total agreement on every detail of this historical event? Not likely. Even though they are writing about an event which occurred within their

lifetime and they have identical backgrounds and education, they still wouldn't be in total agreement.

Let's see how this compares to what we find in the Bible. Consider the following:

• There were about forty different human authors of the Bible.

• They had greatly varying backgrounds (king, fishermen, doctor, etc.).

• They wrote in three different languages (Hebrew, Aramaic, Greek).

• They wrote from three different continents (Africa, Asia, Europe).

• They wrote in different settings (palace, prison, wilderness, etc.).

• They lived and wrote over a period of 1,600 years.

With all of this in mind, it is truly miraculous that the Bible has complete cohesion among its human authors from cover-to-cover. If these authors were simply writing what they felt to be true or important, we would not see the incredible unity that we do.

This naturally leads to the whole topic of "contradictions in the Bible." To do this justice would require an entirely separate book, but I do wish to comment briefly regarding this area.

I personally believe there are numerous apparent contradictions in the Bible. However, they are only alleged contradictions and not actual inconsistencies. There are a number of principles that must be kept in mind when examining any alleged contradiction. I will list just a few for your consideration.

1. *Innocent until proven guilty.*

   Great attempts have been made to clear up apparent discrepancies of the great Greek and Latin classics, because people wanted to believe in them. However, many people are quick to assume the Bible is fallacious, before doing any sort of credible research. Their motto is "Guilty until proven innocent."

2. *A mere difference does not constitute a contradiction.*

   Differences actually support the independence of the writers, showing that they were not in collusion. An example of a "difference" not being a contradiction is explained in the next point.

3. *Don't confuse supplementation with contradiction.*

Fairly often one writer will include additional information, but this does not make it contradictory. For example, someone may refer to John as a father, while someone else says that he is a husband. These are two different details about the same person; they do not constitute a contradiction.

4. *Study the context.*

It's been stated that a text without a context is a pretext! This simply means that we must always be aware of the context of the passage we are examining or we might easily misinterpret it, or even conclude that is contains a contradiction. One skeptic claimed that the Bible couldn't possibly be true because it contains so many crazy stories. His only example was that when the Hebrew people were released from being slaves in Egypt, they wandered in the wilderness for forty years, the entire time carrying the ark on their backs. What this skeptic did not realize is that the passage in Exodus was referring to the ark of the covenant, not Noah's ark!

5. *Parabolic, symbolic and phenomenological language.*

The Bible often uses symbolic and poetic language and we know not to take those statements literally. For example, "Oh LORD, my rock. . ." (Psalm 28:1, KJV) and "the shadow of thy wings" (Psalm 63:7, KJV). We do not believe that God is actually a piece of granite or that He is some kind of bird with wings. Moreover, when the Bible speaks of the rising of the sun (Isaiah 45:6), we know that it is very similar to today's television meteorologist telling us what time sunrise was this morning. In neither case is it being implied that the sun orbits around the earth.

Before moving on, I will share one actual example of an alleged contradiction along with its proper resolution. It has been claimed that the Bible gives contradictory accounts of the timing of the crucifixion. According to Mark 15:25 (KJV), "it was the third hour, and they crucified him. . ." However, John 19:14 (KJV) indicates that Jesus was still on trial ". . .about the sixth hour." How could Jesus be crucified the third hour (Mark) if He was still on trial the sixth hour (John)? Here's the solution. Mark wrote using the Jewish time system. The Jews measured their days from evening to evening (6:00 PM one day until 6:00 PM the next day). The third hour of the morning in that system would have been between 8:00 and 9:00 AM. John, on the other hand, wrote following the Roman system that we use today (from midnight to midnight). The sixth hour would be between 5:00 and 6:00 AM. Therefore, Jesus was still on trial early in the morning and then crucified a few hours later. Problem solved!

HISTORICAL ACCURACY

The historical accuracy of the Bible has often been called into question. However, a great deal of the criticism has been based on a lack of evidence, rather than on anything that was actually discovered. In other words, because archaeologists had not yet discovered anything that would confirm a particular account in the Bible, they assumed that it never happened.

It's been humorously said that "every time a spade is dug into the ground, another atheist dies." Archaeology has repeatedly verified many events and locations found in the Bible, giving an ever-growing confidence in the accuracy and inspiration of God's Word. We'll briefly review two examples.

The Hittites

The Hittites are mentioned numerous times in the Bible (e.g., Genesis 15:20, Exodus 3:8, Joshua 1:4) and are stated as having inhabited the land of Canaan. The most famous Hittite was Uriah, the husband of Bathsheba. Skeptics scoffed at the idea that the Hittites ever even existed, but through a series of discoveries starting in 1876 (by British scholar A.H. Sayce), their existence was confirmed. This discovery proved to be one of the greatest finds in the history of archaeology. In addition to confirming the biblical narrative, we have a much greater understanding of not only the history of our language, but also the religious, social and political practices of the ancient Middle East.

The Battle of Jericho

Another favorite of the skeptics is the story of the battle of Jericho. The first city that the Israelites were instructed to take over after entering into the "promised land" (subsequent to their release from Egyptian slavery and ensuing wandering in the wilderness) was that of Jericho. What makes this story especially interesting is that Joshua (leader of the Israelites after Moses died) quietly led the people in a march around the city for six days in a row and on the seventh day, they circled seven times, after which they blew ram's horns and shouted. And we know what happened next, "the walls came a-tumblin' down." Joshua 6:20 (NIV) states that "the wall collapsed; so every man charged straight in, and they took the city."

What does archaeology have to say about this fanciful story? Beginning in the early 1900s, a number of prominent archaeologists discovered some very interesting details from the site of this ancient city. A fifteen-foot high retaining wall was discovered, supporting an additional eight foot wall. The evidence strongly shows that the walls fell outward, leaving a pile of stone and bricks, which enabled the ensuing army to easily climb over the fortification and attack the inhabitants.

Rahab (the woman who helped the Israelite spies escape while they were originally scouting out the city) lived in a house that was a part of the wall surrounding the city. The biblical account (Joshua 2:1-21) mentions that she and her family were to be saved during the siege of the city. Excavations in the early 1900s found that a short span of the north wall had not fallen and there were houses built against it. This is completely consistent with the biblical story.

An additional detail regarding the destruction of Jericho is that the entire city was burned (Joshua 6:24a). Archaeologists discovered layers of ash and debris three feet thick! Of particular interest is the fact that much grain was found in the ruins, which normally would have been seized by the attacking armies, having been such an important commodity for consumption and bartering. The Bible, however, only mentions that the Israelites took gold, silver, bronze and iron to put into "the treasury of the Lord's house" (Joshua 6:24b). This find is another testament to the veracity of the Scriptures.

In light of these previous examples, it is interesting to contrast the archaeological confirmation of the Bible with that of the Book of Mormon. Mormon officials have stated that the Smithsonian Institution and National Geographic have used the Book of Mormon as an archaeological guide. Both of these entities have denied any such actions and further state that the Book of Mormon has "no connection with archaeology of the New World."

Ethnologist Gordon Fraser:

> Mormon archaeologists have been trying for years to establish some evidence that will confirm the presence of the [Mormon] church in America. There still is not a scintilla of evidence either in the religious philosophy of the ancient writings, or in the presence of artifacts, that lead to such a belief.[1]

Archaeology continues to confirm history as recorded in the Bible, passing the second test regarding historical accuracy.

SCIENCE

Most people who reject the Bible as being completely inspired by God, do so not strictly on the grounds of history or internal inconsistency, but on the assumption that the Bible has been discredited over and over by modern science. In their minds, the Bible has been superseded and stands in stark contrast to the powerful, incontrovertible discoveries of modern science. We will see, however, that rather than disproving the Bible, modern science continues to reveal its divine inspiration.

There are two major categories when it comes to science and the Bible. The first category focuses on "origins," specifically, the creation account. The second deals with "scientific foreknowledge." Since this book already deals with the creation/evolution origins debate, we will limit this section to amazing scientific foreknowledge in the Bible (which conveys scientific phenomenon well before the advent of modern science).

GENERAL HEALTH PRACTICES

Acts 7:22 states that "Moses was educated in all the wisdom of the Egyptians. . ." (NIV). We also know that Moses was the author of the first five books of the Bible. It would logically follow then that we could expect to see some of this "Egyptian wisdom" in his writings.

The Egyptians were renowned for their supposed highly advanced medical practices. The Ebers Papyrus (1550 BC) contained over 800 magical formulas and remedies practiced by the Egyptians. Here's just one example. The remedy for a splinter: apply worm blood and donkey dung! It is obvious to even the most casual reader that this would be far from a great antidote, particularly donkey dung, which is full of tetanus spores. Tetanus (also referred to as lockjaw) causes involuntary muscle spasms, particularly in the jaw, and can cause difficulty in swallowing and even lead to death.

Let's contrast this "advanced medical practice" with an example from the writings of Moses. Consider Numbers 19:11-12:

> Whoever touches a human corpse will be unclean for seven days. They must purify themselves with the water on the third day and on the seventh day; then they will be clean (NIV).

What exactly is the "water?" We find the answer in Numbers 19:6,

> The priest is to take some *cedar wood, hyssop* and *scarlet wool* and throw them onto the *burning heifer* (NIV; emphasis added).

Now, let's take a look at what modern science has discovered about each of these elements.[2]

- Heifer ashes + cedar wood produces lye (caustic soda). For many years, lye was used to make soap, which works well as a cleaning agent.

- Hyssop is a blue-flowered plant that is native to the east Mediterranean. It can be converted into thymol, which is an isopropyl alcohol that kills bacteria.

- Scarlet wool forms a gritty abrasive substance that is useful for getting into every crevasse to aid in thorough cleansing.

- The mention of the third and seventh day (in verse twelve) relates to the fact that bacteria thrive in damp environments. So you have a few days to dry (hampering bacterial growth), then apply the waters, allow to dry again for a few more days and then re-apply.

This amazing remedy evidences inspiration, but is in stark contrast to the Egyptian's remedy for a splinter.

There are numerous other health practices in the Bible, but we will not take the time to detail each one.

- Wound, skin, and discharge precautions (Leviticus 15:2-11, 17:11)

- Postpartum precautions (Leviticus 12:2-3)

- Burial precautions (Numbers 19:14-16,19,22, Leviticus 11:24-28, 40)

- Isolation and quarantine (Leviticus 13:1-14:57, Numbers 5:2-4, Deuteronomy 23:10)

- Waste disposal (Deuteronomy 23:12-14, Leviticus 11:33, 13:47-58, 15:12)

One final example that I will share has to do with a particular Jewish tradition. Genesis 17:12 (NIV) states, "For the generations to come every male among you who is eight days old must be circumcised. . ."

As part of God's singling-out of the Hebrews as his chosen people, He instructed that each male child should be circumcised. The Bible does not tell us why God chose this particular sign, but it does say that it was to occur on the eighth day. Why the eighth day? Why not the eighth month or the thirteenth year? Once again, modern science reveals some very interesting facts that shed further light on this verse.

When we experience any type of cut, our blood automatically clots or thickens in the area of the cut in order to stop the bleeding. There are two crucial elements in our blood that are necessary for clotting to occur: vitamin K and prothrombin.[3] Scientists discovered that vitamin K starts to develop in a newborn anywhere between days five and seven. Prothrombin exhibits the following levels:

Day 1   = 90%

Days 2-5   = 30%

Day 8   = 110%

You can see that if any type of surgical procedure is performed, the ideal day would be the eighth day, because vitamin K is definitely present by then and prothrombin is at a level higher than 100% of its normal level. It will actually will never be that high again the rest of an individual's life! That Moses must have been a pretty smart cookie to have had such advanced medical knowledge; or just maybe he was actually inspired to write what he wrote, even though he did not personally understand all the details. (You'll have to decide which seems more plausible.)

An interesting side note has to do with modern day circumcisions. Just before my son was born, my wife and I attended a few birthing classes so that we would be prepared for the arrival of our first child. They were very helpful and I'm glad we went. However, during one of the classes, the one in which they mentioned the option of having your son circumcised if you chose to do so, I became a bit concerned. They said if anyone was interested in that option, they would simply take the baby down the hall for the procedure. I couldn't help but think about "the eighth day" mentioned in the passage we are discussing. Should I have been worried? Wouldn't this still be valid for today? Should I make plans to come back a week after our son is born and have the circumcision at that time? In the course of sharing other details, the nurse mentioned something about giving the baby a shot in the heel. Someone else in the class raised their hand and asked, "What is this shot you are giving the baby?" The nurse responded by saying that it was vitamin K! They artificially introduce vitamin K to aid in blood clotting before it is naturally produced on its own. No need to come back a week later! (And Prothrombin is at 90% of its normal level on day one, so it's not an issue.) I took the opportunity to share with the rest of the class what I knew about blood clotting and what the Bible said about circumcision. I don't know if any of them were impressed, but I just had to tell them.

PROPHECY

Of all the lines of evidence for inspiration, prophecy arguably presents the strongest case. Predicting the future is risky business. Numerous people throughout history have made predictions and occasionally they seem to be impressive. What is generally not published is the extensive list of predications that did not come true. When all is considered, much of the successful prophecies would be considered statistically probable. In other words, if you make enough predictions, you are bound to get at least a few of them right. Other times, the predications are regarding something that is fairly likely to happen anyway, so predicting it isn't very impressive. For example, if it were predicted that a certain Hollywood couple was going to get divorced within the next two years, or that they were going to have a child (or even both), that is not much of a prophecy because of how likely that is to happen all on its own.

Isaiah 46:10 (NIV), speaking of God, states, "I make known the end from the beginning, from ancient times, what is still to come. I say: My purpose will stand, and I will do all that I please." It is God alone who can truly predict the future, because He is outside of time, seeing the past, present and future all at once. "Before the mountains were born or you brought forth the whole world, from everlasting to everlasting you are God" (Psalm 90:2, NIV).

God often spoke to people through His prophets, but how did the people know if someone was truly a prophet of God? The following passage answers this for us:

> I will raise up for them a prophet like you from among their brothers; I will put my words in his mouth, and he will tell them everything I command him. If anyone does not listen to my words that the prophet speaks in my name, I myself will call him to account. But a prophet who presumes to speak in my name anything I have not commanded him to say, or a prophet who speaks in the name of other gods, must be put to death. You may say to yourselves, "How can we know when a message has not been spoken by the LORD?" If what a prophet proclaims in the name of the LORD does not take place or come true, that is a message the LORD has not spoken. That prophet has spoken presumptuously. Do not be afraid of him (Deuteronomy 18:18-22, NIV).

Nostradamus was a sixteenth century physician and astrologer. Many people are under the impression that he was able to predict the future and will often mention his name in order to down play the prophetic nature and uniqueness of the Bible. However, upon closer examination of his writings we find the following:

• He made numerous false prophecies.

• His prophecies were so vague and unclear that they have no single "correct" interpretation.

• He confessed that the vague manner in which he wrote his prophecies was so that "they could not possibly be understood until they were interpreted after the event and by it."[4]

• Not a single genuine prophecy has ever been proved.

Shortly after the tragic terrorist attacks on the World Trade Center (September 11, 2001), the internet was flooded with claims that this calamity was predicted by Nostradamus. However, a further investigation showed that not only were people greatly reading things into the vague prophecy, but they were also embellishing it to make it more closely match the actual event!

Poor Track Record

In stark contrast to the Bible, you will not find even a single prophecy in the writings of Buddha, Confucius, the Hindu vedas, the Bhagavad Gita, or the Book of Mormon. The Quran (holy book of Islam) contains only one prophecy, which is actually self-fulfilling, regarding Muhammad returning to Mecca. In this case, all Muhammad had to do was to go back to Mecca, and "poof," the prophecy is fulfilled! Not very impressive.

Although there are no prophecies directly in the Book of Mormon itself, there have been many prophecies in other allegedly inspired Mormon writings. Let's examine a few.

Inhabitants on the Moon and Sun

Claims were made by Joseph Smith (founder of Mormonism) and Brigham Young (subsequent president of the Mormon Church) in their *Journal of Discourses* regarding inhabitants living on the moon and the sun, allegedly living to an age of a thousand years, being about six feet tall and dressing like Quakers![5] Well, we've been to the moon a few times and are pretty confident these individuals don't exist!

President of the United States

It was predicted that Brigham Young was to become the President of the United States.[6] That obviously never happened.

The Jehovah's Witnesses have made repeated predictions as to the return of Christ. Charles Taze Russell was the first president of the Watchtower Bible and Tract Society, which is the official organization of the Jehovah's Witnesses. Russell claimed that in 1914 the world would end (in the battle of Armageddon). This was to be followed by the millennium. When 1914 came and went without the advent of Armageddon, he revised the date to 1916 and eventually to 1918. J.F. Rutherford (the second president of the society) set 1925 as the year for Christ's return. Later he said that it would occur around 1940.

Many other false prophecies could be listed, but these will suffice in showing that the Jehovah's Witnesses do not have a good track record when it comes to claiming prophetic inspiration.

THE BIBLE ON THE OTHER HAND. . .

We will now examine the prophetic nature of the Bible. Unlike any other religious book in existence, approximately twenty-seven percent of the Bible is prophetic in nature, covering some 700 topics. That's incredible, especially considering that it contains over 31,000 verses. Many of the prophecies are intricately detailed, as well as depicting strange and highly unlikely events. We will highlight a few here to give you a feel for the kind of prophecy found in the Scriptures and how they are strong evidence of divine inspiration.

City of Tyre

Prediction:	Failure of Tyre's fortresses (Amos 1:9-10).
Fulfillment:	This was fulfilled by Nebuchadnezzar when he attacked the mainland of Tyre, and later by Alexander the Great when he attacked the island city of Tyre.
Prediction:	Attacked by many nations (Ezekiel 26:3).
Fulfillment:	Tyre was attacked by the Babylonians, Greeks, Romans, the Crusaders and the Muslims.
Prediction:	The city's stones, timber and soil would be thrown into the sea (Ezekiel 26:12).
Fulfillment:	History tells us that Alexander the Great took all of the rubble from the mainland city of Tyre and cast it into the sea in order to build a bridge over to the island city of Tyre to attack the inhabitants (not having ships capable of floating a significant army). That land bridge still stands today.
Prediction:	Tyre will be covered by ocean waters (Ezekiel 26:19).
Fulfillment:	In 1170 AD it was reported that the city was under water and one could view the ruins from a boat.

Prediction: Tyre would never be found/built again (Ezekiel 26:14, 21).

Fulfillment: Although there exists a city today named "Tyre" near the general area of this biblical city, it has no relation to the original Phoenician city or people. Alexander the Great, conquering Tyre (in 332 BC), brought a permanent end to the Phoenician empire, and to this day it has never been rebuilt.

This was certainly not a vague prophecy that was very likely to happen naturally. Once again, we see fingerprints of divine inspiration.

Called By His Name: Cyrus

In approximately 700 BC, the prophet Isaiah foretold of the rebuilding of Jerusalem and the temple (Isaiah 44:28; 54:1). What makes this prediction strange is that at the time, both Jerusalem and the temple were standing strong. Further details of this prophecy tell of the conquering of Babylon, which was virtually impenetrable (having moats, walls that were over 70 feet thick and 300 feet high, and having 250 watchtowers). Isaiah even mentioned by name the Persian king (Cyrus) who would lead this invasion, all 100 years before this king was even born! He further stated that Cyrus would allow the exiled Israelites to go free, without asking for any ransom money (contrary to common practice). Cyrus was also predicted to be the one to issue the decree for the rebuilding of Jerusalem and the temple.

This is exactly what happened in history. In 586 BC, Jerusalem and the temple were destroyed by King Nebuchadnezzar (king of Babylon). The Israelites were taken captive. Around 539 BC, a Persian king named Cyrus conquered Babylon, freeing the Israelites and giving the decree to begin the rebuilding of Jerusalem and temple.

The Messiah

The final prophetic example that we will examine has to do with the Old Testament's prediction of the coming Messiah. The central focus of the entire Bible is without question, Jesus Christ. There are over 300 prophetic references regarding the life, death and resurrection of the Messiah, consisting of 60 major predictions and 270 ramifications, all of which were made over 400 years in advance. Jesus proved beyond any doubt that He was truly this long-awaited savior, by fulfilling every single one of them. Having to accurately fulfill so many prophecies made it quite impossible for anyone else in history to legitimately lay claim to being the Messiah, although many have tried. The following table lists just a few examples of these prophecies:

Prophecy	Predicted	Fulfilled
Born of a virgin	Isaiah 7:14	Matthew 1:18, 24-25
Born in Bethlehem	Micah 5:2	Matthew 2:1
Herod kills children	Jeremiah 31:15	Matthew 2:16
Preceded by a messenger	Isaiah 43	Matthew 3:1-2
Resurrection	Psalms 16:10	Acts 2:31
Betrayed by a friend	Psalms 41:9	Matthew 10:4
Sold for 30 pieces of silver	Zechariah 11:12	Matthew 26:15
Silent before his accusers	Isaiah 53:7	Matthew 27:12
Crucifixion	Psalms 22:16	Luke 23:33
Crucified with thieves	Isaiah 53:12	Matthew 27:38
Bones not broken	Psalms 34:20	John 19:33
Buried in a rich man's tomb	Isaiah 53:9	Matthew 27:57-60

Some skeptics claim that all of the prophecies were "self-fulfilling," meaning that Jesus knew what was written and simply set out to purposely fulfill them all. This criticism is not well founded, considering the nature of some of the prophecies. How would Jesus have been able to control where he was born? And how would Jesus, when he was not even two years old, convince King Herod to kill all male children who were two years old or younger? And how would He contrive the amount of money He would be "sold for" just before his death and also determine His own execution style? He would also have had to ensure that none of His bones would be broken (which was contrary to current crucifixion customs).

An interesting and powerful exercise is to calculate the probability of someone "accidentally" fulfilling these prophecies. In other words, assume Jesus wasn't really the Messiah, He just happened to be in the right place at the right time, so to speak, and also did all of the right things. We will not look at the probability for *all* of the prophecies, just a portion of them. The figure we will use comes from Professor Peter Stoner (1888-1980). Dr. Stoner was chairman of the departments of mathematics and astronomy at Pasadena City College and later chairman of the science division of Westmont College. He published his findings in his book, *Science Speaks: Scientific Proof of the Accuracy of Prophecy and the Bible* (Moody Press, 1963). The American Scientific Affiliation even gave his work their stamp of approval (reproduced in the forward on Stoner's book):

> The manuscript for *Science Speaks* has been carefully reviewed by a committee of the American Scientific Affiliation members and by the Executive Council of the same group and has been found, in general, to be dependable and accurate in regard to the scientific material presented. The

mathematical analysis included is based upon principles of probability which are thoroughly sound and Professor Stoner has applied these principles in a proper and convincing way.

Stoner calculated that the chances of just 48 details being fulfilled is equal to—not one in a million; not one in a billion—but one in ten million, million, million, million, million, million, million, billion, billion, billion, billion, billion, billion, trillion, trillion, trillion, trillion, trillion, trillion (that's a "1" followed by 157 zeros!).

Since that number is so unbelievably huge, let's compare it to something that we are more familiar with. In chapter 4 we used the example of solving a Rubik's Cube blindfolded. We'll do the same here as well. Solving the enigmatic puzzle can be quite challenging and certainly doesn't happen by mistake. You may recall that there are over ten million trillion possible combinations, meaning that if you were blindfolded, you would have less than one chance in ten million trillion of getting it right! (The exact number is 43,252,003,274,489,856,000.)[7]

Let's compare solving the Rubik's Cube purely by chance (being blindfolded and spinning randomly) with the probability of someone in history just happening to fulfill forty-eight of the prophecies ascribed to the Messiah, with no supernatural intervention involved. It would be less likely than someone haphazardly solving the Rubik's Cube eight times in a row! This is not only very strong evidence for the inspiration of Scripture, but also virtual proof that Jesus Christ is the Messiah, the Savior of the world!

CONCLUSION

We've just completed a whirlwind tour, discussing a few of the evidences for the inspiration of the Bible. Certainly much more could be written, but this will at least give you a feel for the kind of characteristics we might expect to see if the Bible truly is the inspired Word of God. What can we conclude from all of this? Simply this: if the Bible is truly the Word of God (which is what we believe and is what our examination strongly indicates), then the biblical account of creation must necessarily be true, independent of whatever view might be popular among modern-day scientists. It is also comforting, however, to know that true science also supports the biblical record, which is further highlighted throughout the rest of this book.

I would like to mention two final points in closing this chapter. First of all, those of us who consider ourselves to be Christians must be careful that we are not of the mindset that we are out to "prove" that the Bible is true. That would essentially imply that there is a higher authority by which the Bible must be judged. If it truly is the Word of God, then the Bible is the final authority to which everything else must stand in judgment. We have two choices. We can either exercise reasonable faith and accept that the Bible is the final authority in all matters, or we can choose to live life tenuously, always wondering what the basis is for our moral compass and ultimate source of truth. Presuppositional apologetics actually shows us that our Christian worldview is correct, without getting bogged down in these various evidences.

The second closing point is that while it is very important to believe that the Bible is the divinely inspired Word of God, it is even more important to commit your life to following its precepts. With all of the exciting evidence for Christianity, creation and the Bible, it is all too easy to get caught up in the evidence and ignore the development of our personal, daily relationship with Jesus Christ. Commit yourself to reading God's Word daily and ask Him to reveal to you areas in which you need growth. James 1:22 (NIV) warns us by stating, "Do not merely listen to the word, and so deceive yourselves. Do what it says." If you do so, you will be in a much better position to share your faith and you will, "always be prepared to give an answer to everyone who asks you to give the reason for the hope that you have. But do this with gentleness and respect" (I Peter 3:15, NIV).

ENDNOTES

1.   Fraser, Gordon, *Is Mormonism Christian?* Moody Publishers, 1995, pp. 143-145.

2.   Butt, Kyle, "Scientific Foreknowledge and Medical Acumen of the Bible," Apologetics Press: *Reason & Revelation*, December 2006-26[12]:89-95, also: http://www.apologeticspress.org/articles/3159—*last accessed 9/19/10.*

3.   Thompson, Bert, "Why The EIGHTH Day?" Apologetics Press: Bible Bullets, http://www.apologeticspress.org/articles/1615—*last accessed 9/19/10.*

4.   Randi, James, "Nostradamus: The Prophet for All Seasons," *The Skeptical Enquirer* (Fall 1882), p.31.

5.   Huntington, O.B., *Young Women's Journal*, Vol. 3, p. 264, 1892) & (B. Young, *Journal of Discourses*, 1870, Vol. 13, p. 271.

6.   *Journal of Discourses*, Vol. 5, p.219.

7.   http://en.wikipedia.org/wiki/Rubik%27s_Cube—*last accessed 9/8/10.*

Chapter Nine

A Time Bomb:
The Old Earth/Young Earth Debate

If you've made it this far through the book and are feeling like there just hasn't been enough controversy for your liking. . . you've come to the right place! Arguably, no other topic within the creation/evolution debate is as potentially explosive or evokes as much emotion and argumentation among Christians as the age of the earth. For many, talking about the age of the earth. . ."Well, them's fightin' words!" Addressing this issue is not an effortless task. My goal with these next few chapters is five-fold:

1. Help you understand the significance of this issue within its context.

2. Give you a better understanding of what the Bible actually says related to the age of the earth.

3. Clarify what we actually learn from science on this issue, as well as its limitations.

4. Encourage you to have your own, educated, Spirit-led opinion (as opposed to simply accepting someone else's, including mine!).

5. Assist you in graciously conveying this information in an encouraging way, ultimately to strengthen the faith of others in the authority of God's Word and most importantly the gospel message.

IS ANYTHING LESS IMPORTANT?

Many people react to this issue by saying that the age of the earth is so insignificant it doesn't even warrant discussion, let alone argument. It's certainly not a salvation issue, is it?

Romans 10:9 states:

> That if you confess with your mouth, "Jesus is Lord," and have the correct view regarding the age of the earth, you will be saved.

This is not from the KJV (King James Version), but from the JKV—the "Just Kidding Version." Most of you are probably very familiar with this passage, which when correctly quoted states:

> That if you confess with your mouth Jesus is Lord and believe in your heart that God raised him from the dead, you will be saved (NKJV).

Clearly, a person's salvation is not dependent upon their opinion regarding the age of the earth. However, that does not mean that it is not of any importance. There are numerous issues in the Bible that, while not being essential for salvation, are still quite significant.

IT GOES WITHOUT SAYING

Certain things in life seem obvious; it's darker at night than during the day, fire is very hot and chocolate ice cream is much better than vanilla. (Okay, that last one might be debatable—maybe.) Within this list of obvious things many people would also include the idea that the earth is very, very old—in the billions of years.

Most people's opinions are based not on personal knowledge, but on assumptions that a certain view has already been proven beyond question. I also believe that our own pride often keeps us from humbly being open to hearing things that go against our presuppositions. One appropriate adage might be, "If you don't have facts on your side, get emotional." Most people have some opinion regarding whether the earth is relatively young or very old, but very few have any substantial reasons in defense of their view. I believe the number one reason for the lack of knowledge regarding this subject is the pervading view that it really doesn't matter one way or the other. This is where I would part company. I believe it does matter, for one simple reason: the Bible comments on it. I would be the first to agree that if the Bible doesn't comment on a particular subject, then we should not be too eager to make a big deal out of it. On the other hand, if it does, then we should pay close attention and learn as much as we can about what God is trying to convey regarding that particular topic.

Although I attended a non-denominational Bible church throughout my entire youth, I grew up believing that the earth was billions of years old; but it was solely because of what I was taught (from public school and the media), as opposed to being based on any personal knowledge of the subject. Since I didn't spend enough time critically thinking through my faith, I didn't see the age of the earth as being a very important issue one way or the other. You may have a similar opinion.

Even the most casual reader would recognize that there exists a significant amount of tension between a straight-forward literal reading of the Genesis creation account and what most modern scientists believe about the age of the earth. The literal six-day creation account indicates that the earth is in the range of thousands of years old (perhaps 6,000 or so), while current thinking in astronomy and geology conveys a figure of 4.6 billion years for the earth (and about 13.7 billion years for the universe). There is one thing for certain: both cannot be correct.

The intention of this chapter is to take a closer look at this issue, and in the process, expose the reader to some information that will hopefully challenge their thinking and increase their respect for the authority and inspiration of God's Word.

TWO OPTIONS

There really are only two feasible options regarding the age of the earth. Either the earth is about as old as many scientists tell us it is (about 4.6 billion years old) or it is relatively young (in the ball-park of 6,000–7,000 years old). Most values in between just don't cut it with either side. For instance, secular scientists would not be satisfied if it were presented to them that the earth was 100 million years old. On the other hand, most Christians (scientists included) who believe the Bible speaks of a "young Earth" would not be appeased if they were told the earth is 345,000 years old. So for our discussion, we will be focusing on whether the age of the earth is closer to 4.6 billion years or roughly 6,000. These two options are so diametrically opposed that no sane person could imagine both to be true.

LIMITING FACTOR OF PRESUPPOSITIONS

It is interesting to note that those who believe God created the universe and everything in it, at least theoretically have various options available regarding the earth's age. It could be relatively young, extremely old or anywhere in between. This naturally follows from the belief that God is all-powerful and could create anything in any amount of time, be it great or small. (More on that a bit later.) On the other hand, those who preclude the idea of the supernatural, are stuck with one option—a very, very old earth. (There is another option that we are ruling out for the time being, but will be explored in a bit more depth later; that of an infinitely old universe—one that has always existed.)

Given this situation, it becomes apparent that when an atheistic scientist examines evidence regarding the age of the earth, he/she automatically rules out evidence that would indicate anything other than a very old Earth (in the billions of years).

There is an interesting quote from Professor George Wald, written about a year after the famous Miller-Urey origin of life experiment, which purportedly helped explain how life originally formed on the primeval earth. (You can read more on this experiment in chapter 4).

> The important point is that since the origin of life belongs in the category of "at-least-once" phenomena, time is on its side. However probable we regard this event, or any of the steps it involves, given enough time it will almost certainly happen at least once. And for life as we know it. . .once may be enough. Time is the hero of the plot. What we regard as impossible on the basis of human experience is meaningless here. Given so much time, the impossible becomes possible, the possible becomes probable, and the probable becomes virtually certain. One only has to wait, time itself performs the miracles.[1]

This reveals a number of interesting points. (Note: At the time of this statement, secular scientists believed the earth to be about 2 billion years old, as opposed to the current value of 4.6 billion.) We'll look at selected portions of this quote one section at a time.

> *the origin of life belongs in the category of "at-least-once" phenomena.*

> > This is simply assumed with no actual evidence or reasoning. The reader is expected to merely ingest and move on. In reality, there is no compelling reason to believe that the origin of life is an "at-least-once" phenomena (i.e., naturalistically inevitable).

Time is the hero of the plot.

In this statement *time* is actually given *power* when in reality time never does anything other than allow events to occur which naturally will happen if *time* does continue. For example, if you roll a ball down a hill, if time continues long enough (for this analogy we're pretending that time could possibly not continue) the ball will eventually roll all the way down to the bottom of the hill, assuming that no outside forces intervene. On the other hand, it is not logical to say that if enough time occurs the ball will eventually roll back up the hill. That event is not just improbable, it is impossible, according to the laws of physics, which is what we are limited to when not considering the supernatural. Time does not help counteract the laws on nature.

What we regard as impossible on the basis of human experience is meaningless here.

In other words, forget everything you know (i.e., human experience). Don't use logic right now because that would lead you to conclude that life could not form by accident and that's not what we want you to believe.

Time itself performs the miracles.

Time is given power to do the miraculous. It is paradoxical that schools can teach about miracles as long as they aren't miracles enacted by God! If you say, "God performs miracles" you will be censored from the classroom, but if you say, "Time performs miracles" you will be heralded as a brilliant scholar.

By now, you are beginning to see just how important *time* is to the committed evolutionist. It's a non-negotiable. All modern evolutionists would admit that evolution wouldn't even be thinkable if the earth were not at least billions of years old. (This is not to say that if the earth truly is billions of years old that evolution is automatically possible, because there are so many other issues involved, as elucidated throughout this book.)

Physically speaking, since God is all-powerful He could have created the universe over sixty trillion years, in sixty trillionths of a second, or anywhere in between. He is not at all limited—*kind of*. Why would I say kind of? How can that be? It doesn't seem to make any sense. It reminds me of former major league baseball player and manager Yogi Berra's response to a question about baseball years ago. He was asked if he *always* attended *every* game. His response was, "Usually." (I found that fairly amusing.) What I mean by limited is not that He is insufficient in any way that would keep Him from being able to accomplish something, but rather, that He cannot lie (Titus 1:2)—it is against His nature. Therefore, it logically follows that the all important question is not, "What could He have done?" because He is all-powerful, but "What did He *say* He did?" It also logically follows that His acts of creation are limited to what He told us He did.

HISTORICALLY SPEAKING

Before we get to the next two chapters which contain slightly more technical matters, let's take a brief look at how our views regarding the age of the earth have changed over time. Historically, prior to the rise of modern science, there were two dominant views. One view, largely based on the Bible, held that Earth was relatively young, having been created by God in approximately 4,000 BC or at least within the past few thousands of years. The other view posited was that the universe is infinitely old, having always existed. The latter view was essential and convenient for anyone wishing to avoid the religious implications of a creator and an associated beginning. No beginning, no "beginner" necessary.

Advances in science during the early and mid-1900s seemed to indicate that the universe did indeed have a beginning and was thus, not infinitely old. The concept of the big bang was birthed and has been the reigning view among secular cosmologists (and even a number of Christian cosmologists) all the way up to the present. (For more information about the big bang, please refer to chapter 3). Since the majority of scientists from both evolutionist and creationist camps have determined that the universe is not infinitely old, we can singularly focus on determining its approximate age.

This chapter focuses on the historical change in views regarding the age of the earth—having changed from that of a relatively young Earth (thousands of years) to an ancient Earth (billions of years). The concepts of young and old are certainly relative in nature. For instance, when I was in grade school I thought than anyone who was thirty-five was "old." Now that fifty is not too far off for me, thirty-five seems fairly young! In reality, I actually think that a 6,000 year-old Earth would be a very old Earth! A lot can happen in that amount of time. Consider what has happened in our own country in just the last 200 years—it boggles the mind. Imagine what could happen in thousands of years! So when we speak of a "young" or "old" Earth, these terms are certainly relative and subjective.

Within the Christian church, the dominant opinion was that the Genesis creation account took place over a period of six solar days, within the memory of mankind, a number of thousands of years ago. This view, however, experienced a major change just before the lifetime of Charles Darwin.

There were a number of significant personalities in the eighteenth and nineteenth centuries that paved the way for the widespread acceptance of millions of years, as opposed to the traditional biblical view. One of the more prominent figures was James Hutton (1726-1797), a Scottish geologist. He was insistent on not invoking the supernatural as any kind of explanation for the geologic features of the earth:

> The past history of our globe must be explained by what can be seen to be happening now. . .No powers are to be employed that are not natural to the globe, no action to be admitted except those of which we know the principle.[2]

Hutton felt there was evidence of repeated cycles of decay and repair that in succession obliterated previous cycles from the historical geologic record. Therefore, in his mind "we find no vestige of a beginning—no prospect of an end." He believed the earth was at least millions of years old, but that there was no way of telling just how much older it might be.

Hutton   Lyell

Another prominent figure was Charles Lyell (1797-1875), a Scottish lawyer who eventually became a geologist. In brief, Lyell drew upon works of his predecessors (Hutton, in particular) to write a three-volume treatise entitled *Principles of Geology*, in which he claimed that no worldwide or even continental floods have ever occurred in the history of our globe. He insisted that the rock record must be explained by the same gradual processes that we observe today. This principal became known as uniformitarianism, "that the geologic processes observed in operation that modify the earth's crust at present have worked in much the same way over geologic time."[3] Therefore, it would have required multiplied millions of years to account for the vast geologic formations that we currently observe.

Lest you be led to believe that Lyell was simply following the conclusions of empirical science and that the creationists were merely exercising blind faith in the Bible, consider the following quote by Stephen J. Gould (who was one of the world's leading evolutionists until his death in 2002, and no friend of creationists):

> Charles Lyell was a lawyer by profession, and his book is one of the most brilliant briefs published by an advocate. . .Lyell relied upon true bits of cunning to establish his uniformitarian views as the only true geology. First, he set up a straw man to demolish. In fact, the catastrophists [i.e., biblical creationists] were much more empirically minded than Lyell. The geologic record does seem to require catastrophes: rocks are fractured and contorted; whole faunas are wiped out. To circumvent this literal appearance, Lyell imposed his imagination upon the evidence. The geologic record, he argued, is extremely imperfect and we must interpolate into it what we can reasonably infer but cannot see. The catastrophists were the hard-nosed empiricists of their day, not the blinded theological apologists."[4]

While there certainly were other scientists around who opposed Lyell's views, a more significant phenomenon was occurring within the church itself. Many Christian leaders, feeling somewhat intimidated, deemed it was necessary to accommodate these "new scientific discoveries" by re-evaluating the traditional view of Genesis. One attempt, the gap theory, was developed in 1814 by Thomas Chalmers, a Presbyterian minister. This view holds that all of the newly discovered millions of years can be inserted in between Genesis 1:1 and 1:2. There are a few different versions of the gap theory, but the following summarizes the standard view:

> In the far distant, dateless past God created a perfect heaven and perfect earth. Satan was ruler of the earth, which was peopled by a race of 'men' without any souls. Eventually, Satan, who dwelled in a Garden of Eden composed of minerals (Ezekiel 28), rebelled by desiring to become like God (Isaiah 14). Because of Satan's fall, sin entered the universe and brought on the earth God's judgment in the form of a flood (indicated by the water of 1:2), and then a global ice age when the light and heat from the sun were somehow removed. All the plant, animal, and human fossils upon the earth today date from this 'Lucifer's Flood' and do not bear any genetic relationship with the plants, animals and fossils living upon the earth today.[5]

Another theory, especially espoused by George Stanley Faber, an Anglican theologian, was the day-age theory, which is somewhat self-explanatory. It purports that each "day" of creation was actually a period of multiplied millions of years, drawing popular biblical support from II Peter 3:8, which states that a "day is as a thousand years." See also Psalm 90:4.

It is not within the scope of this book to address the numerous biblical and scientific faults with each of these theories, but the reader should at least be aware of these beliefs, because of how prevalent they are within the church, even today. I believe that by exposing the lack of credible scientific support for the idea of millions and billions of years and discussing the associated theological problems introduced by accepting long periods of time, the reader will see there is no justifiable basis for deviating from the straightforward six solar-day creation account. I would also like to re-emphasize that the issue of the earth's age, while being significant, is not something I put at the top of my list when discussing Christianity with skeptics. Furthermore, I certainly do not call into question any believer's salvation or sincerity if they differ with me on this issue.

YOU MUST BE CRAZY!

To even suggest that the earth might actually only be thousands of years old generally causes many people to think that you have lost all sense of reason and are out of touch with reality. It may be accompanied by statements such as, "Oh, I guess you've never heard of 'science'?" and "I'll bet you also think the world is flat, don't you?" These types of *ad hominem* responses in which one's character is attacked instead of directly dealing with the actual issue are often effective enough to end the conversation, with the person believing in a young Earth walking away in defeat.

The average "man on the street" assumes the earth is billions of years old and probably doesn't give it much thought beyond that. Even within the church, many have the same belief, also feeling that it is such an insignificant issue that spending any time debating is a complete waste of time and only causes division within the church. As I mentioned earlier, I personally believe that if the Bible doesn't address something, either directly or indirectly, then we shouldn't make much of a fuss over it. I am convinced, however, that the Bible does address the age of the earth and that what we believe about it has a very significant affect on how we interpret many other significant portions of the Bible, as well as affecting our view on the authority and inspiration of Scripture as a whole.

There is inherently nothing that makes an old Earth more spiritual than a young Earth, or vice versa. That's certainly not the point here. It is much more a matter of interpreting Scripture using grammatical and historical contexts, as opposed to using outside sources (e.g., modern science) to force an unnatural interpretation of the text. God, being all-powerful, could have created the universe over billions of years. He could also have created it in a trillionth of a second. The primary question again is not what He could have done, but what He said He did.

TWO RECORDS

There are two primary sources for trying to get a handle on the actual age of the earth: (1) theology, via the Bible, and (2) science, what used to be referred to as "natural theology."

Many people would downplay the Bible in favor of science, because the age of the earth seems to them like much more of a scientific issue than a religious one. The claim is often made that "the Bible is not a science textbook!" My response is that I'm glad it isn't! Science books have to be constantly updated and re-written! It is interesting to note, however, that science is actually incapable of determining exactly how old the earth is. There are too many assumptions involved in every conceivable method we might use. It is only useful in determining likely upper limits to the earth's age as we will see in chapter 11. The Bible, on the other hand, declares that it is an eye-witness account from the One who created the universe itself! Reason alone would tell us that if the Bible is the infallible Word of God, then it is more capable of rendering an accurate age for the earth than science, which is simply a body of conclusions drawn by imperfect humans who don't know everything, were not present at the beginning, make mistakes, sometimes even lie and who are observing a fallen/cursed world. We have already discussed the difference between observational and historical science and this difference plays a significant role in the issue of the age of the earth, as we will shortly see.

While our eternal destiny is certainly not dependent upon our belief regarding the age of the earth, a careful and reverential study of the Bible warns against being too quick to adopt the conventional secular thoughts in geology and astronomy, especially when they appear to oppose the straightforward reading of God's Word. "Let God be true, but every man a liar" (Romans 3:4, KJV).

With this background, let's move on to discussing the biblical implications of a young Earth versus an old Earth debate.

ENDNOTES

1.   Wald, G., "The origin of life," *Scientific American* 191:45, August 1954.

2.   Hutton, J., "Theory of the Earth," Transactions of the Royal Society of Edinburgh, 1785.

3.   Definition of "The Principle of Uniformitarianism," *New World Encyclopedia (online)*, http://www.newworldencyclopedia.org/entry/Geology —last accessed 8/21/12.

4.   Gould, S.J., *Natural History,* February 1975, p. 16.

5.   Fields, Weston W., "Unformed and Unfilled," (Collinsville, IL: Burgener Enterprises, 2005), p. 7.

The Age of the Earth: Biblical Considerations

In this chapter we will specifically be looking at what the Bible itself tells us about the age of the earth and whether or not it really even matter what we believe.

A recent *CNN Opinion* author offered an interesting comment germane to our topic:

> Although few of us would turn to the Old Testament or the Quran to determine the age of the earth, too many of us still turn obediently to these books (or their secular copies) as authorities about morality.[1]

Setting aside the message regarding the source of our moral code for this particular discussion, this quote conveys the common attitude towards the Bible and its lack of relevance to the "real world." The underlying point is that no one would seriously look to the Bible when considering a question such as the age of the earth, which according to the article's author (and probably most people in general) is obviously better left to science.

Many people think that the Bible does not even address the age of the earth and therefore, we shouldn't be concerned about it either. While it's true that you will not find anywhere in the Bible a verse that states something like "God created the earth 'x' number of years ago," it does give us enough information to have a reasonable idea of approximately when creation took place. In particular, there are enough passages that help us quickly determine whether we're talking about thousands or billions of years.

Let's start with looking at the big picture. God tells us that He created everything in six days (Genesis 1, Exodus 20:11). Immediately some will ask, "But how do we know those were actual solar days?" That's a great question and one we'll examine in detail shortly. I have been studying this for over twenty-six years now and I am fully convinced that a "day" in the creation account is a normal solar day similar to what we currently experience. Do my credentials and extensive research automatically make me right? Of course not. It simply means that I really should have an opinion one way or the other by now. It reminds me of a comedy sketch I saw back when I was in junior high school. The setting was that of a very serious television news program in which a couple world-renowned authorities were being interviewed about a particular subject. The host turned to one of the guests and said, "Dr. Winston, you have two PhDs from Oxford University, have written five books and sixty-two articles on this matter, and have been researching this issue for over forty years. What are your thoughts on this situation?" The reply came, "I think it's too early to tell." It's one of those things that you had to see to truly appreciate, but I thought it was funny. Ultimately, I urge you to study the Bible for yourself and allow the Holy Spirit to guide you to the truth. If we both do that and still end up disagreeing, we can still embrace each other as fellow Christians as the God continues to work in both of our lives, maturing us and conforming us to the image of His Son, Jesus Christ.

KEEPING IT IN CONTEXT

Realtors sometimes humorously say that the three most important things to consider when buying or selling a home are:

Location, Location, Location.

The point is clear; the location of your home or property is extremely important when buying or selling. In biblical interpretation, we could somewhat humorously say that the three most important factors are:

Context, Context, Context.

We must interpret Scripture by looking at its grammatical, historical and textual context.

KEEPING IT SIMPLE

Simple solutions are always refreshing. William of Ockham (English logician and Franciscan friar, fourteenth century) is famous for establishing a principle that today is referred to as "Occam's Razor" (or "Ockham's Razor"). In essence, it states that the best solution to a particular situation is most often the one which is the simplest or most straight-forward. Our apparent dilemma is that most secular scientists believe the earth and universe are billions of years old, but the Bible talks about creation "in six days." For many people, interpreting the "days" of Genesis as vast ages is the simplest, easiest and best solution. At first glance, it may seem brilliant and appear to resolve the conflict. Many people are bothered by the alleged notion that science and the Bible are at odds with each other and in constant battle. It's uncomfortable to have to choose between the two. On one hand, if you choose "science," you are left with a nagging feeling of guilt, that somehow you are rejecting God's Word and that your faith is weak. On the other hand, if you choose the Bible, you feel that you are broadcasting to the world that you have no real intelligence and are going to cling to your blind faith no matter what anyone says and no matter what science discovers. Both responses are unsatisfying. If there were just some way to resolve this tension it would be welcomed with open arms. Unfortunately, most people's "solutions" have come at the expense of fidelity to God's Word, rather than to question or reevaluate the conclusions of modern scientists.

When we are not careful in our biblical interpretation, we are in danger of taking a difficult situation and making it even worse. I believe that is what happens when we accept many of the current "middle ground" positions. We actually end up taking a fundamentally poor scientific theory (unbeknownst to many) and marrying it to what then has become bad theology. How could that possibly be a good solution?

COMPROMISE

Compromise can be a great thing. If your children are arguing over which restaurant to visit for lunch after church, a compromise might be in order. Today Tori gets to choose and next week it's Taylor's turn. It often works the same way in marriage; each partner may have to make slight compromises in what they desire in order to maintain harmony. What happens if we apply this principle to our apparent Bible versus science dilemma?

You might ask, "Do we really want to compromise science? I really don't think that I would want my doctor compromising his procedures when diagnosing an illness or performing an operation. We certainly wouldn't want NASA scientists knowingly compromising on acknowledged scientific principles when designing the space shuttle. At this point, it doesn't seem logical to ask science to compromise, so our only other choice is to come up with some sort of compromise related to Scripture." While this may not seem like an ideal option for many Christians, it appears more palatable to them than messing with science, which they generally feel inadequate and unqualified to do. Most importantly, many have convinced themselves that how we interpret the Bible doesn't really matter anyway. They reason, "Who really cares how or when God created, as long as we at least agree that He is ultimately the creator of all?"

A NOVEL IDEA

Instead of accepting ideas such as the gap theory or the day-age theory, which I believe are unhealthy attempted and problematic solutions, I would like to propose a resolution that actually does not ask either science or the Bible to compromise. How in the world is that possible? It's actually very possible (and quite natural) when we understand three basic concepts:

a) There is a very important distinction between "operational science" and "historical science."

b) There is a very important distinction between "science" and "scientist's opinions."

c) The Bible is the infallible Word of God.

Let's expand on these very briefly:

(a). We've previously covered "operational and historical science," so we will not repeat that discussion here. (See chapter 2 for a review)

(b). As an example, it is *science* that *proves* there are fossils in various layers of the earth; when and how they got there is a matter of "scientists' opinions," which are fallible and subject to change with the discovery of additional data. These conclusions were made by men and women who were not there at the beginning, don't know everything, sometimes make mistakes, sometimes are dishonest with their findings—*driven by their own agendas*—and who are ultimately studying a "fallen" world which is not the same as it was originally created. This holds true for Christians as well, so we should keep this in mind as we do our own scientific research regarding origins.

(c). Considering the limitations of science and the ultimate nature of God's Word, we should give precedence to Scripture in any situation where unresolved conflict exists. Even though the Bible is God's first attempt at writing a book, I think He did a pretty good job (just a little humor—no disrespect intended). He is fully capable of telling us exactly what He did without the notion of having to "dumb it down" for the alleged primitive culture of the patriarchs. I believe that God says what He means and means what He says. (Yes, there are passages in the Bible that are poetic and allegorical, but it is always evident by the context. Genesis chapters 1 and 2 were written as historical literature, and thus should be interpreted that way.) Since modern science is a relatively "new kid on the block," it doesn't make sense that it would be required to correctly understand such a fundamental concept as the origin of the life and the universe. If it were required, it would mean that for most of history, the people of God were truly living in the "dark ages," not understanding that God did not really mean exactly what He said and that it is only now (with the advent of modern science) that we are able to figure out that even though He said "six days," He really meant billions of years and natural mechanisms. This doesn't at all seem consistent with God's character and doesn't say much about His ability to communicate. He is not a God of confusion (I Corinthians 14:33).

SO WHAT DOES A "DAY" REALLY MEAN?

Having covered a lot of background information up to this point, we will now delve into the question of what a "day" actually means.

The Old Testament was primarily written in Hebrew, with small portions being written in Aramaic. The Hebrew word for "day" is "יום" or "*yōm*" (using the English alphabet) and can have many meanings.

The same thing holds true for the English word "day." Take for example, the following sentence.

> In my *day*, we had to get up early and work all *day*, so we could save enough money to go on a 5-*day* vacation.

In this sentence, the word "day" is used three different ways. The first occurrence represents a general period of time ("in my day"). The second generally refers to the light portion of a day ("work all day"). The final occurrence is in reference to an ordinary 24-hour, day/night cycle ("5-day vacation"). The context determines the meaning in each case.

We have a similar situation with the use of the Hebrew word for "day" in Genesis. It can have any of the following meanings:[2]

- an ordinary solar day (~twenty-four hours),

- the light portion of an ordinary solar day,

- a general/vague period of time,

- a specific point in time, or

- the period of one year (in prophetic passages).

Although it can mean a general period of time, it is never used to refer to a long period of time with a definite beginning and distinct, marked ending (such as the ending of a millennium and the distinct beginning of the next).

Is there anything in the immediate context of Genesis 1 that would assist us in determining the meaning in each case? The answer is yes: there are actually a number of indicators.

GOD DEFINES HIS TERMS

The first time we see *yōm*, it is defined for us quite simply: "And God called the light Day, and the darkness he called Night" (Genesis 1:5, KJV). If a "day" is actually millions or billions of years long, then what is a "night"? I guess that would have to be millions or billions of years in duration, as well.

Dividing and Ruling over the Day and Night

God tells us that He made two major lights in the sky to "divide the day from the night" (Genesis 1:14). This obviously refers to the sun and moon. (We certainly understand that the moon does not create its own light, but simply reflects the light of the sun onto the earth.) This passage only makes sense if these are normal solar days. How would the sun divide the "day" from the "night" if each is really millions of years long?

Similarly, God tells us that the sun would "rule the day" and the moon would "rule the night" (Genesis 1:16). Once again, this only makes sense in the context of normal solar days.

Association with a Number

Everytime we see the word *yōm* (day) outside of Genesis 1 associated with a number (e.g., the fifth day, day ten, etc.) it is in reference to an ordinary day. That is exactly what we have in Genesis 1: "And the evening and the morning were the *first day*," and "And the evening and the morning were the *second day*." If it is a normal day everywhere else in the Old Testament, what is the textual basis for interpreting it differently in Genesis 1?[3]

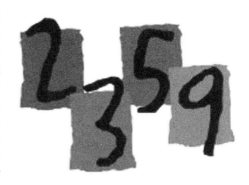

Evening and Morning

Everytime we see the word *yōm* (day) outside of Genesis 1 associated with the word "evening" or "morning" or the phrase "evening and morning" it refers to an ordinary day.[4] Again, that is exactly what we find in Genesis 1: "And the *evening and the morning* were the first day," "And the *evening and the morning* were the second day," etc. Additionally, it is interesting to note that the Hebrew people measured their days beginning in the evening and continuing on through the morning, ending with the beginning of the next evening. They literally had an evening and then a morning. This Scripture was originally given to the Jews (Hebrews) and that's exactly how they would have understood it—a normal solar day!

Days and Years

Referring to the sun and stars, God said, "let them be for signs, and for seasons, and for days, and years" (Genesis 1:14, KJV). If a "day" really means multiplied millions of years, what does a "year" mean? This verse would then be interpreted to read something like the following: "let them be for signs, and for seasons, and for millions of years, and years."[5] This is a senseless statement.

Plural Form: "Days"

How do we measure the length of a day? It comes from the time it takes the earth to rotate once on its axis. How about the length of a month? Roughly the time it takes for the moon to orbit once around the earth. How about a year? The time it takes the earth to orbit once around the sun. And how about a week? (Are you stumped?) Each of the previous time periods (day, month and year) are based on astronomical measurements. The concept of a seven-day week originated in the Bible in the Ten Commandments, specifically the fourth commandment (Exodus 20:8-11; KJV, emphasis added):

> Remember the sabbath day, to keep it holy. Six days shalt thou labour, and do all thy work: But the seventh day is the sabbath of the LORD thy God: in it thou shalt not do any work, thou, nor thy son, nor thy daughter, thy manservant, nor thy maidservant, nor thy cattle, nor thy stranger that is within thy gates: *For in six days the LORD made heaven and earth, the sea, and all that in them is*, and rested the seventh day: wherefore the LORD blessed the sabbath day, and hallowed it.

Virtually all cultures today observe a seven-day week. France, at the end of the eighteenth century, tried changing to a ten-day week, but changed back to seven because it was not working out.[6] The Soviet Union (from 1929-1931) experimented with a five-day week, then a six-day week, but also returned to seven after their attempts were unsuccessful.[7]

The point we are making here is that if a "day" is actually millions of years in length, then the Sabbath becomes meaningless. Are we supposed to work for six periods of undetermined millions of years and then rest for an additional period of undetermined millions of years? I'm sure we'd all enjoy the lengthy period or rest! In reality, that's probably not true. God made us to work (even before Adam sinned), so in avoiding work altogether for long periods of time, we would most likely not feel complete. I know this from personal experience. When my wife and I go to the beach, which is very rare, she loves to sit and relax on the sand. After about three minutes, I say, "So now what do you want to do?" Maybe I'm just a bit too restless!

In each of the 845 occurrences of this word in the Old Testament, it is rendered "days" in the ordinary sense of solar days.[8] Why should it be different in Exodus 20:11?

Note: the passage from the Ten Commandments (among many others) employs the Hebrew plural form of "day" ("days") which is "*yamim*" (ימים).

WHAT DOES GOD TELL US HE DID?

I don't know anyone who would try to argue that an all-powerful God is limited in His ability to create whatever He wishes, however He wishes and whenever He wishes. As previously noted, God could just as easily have created an entire universe in a trillionth of a second as He could over a period of trillions of years. That is certainly not the issue. The question becomes more of "what did He tell us He did?" Consider the following: If God had meant to convey the idea that He created everything over vast periods of time, there are a number of Hebrew words He could have used. A partial list follows:[9]

Qedem	"ancient" or "of old"
Olam	"everlasting," "eternity," "of old" or "forever"
Dor	"a revolution of time" or "an age"
Tamid	"continually" or "forever"
Ad	"unlimited time" or "forever"
Netsach	"for ever"
Eth	general term for time

On the other hand, if He meant to convey the idea of ordinary solar days, there is only one Hebrew word He could have used: *yōm*; which is exactly what He chose!

In concluding this segment on what the Hebrew text actually means, it is insightful to read the words of James Barr (a world-renowned Old Testament scholar from Oxford University). Keep in mind that Barr does not believe in Genesis, but he is an expert on the Hebrew language. This makes him what we call a "hostile witness," which means that his comments are of special importance because he has no interest in assisting those who hold to the historical accuracy of Genesis. In fact, quite the contrary. Here's what he said about the Genesis creation account:

> Probably, so far as I know, there is no professor of Hebrew or Old Testament at any world-class university who does not believe that the writer(s) of Genesis 1-11 intended to convey to their readers the ideas that (a) creation took place in a series of six days which were the same as the days of 24 hours we now experience. Or, to put it negatively, the apologetic arguments which suppose the "days" of creation to be long eras of time, the figures of years not to be chronological, and the flood to be a merely local Mesopotamian flood, are not taken seriously by any such professors, as far as I know.[10]

FROM THE BEGINNING OF THE WORLD

Let's briefly consider our own place in the world, as taught by currently accepted theories. The following table represents a typical big bang / evolutionary timeline:

Event	Years Ago (in Billions)
Big Bang	13.7
Formation of Earth	4.6
Origin of Life	3.8
Arrival of Man*	0.0002
*Modern Man ~ 200,000 years ago	

We are told that mankind began evolving somewhere between six and ten million years ago (from ape-like creatures). Modern man is supposed to have appeared somewhere beginning around 100,000 to 200,000 years ago. Even though this seems like a long time ago (and indeed it would be), it would actually be considered at the very "end" of the overall timeline, considering that the universe supposedly originated closer to thirteen to fifteen billion years ago. Let's say you told your child that you were leaving for church in an hour, but you wanted them to make their bed *right away*. If they waited until one minute before it was time to go, would you say that they obeyed, or would you say that they put it off until the very end?

To put this into perspective, if all of history (let's assume fourteen billion years) was compressed into one hour with the big bang having occurred at the very beginning of the hour (starting it all off), mankind doesn't arrive on the scene until there is about 0.05 of a second left in the entire hour! That truly would be considered "at the very end." (Alright, some of you are wondering where I came up with those figures. If we take the estimate for the "age of modern man"—two hundred thousand years, and divide it by the estimated age of the universe—fourteen billion years, we come-up with 0.00143%. There are 3,600 seconds in an hour, so we take

0.00143% of 3,600 and end up with approximately 0.05 (= 5/100) seconds. . .that's how long before man would arrive in our compressed 1-hour scenario.)

Does the Bible comment at all about the timing of Adam's arrival? It certainly does and with no less authority than the words of Jesus Himself (who is the creator of all things—see John 1, Colossians 1, Hebrews 1). Most of us are fairly familiar with the Pharisees in the Bible. They were a sect of the Jews who were particularly proud of their knowledge of Scripture. They were overly focused on "keeping the letter of the law" and were very antagonistic towards Jesus because He taught that it was not by keeping the law that anyone would merit favor before God, but through faith in Himself. Because of this, they were constantly trying to trap Jesus and trick Him with their questions, assuming that they could accuse Him of heresy no matter how He responded. In one of their encounters (found in Mark 10:6 and Matthew 19:4) they asked Jesus about marriage and divorce. In His response to the Pharisees Jesus stated, "But *from the beginning of the creation* God made them male and female" (KJV, emphasis added). Why is this significant? The Greek phrase here is very emphatic that "male and female" (Adam and Eve) were created at the *beginning* of creation. This is in stark contrast to what we are taught from anthropology and secular geology. However, if the days in Genesis are ordinary days, then this makes perfect sense, having Adam and Eve created only five days after the creation of the universe itself (day six), all within the first week of the entire history of the world!

That truly would be "the beginning" as opposed to the standard big bang scenario. This is illustrated in the figure below. The top timeline depicts the typical series of events in a big bang/old Earth scenario. On this timeline, modern man would be placed at the far right. On the bottom timeline, representing a relatively recent six solar-day creation, mankind appears at the very left (within the first week of the entire timeline!).

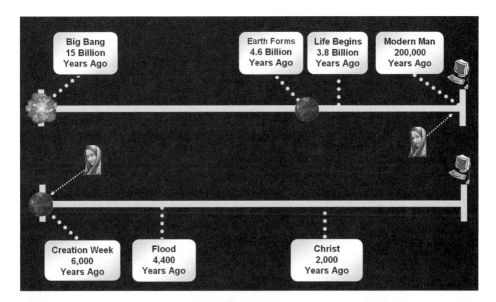

Another point related to "the beginning of the world" is found in Romans 1:20 (KJV), which states:

> For the invisible things of him from the creation of the world are clearly seen, being understood by the things that are made, even his eternal power and Godhead; so that they are without excuse

In this passage, the apostle Paul is stating that "men are without excuse" if they deny the existence of God, because He (God) has made Himself clearly known to them. In this passage we also learn that various attributes of God have been clearly seen "from the creation of the world" (since the beginning of time). The Greek language conveys the concept of rational human thought. This would not make sense in a billions-of-years scenario, since mankind would not have been around anywhere near the beginning of creation to perceive anything! Once again, it only makes sense if Adam and Eve were truly created from the beginning, in a six solar-day, recent creation.

OUT OF ORDER

An additional problem we have when trying to harmonize the Genesis account with millions or billions of years is that the order of events becomes a significant conundrum. Consider the following examples.

Sun/Earth: According to the big bang (and associated "billions of years"), the sun evolved first and then the earth much later. The Bible, however, tells us that God created the earth first (on day one), and the sun later (on day four), which is just the opposite order.

Appearance of Water: According to the standard geologic view involving billions of years, the earth initially cooled down from a molten mass into hard rock. Then millions of years later, water appeared. Genesis, on the other hand, teaches that the earth was initially covered with water and that the dry land did not appear until day three.

Fish/Land Plants: According to the secular biological view involving millions of years, fish evolved/appeared first, then land plants twenty-five million years later. Genesis, however, says that God created plants first (day three), then fish (day five).

Reptiles/Birds: According to the secular biological view involving millions of years, reptiles appeared first and approximately 150 million years later evolved into birds. Genesis says that God created the birds of the air first (day five), then reptiles (day six).

These are just a few examples of contradictions in the order of events that exist when we attempt to harmonize the standard secular model with the Genesis creation account.

THE FLOOD

We are all fairly familiar with the account of Noah's ark and the flood. This is one more area that is greatly affected by deviating from the straight-forward creation account.

If you were to ask most Christians to briefly describe the flood, they would most likely tell you that it was a worldwide cataclysmic event that wiped out all life outside the ark, except for some plants and marine creatures that could survive in the waters. This response would be an accurate description according the Scripture (Genesis 6-8).

However, those who believe that the earth is billions of years old cannot accept this account and still be consistent with their belief regarding the age of the earth. We will now examine the reasoning behind this.

According to modern geology, the earth is approximately 4.6 billion years old and its major geologic features have formed over hundreds of millions of years, prior to the arrival of mankind. Christians who believe that the biblical account of creation *did not* take place in six literal days beginning a number of thousands of years ago do so because they accept the conclusions of modern geology as scientific fact. This, however, causes a problem with the Bible's description of the flood account. As previously mentioned, the Bible describes a flood that was global in nature, but if the major features of the earth (e.g., the Grand Canyon, Mt. Everest, the Rocky Mountains, etc.) were formed slowly over millions and millions of years long before Adam was even created, you can't have a global flood in Noah's day, because it would be catastrophic in scope, disrupting existing features and itself, laying down new layers of sediment all over the earth! Secular geologists believe that any such global event happened after the formation of the earth's major features. Furthermore, it would be nearly impossible to know much about what supposedly happened during the prior hundreds of millions of years, if it was all catastrophically up heaved during the flood of Noah. So what do Christians do who still believe in an old Earth? Instead of questioning the validity of the secular scientists theories that they have accepted as "fact," they simply choose to re-interpret Scripture to align with their views (making the assumption that "science is science and not really open to questioning"). In this case, they tell us that Noah's flood was not a global event, but rather just a local flood in the Mesopotamian area where Noah was living! This makes no sense at all when you read the flood account (Genesis 6-8). Consider the following passage from Genesis 7:19-23 (NIV, emphasis added):

> They [the waters] *rose greatly on the earth*, and *all the high mountains under the entire heavens were covered.* The *waters rose and covered the mountains to a depth of more than twenty feet. Every living thing that moved on the earth perished*—birds, livestock, wild animals, all the creatures that swarm over the earth, and *all mankind. Everything on dry land* that had the breath of life in its nostrils died. *Every living thing* on the face of the earth was wiped out; men and animals and the creatures that move along the ground and the birds of the air were wiped from the earth. *Only Noah was left, and those with him in the ark.*

This was truly a global event! It also brings up a lot of questions. If it was just a local flood:

• Why did Noah spend over one hundred years building the ark? God could have said, "Hey Noah! Here's the number of a good realtor. I suggest you move. I'm going to flood this area!"

• Why did Noah build such a huge ark (over 1.5 million cubic feet of storage space)? All he would have needed to take on the ark would be representatives of the local animals.

• Why did Noah take birds on the ark? They could have just flown away to avoid the flood?

• How were *local* mountains covered to a depth of twenty-two feet without the water spreading out? Water seeks its own level, so a flood could not possibly only cover the local mountains.

• Why did God give Noah the sign of the rainbow as a promise that He would never again flood the earth (Genesis 9:15-16)? If it was a local flood, then God lied. We have had thousands of floods since then, in which hundreds of thousands have lost their lives.

DEATH

One of the biggest issues with interpreting the days of Genesis as anything other than solar days has to do with the entrance of death into our world.

According to secular models of Earth history, the layers that we observe were laid down over multiplied millions of years, long before the appearance of man. The problem occurs when we see that these layers contain literally billions of fossils. Fossils are largely the remains of creatures that were once living. This would mean that death (and disease, pain, suffering, bloodshed, mutations, survival of the fittest, etc.) existed for millions of years before Adam and Eve were even created. The Bible clearly states that it was Adam's sin that brought death into God's world (Romans 5:12). We even have evidence of cancer in dinosaur bones. God pronounced His original creation as "very good," not filled with death and disease. It was man's disobedience that tainted God's creation and brought the curse upon mankind (and all of creation—Genesis 3:14-19, Romans 8:22).

If death existed for millions of years before Adam, then we are not responsible for death (and its associated curse) and therefore, Jesus wasted His time dying for us. Sadly, some have gone as far as to say that Adam and Eve didn't actually exist. . .they are only symbolic. Professor Richard Dawkins (atheist and certainly no friend of creationists) had something to say about this:

Death
Disease
Pain
Suffering

The Fossil Record

Millions of years

Creation Ministries International

> Oh, but of course, the story of Adam and Eve was only ever symbolic, wasn't it? Symbolic?! So in order to impress himself, Jesus had himself tortured and executed in vicarious punishment for a symbolic sin by a non-existent individual. As I said, barking mad, as well as viciously unpleasant.[11]

"A DAY IS A THOUSAND YEARS!"

"Yeah, but the Bible says a day is a thousand years!"

I wish I had a nickel for every time I've heard that response. I'd probably have about $3.75 by now! (On second thought, maybe I should ask for more than just a nickel each time.) What do they mean by this? The intended meaning is that God did not create everything in six solar days and the proof is in the fact that the Bible says "a day is a thousand years."

In response, I always ask, "Where do you find that in the Bible?" The majority of these people respond by saying that they aren't quite sure where it is, they just know it's in there somewhere. I tell them that it really isn't in the Bible, but there's something somewhat similar. I then ask a follow up question to see if they know who penned the passage and they virtually never know that either. I ask a further question: "Do you know the context of that passage?" Again, they respond in the negative. (By the way, I always ask these questions graciously and with respect, just wanting them to think through a few issues.) I then proceed to explain exactly where the passages are found, as well as who the authors were and the briefly discuss their proper context.

The main verse to which they refer is II Peter 3:8 (NIV):

> But do not forget this one thing, dear friends: With the Lord a day is like a thousand years, and a thousand years are like a day.

Peter is referencing Psalm 90:4—"A thousand years in your sight are like a day that has just gone by, or like a watch in the night" (NIV).

The following is a list of reasons why this passage does not support their interpretation (which in reality, is not truly their interpretation of Scripture, it is usually just a regurgitation of a false argument they learned from someone else).

- The verse says that a day is *as* a thousand years—not *is* a thousand years. It is a simile, a grammatical construct in which two dissimilar things are compared: a short period of time (a day) and a very long period of time (a thousand years.) The fact that the Psalmist is also comparing a thousand years to "a watch in the night" implies that the *watch in the night* is about equivalent to a day. If this passage from the Psalms is truly intending to convey the idea that a *day* really means a thousand years, then a *watch in the night* is also a thousand years, but no one is willing to reinterpret other passages that use this phrase as meaning thousands of years (e.g., Psalm 63:6 and 119:148).

- Even if the verse said "is " a thousand years, it would be saying that God created everything in a period of six thousand years since Genesis 1 says "six days." This doesn't appease the modern cosmologists who want 13-15 billion years for the universe and 4.6 billion years for the earth.

- They are taking a word from the Greek New Testament and attempting to define a Hebrew word in the Old Testament, written almost 1,500 years earlier! If this is legitimate, then I guess that Jesus was apparently in the grave for three thousand years, because it says "three days." Most people would say that's ludicrous (and I agree), but at least that would be attempting to define another word within the same language written and within the lifetime of the author. Similarly, Jonah must have been in the great fish for 3,000 years, because the Old Testament states that his ordeal lasted "three days" (Jonah 1:17). Actually, it would have been more like 6,000 years, because it says "three days and three nights." Nights must be about equal to days if we are to be consistent and logical, so we have 3,000 years for the "days" and another 3,000 for the "nights." This would be beyond absurd.

- This verse is being taken out of context as a whole. We need to understand the bigger picture of what Peter was saying, which we will look at next.

Here is the actual passage in its entirety:

> Dear friends, this is now my second letter to you. I have written both of them as reminders to stimulate you to wholesome thinking. I want you to recall the words spoken in the past by the holy prophets and the command given by our Lord and Savior through your apostles. First of all, you must understand that in the last days scoffers will come, scoffing and following their own evil desires. They will say, "Where is this 'coming' he promised? Ever since our fathers died, everything goes on as it has since the beginning of creation." But they deliberately forget that long ago by God's word the heavens existed and the earth was formed out of water and by water. By these waters also the world of that time was deluged and destroyed. By the same word the present heavens and earth are reserved for fire, being kept for the day of judgment and destruction of ungodly men. But do not forget this one thing, dear friends: With the Lord a day is like a thousand years, and a thousand years are like a day (II Peter 3:1-8 NIV).

Peter is urging his readers to remember something he assumes they already know; hence the phrase "I want you to recall" (v 2). He goes on to warn that in the "last days" skeptics would arise, doubting the return of Christ. They would boastfully state that even though Christians claim Christ is returning, in reality, He hasn't come yet and He never will. Peter then responds by telling us that these "scoffers" (of which there are many today) are deliberately ignoring two things: (1) that by the word of God the heavens and Earth were created and that (2) God judged the entire earth with a global flood because of sin.

In this context we find the two very interesting points:

- What the skeptics wanted to see happen immediately (the return of Christ), God can take a thousand years in doing.

- What they think would take "thousands of years" (the creation of the world), God can do in a day!

The whole point of the passage is that God is outside of time—not constrained by it in any way. He sees all time: past, present and future, simultaneously. This Greek passage has nothing to do with defining a Hebrew word in the Genesis creation narrative, but most who use it to do so are completely unaware of the previous comments. As is often quoted, "A text without a context is a pretext for a proof text." This simply means that when we take something out of context, we will be erroneously using it to *prove* a point that we have ulterior motive for promoting.

DETERMINING A BIBLICAL AGE

So how old is the earth according to the Bible? Understanding now that the days in the creation account are truly literal days, we note that God said He created the earth on day one and Adam on day six; that's a five day difference. If we could get a feel for about when Adam was created, we would then know about how old the earth is, having been created just five days prior.

It is a matter of fact that Jesus lived roughly 2,000 years ago. (Even skeptics who deny the deity of Christ acknowledge that there was a person named Jesus who lived about 2,000 years ago and whom Christians believe was the Son of God.) When we study Scripture, we find that Abraham live roughly 2,000 before Christ (~2000 BC). This is also generally accepted, even by secular historians. So it is about 4,000 years from our time back to Abraham. How long was it from Abraham back to Adam? Taking a look at the biblical genealogies between the two, we come up with roughly another 2,000 years. This takes us back to approximately 4,000 BC, or 6,000 years ago. Some critics make the argument that these genealogies are not straight-forward (i.e., names are often added, omitted, or changed in form). However, there exists no firm basis for these claims, so the straight-forward reading should be the default until compelling contextual evidence arises to think otherwise.[12]

With all of this considered, the age of the earth would be approximately 6,000 years. "So, it could it actually be 6,500 or 7,000 years old?!" Perhaps this might be true, and the exact age is certainly not the issue. But could it be 4.6 billion years old? Not according to the text.

Carl Sagan (atheistic astronomer and astrophysicist, famous for the 1980 television series, *Cosmos: A Personal Voyage*, stated:

> If God is omnipotent and omniscient, why didn't he start the universe out in the first place so it would come out the way he wants? Why is he constantly repairing and complaining? No, there's one thing the Bible makes clear: The biblical God is a sloppy manufacturer. He's not good at design, he's not good at execution. He'd be out of business if there was any competition.[13]

While I certainly recognize the irreverence exuded in this quote, I think there is some validity to the questions posed. Of course, all of this goes away *if the universe indeed is not that old and you take into account the affects of curse due to Adam's sin.*

CLOSING COMMENTS

While it's certainly true that one's eternal destiny is not dependent upon their view on the age of the earth, it does affect the way we view the authority of Scripture and also the way we share our faith. I believe there are two crucial elements necessary for understanding God's truths: (1) His Word—the Bible and (2) the Holy Spirit. We don't want to fall into the trap of feeling woefully incapable of understanding His Word because of a lack of academic credentials (not having a PhD in astrophysics, microbiology, geology or even Greek and Hebrew). God is perfectly capable of communicating to us through the Scriptures with the aid of the Holy Spirit. When we have to rely on "experts" telling us that certain passages mean something other than what they appear to say, we are often on dangerous ground. This is not to say that we have never had our understanding of God's Word enhanced by those who hold such degrees, but it should always be accompanied by a spirit of humility, graciousness and in consistency with the rest of the Bible.

We also have to keep in mind that for the vast majority of history, we did not have modern science. If it is only now, through these new so-called "discoveries" that we can finally understand that God didn't *really* mean six days and a global flood, but rather a big bang, fourteen billion years, a local flood, death before sin, etc., then all of those who have come before us were truly living in the "dark ages."

It also puts God in the position of thinking something along the lines of, "I know I said six days and global flood. . .and they actually believed Me, but when they finally get around to developing more advanced science, they will realize that I never meant for them to take it literally. I just hope that they aren't too upset when they find out how wrong they were when they took Me at my word."

We need to trust the authority of God's Word and be a bit less concerned about the "wisdom of man" which is foolishness to God (I Corinthians 3:19), and God's "foolishness" is wiser than man (I Corinthians 1:25).

ENDNOTES

1. Brook, Yaron, and Ghate, Onkar, "Our moral code is out of date," *CNN Opinion*, September 16, 2010, http://www.cnn.com/2010/OPINION/09/16/brook.moral.code.outdated/index.html?hpt=T2—*Last accessed 9/20/10.*

2. Sarfati, Jonathan, *Refuting Compromise*, Master Books, 2004, p.68.

3. Ibid, pp.73-80.

4. Ibid, pp.81-82.

5.   Ibid, pp. 69-70.

6.   http://creation.com/images/pdfs/CFK/cfk29(2).pdf—*last accessed 9/23/10.*

7.   Ibid.

8.   Sarfati, Jonathan, "D. Russell Humphreys' Cosmology and the 'Timothy Test': A Reply," *Creation Ex Nihilo Technical Journal*, vol. 11, no. 2, 1997, (online) http://creation.com/images/pdfs/tj/j11_2/j11_2_195-198.pdf—*last accessed 9/23/10.*

9.   Sarfati, Jonathan, *Refuting Compromise*, Master Books, 2004, p.68.

10. Barr, James, in a letter to David C.C. Watson, Oxford University, England, 23 April 1984.

11. Dawkins, Richard, *The God Delusion*, Bantam Press, 2006, p. 287.

12. For more information regarding alleged "gaps," see http://creation.com/biblical-chronogenealogies—*last accessed 9/1/10.*

13. Sagan, C., *Contact*, (New York: Simon & Schuster, Inc., 1985).

Chapter Eleven

The Age of the Earth: Scientific Evidence

[Author's Note: If you're like me, you tend to skip around when reading non-fiction books. If you have not yet read either of the two previous chapters, you are missing a great deal of material that is foundational to this particular chapter.]

Alright, the scientific evidence. . .we're finally getting somewhere. I suppose that might be the feeling of many people at this point, having waded through a lot of background information and biblical commentary in the previous two chapters. The thinking process is that since science is so "black and white," so objective, so precise, we'll finally have a definitive answer regarding the age if the earth; right? Wrong! It's not that simple. As has been previously discussed, science is fascinating, but definitely has its limits. This we will see very quickly when trying to determine the age of the earth.

Science does not directly supply us with any actual "clocks," just physical processes, which we then turn into clocks based on certain assumptions we make. As an overly simplistic example, let's say a neighborhood child wants you to time him as he races across his yard and up the slide on the playground. You don't have a watch, but you happen to notice there's a bird in a tree chirping away. It also just happens to be the kind of bird that someone told you typically chirps once per second. Now, this bird is not a stopwatch, but you can use its chirping to measure time. You subsequently observe that the bird chirped for the tenth time as the neighbor boy victoriously arrived at the top of the slide. You

can then conclude that it took him ten seconds to reach the "goal line." This, of course, is a rough figure and also based on the assumption that the bird is true to form and not chirping a bit slower from being up too late the night before or chirping faster because he had too much coffee. This will all make much more sense (and become much more relevant) as we delve further into this subject.

This chapter is divided into two sections: (1) a brief description of radiometric dating and (2) examples of evidence for a young Earth.

RADIOMETRIC DATING

While it's true that the research and literary works of Hutton and Lyle had a tremendous influence on the estimated age of the earth (as mentioned in chapter 9), it was the advent of radiometric dating in the early twentieth century that appeared to give the notion of an ancient Earth much more scientific credibility (and even absolute proof, in the minds of many). I've heard it countless times: "Of course the earth is billions of years old! Come on! Haven't you heard of radiometric dating? Where have you been living?" With such strong and often condescending statements as these, it pays to examine this a bit further. I promise not to get too technical, so even if you don't consider yourself to be a "science person," you'll be able to grasp this, and hopefully it will make this subject be much easier to understand.

Radiometric dating involves the decay of unstable or "radioactive" elements into stable, non-radioactive elements. One such example is that of uranium decaying into lead (e.g., ^{238}U into ^{206}Pb). It can be much more complicated, but in its simplest form the estimation process works like this:

- Measure how fast ^{238}U decays into ^{206}Pb.

- Determine the current amount of ^{206}Pb in the rock being dated.

- Calculate the age of the rock from these two figures (how long would it take the discovered amount of ^{206}Pb to be produced from the decay of ^{238}U).

Let's use a very simplistic example that we can more easily relate to: that of grapes "decaying" into raisins. On the counter in your kitchen is a large bowl filled with grapes. How could we tell how long the grapes have been in the bowl? We could do the following:

- Measure the rate at which grapes turn into raisins.

- Determine the amount of raisins currently in the bowl.

- Calculate the time it took to accumulate that amount of raisins using the two previous figures.

Seems simple enough. Let's say that we determine that three grapes "decay" into raisins every day and that there are currently twenty-one raisins in the bowl. We simply divide the amount of raisins (twenty-one) by the "decay rate" (three raisins per day) to find out how long the grapes have been there. In this case the answer is seven days. Case closed; right? Not quite. In order to use the method we just employed, three assumptions are necessary, and you are probably not even consciously aware of them. We'll list them, using semi-technical language and then briefly explain each one.

- Constant decay rate

- Closed system

- Zero initial daughter element

You're probably thinking (and with a degree of sarcasm), "You're right, I wasn't thinking about any of those things during the previous exercise." Let's look at each one of these assumptions, in reverse order.

Zero Initial Daughter Element: This assumption probably sounds the strangest, but it's very easy to understand. When our grapes decay into raisins, we call the grapes the "parents" and the raisins the "daughters." This assumption simply means that we are presupposing that when the system began (the bowl of grapes) there were only grapes in the bowl—no raisins (zero daughters). So, what if when the bowl was first placed on the counter it contained thirty grapes and thirty raisins? We would enter the room shortly after and proclaim that the grapes had been there ten days (at a rate of three raisins produced per day). We would also be very wrong, because of an erroneous assumption. More

recent advances in radiometric dating (such as using the isochron method) have been developed to significantly reduce problems associated with this assumption.

Closed System: A second assumption that was made in our grapes-to-raisins scenario was that no additional raisins from outside our "system" entered into the bowl in the past and that all of the raisins that did decay, stayed in the bowl and were not removed by anything or anyone. Again, we were not around to see what happened. What if someone walked by and emptied a box of raisins into the bowl, just before we walked into the kitchen? We would conclude that the grapes must have been there a very, very long time in order to produce all those raisins! With radiometric dating, it's a similar situation. Let's take Potassium-Argon dating, which is one of the more commonly used methods. Argon (the daughter product—like our raisins) is a gas and can easily be leached in and out of rocks through the simple flow of groundwater. To say that the rocks we are dating sat there for multiplied millions or even billions of years and were never affected by any outside influences is not only an assumption, it's a very unreasonable one in many cases. However, as was with the zero initial daughter element assumption, using methods such as the isochron method can also reduce the potential affects of this assumption.

Constant Decay Rate: This is the assumption that the grapes have always "decayed" at the rate we presently observe. However, we were not around from the beginning (whenever that was) to make measurements all along the way, so we really don't know for sure what the rate was in the past. We can only make logical or reasonable guesses and assume, for instance, that it was the same. What if the rate was much faster in the past? We would look at the bowl today and say, "Wow, there are quite a few raisins; the grapes must have been here for a very long time." In reality, they may have only been around a fairly short period of time, with most of the raisins having been produced much faster than we now observe.

In the case of radiometric dating, there is no way to be confident that decay rates have always been constant. In fact, much research has been conducted providing very strong evidence that rates have *not* been constant. The Institute for Creation Research and the Creation Research Society initiated a joint project called RATE,[1] an acronym for **R**adioisotopes and the **A**ge of **T**he **E**arth. It consisted of a team of credentialed and competent scientists working over a period of eight years, whose goals were to better understand the intricacies of radiometric dating and specifically to address apparent discrepancies between the currently observed slow rates of decay and the view of a relatively young Earth.

One of their findings was that there is solid evidence that the earth has experienced a period (or periods) of greatly accelerated decay in the past, possibly up to one billion times the rates observed today.[2] This would significantly throw off (to put it mildly) dates of billions of years that are so commonplace in radiometric dating. Some of their research focused on the leak rate of helium found in zircon crystals. (I know what you are thinking: "Where can I get the book and when will the movie be in the theaters?" I know sarcasm when I hear it. However, it actually is very interesting and it provides very powerful evidence of accelerated decay rates. And yes, there is a book, actually a few books,[3] and a DVD[4] in case you are interested in more of the technical details.) In summary for now, what this research means is that a rock that most geologists believe to be a billion years old, could actually have been formed in the period of only one year, most likely during the year-long flood! We'll revisit this briefly later in the chapter.

Known Errors

There are numerous examples of dating errors that have come from attempting to date rocks of known ages (e.g., rocks formed as the result of relatively recent, observed volcanic eruptions). One such instance is that of a lava flow in Hawaii, known to have taken place between 1800 and 1801. The rocks were dated using the Potassium-Argon method yielding an "age" just shy of 3 billion years old![5] There are many other examples that could be listed, but the all-important question is, "If these dating methods yield significant errors on rocks of known ages, how can scientists be so confident they are accurate for rocks of unknown ages?" The simple answer is: they can't!

Conflicting Results

Not only are we aware of erroneous results regarding rocks of known ages, but the various methods used by those claiming the earth is billions of years old often are in conflict with each other. One example is that of rock samples from the Bass Sills in the Grand Canyon. The Potassium-Argon (K-Ar) method yielded an age of approximately 842 million years. However, Samarium-Neodymium (Sm-Nd) method yielded an age of approximately 1.379 billion years! That's a difference of 537 million years! So which date is correct? How would we know either date is accurate? I suggest that they are both wrong. We could go on for page upon page with similar examples, but the main point is that since there exists so much discordance between the methods that are deemed to be generally reliable by evolutionists, there is sound reason to reject their accuracy and question the assumptions behind the methods.

A great resource regarding the results of the RATE team research (written in less technical detail than the book I previously referred to) is *Thousands not Billions: Challenging the Icon of Evolution, Questioning the Age of the Earth*, by Dr. Donald DeYoung.[6] Further information can also be found on their website: www.icr.org/rate.[7]

A short story related by Dr. Tas Walker (PhD—University of Queensland, now mechanical engineer and geologist with Creation Ministries International, Australia) sheds some further light on the reliability of radiometric dating:

> Recently, I conducted a geological field trip in the Townsville area, North Queensland. A geological guidebook, prepared by two geologists, was available from a government department. . .

> The guidebook's appendix explains "geological time and the ages of rocks." It describes how geologists use field relationships to determine the relative ages of rocks. It also says that the "actual" ages are measured by radiometric dating—an expensive technique performed in modern laboratories. The guide describes a number of radiometric methods and states that for "suitable specimens the errors involved in radiometric dating usually amount to several percent of the age result. Thus. . .a result of two hundred million years is expected to be quite close (within, say, four million) to the true age."

> This gives the impression that radiometric dating is very precise and very reliable—the impression generally held by the public. However, the appendix concludes with this qualification: "Also, the relative ages [of the radiometric dating results] must always be consistent with the geological evidence. . .if a contradiction occurs, then the cause of the error needs to be established or the radiometric results are unacceptable". . .

> Radiometric dates are only accepted if they agree with what geologists already believe the age should be.[8]

EVIDENCE FOR A YOUNG EARTH

As was mentioned in chapter 9, science can never tell us exactly how old the earth is, because every method available involves improvable assumptions. Creationists who believe the earth is relatively young often do not feel that all three assumptions we've just reviewed are valid. However, for argument's sake, they point out that even if these assumptions were justifiable, there are many more methods (over 100) that yield ages far too young for the standard geological and biological stories to be plausible.[9] The main point in examining these is not to determine the exact age of the earth, but rather to draw a general conclusion of whether we are talking about millions and billions of years, or thousands of years. In each case, the age yielded represents a reasonable upper limit, not an actual age. In most instances, the actual age could easily be much less than the determined age if we could somehow correct our assumptions to be more accurate (e.g., historical decay rates, initial conditions, etc.).

Earth's Magnetic Field

The earth is like a giant magnet and scientists have been measuring its strength for over 170 years. From these measurements, they have determined that the earth's magnetic field has a half-life of about 1,400 years. This simply means that every 1,400 years it loses half of its existing strength. The most interesting aspect of this phenomenon is not related to the future of the field, but to its past. About 1,400 years ago (according to its decay rate) the magnetic field of the earth would have been twice as strong as it is today. Going back another 1,400 years (~ 788 BC) would make it four times as strong. A greatly increased magnetic field means a greatly heated core in the earth (due to frictional effects of electrical currents within the core). So how far back could we possibly go? According to various calculations, a plausible limit is about 10,000 years. Much beyond that the earth's structure would not be able to withstand the heat! So could the earth actually be billions of years old? Not according to the decay of the earth's magnetic field. Could it be less than 10,000 years old? Certainly. (Note: some have attempted to counter this by reference to "magnetic reversals." However, the actual evidence shows that these reversals happened relatively quickly, related to the flood, and are in no way a valid counter-argument.) Dr. Thomas Barnes (professor of physics) conducted the initial work in this area back in the 1970s. More recently, additional conformational work has been done by Dr. Russell Humphreys (PhD—physics)[10] and Dr. John Baumgardner (PhD—geophysics and space physics).

Radiohalos

When uranium-238 (^{238}U) decays into its final daughter element, lead-206 (^{206}Pb), it does so indirectly by going through a series of thirteen intermediary steps along the way. For example, ^{238}U decays directly into thorium-234 (^{234}Th), which then decays into protactinium-234 (^{234}Pa) and so on until it reaches lead-206 (^{206}Pb) which is stable and no longer decays. The half-life of ^{238}U is about 4.5 billion years. Once again, this just means that at the rate we measure it decaying today in the laboratory, it would take about 4.5 billion years to decay to half of its current amount. With this slow decay rate, the amount of ^{206}Pb found in certain rocks

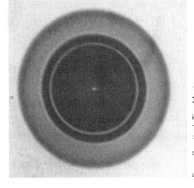

From Creation's Tiny Mystery

theoretically should take billions of years to accumulate if it all came from the decay of ^{238}U. However, there is strong evidence that the decay rate has not been constant, as we shall shortly see.

Three of the intermediate elements produced during the decay of ^{238}U are isotopes (versions) of an element called polonium (^{218}Po, ^{214}Po and ^{210}Po). Unlike uranium, polonium decays very rapidly. These three polonium elements have half-lives of just 3.1 minutes, 164 micro-seconds and 138 days, respectively. What does that mean? It means that these elements decay very quickly, not over millions or billions of years, but in days, minutes or fractions of a second (depending upon which isotope is under consideration). Why does any of this matter? Scientists have discovered numerous examples of polonium "halos" within granite rocks. When polonium decays, the radioactivity damages the surrounding structure (biotite—a mica mineral) leaving a spherical pattern. The general term for these patterns is "radioactive halos" or "radiohalos" for short. Polonium halos are radiohalos specifically formed by polonium decay. So where is this all leading? The existence of polonium halos indicate that it should supposedly have required (by standard geologic theory) 100 million years for the uranium decay to produce enough polonium to create these halos. However, since polonium decays so quickly, it could not have left any record in the rocks, because they supposedly were still in the process of cooling for millions of years. But the halos *are* there! This is evidence of greatly accelerated radioactive decay rates. In other words, it appears that 100 million years worth of decay took place in a number of days![11] This would account for the appearance of the halos and also indicate that uranium decay was accelerated approximately one billion times faster than the current measured rate. With this in mind, these radiohalos are evidence for a young Earth and strong reason to doubt the assumption of constant decay rates.

Helium Abundance in Minerals

Another by-product of ^{238}U decay is the element helium (He), a gas with which you are most likely very familiar with because it is commonly used in balloons to make them float. At eight different times during the decay process of every ^{238}U atom a helium nucleus is ejected into the surrounding mineral structure. This gas is kind of "slippery" (meaning that it doesn't often react with other elements) and easily escapes from the rock in which it was produced, out into the atmosphere. If the rocks are millions or billions of years old we should not expect to find much helium within them, because it would have escaped long ago. Conversely, we should find a fair amount of helium in our atmosphere, since most helium atoms cannot reach the necessary velocity to escape the earth's gravitational pull. In reality, we find much more helium in the rocks than would be expected by the evolutionists and not nearly as much as expected in the atmosphere! Recent research on this (by the RATE group) has shown that not only does this limit the age of the rocks and atmosphere to a number of thousands of years, but it also shows evidence of accelerated radiometric decay—billions of years worth within a very short burst of time, or a few bursts of time, similar to the previous "radiohalo" example).[12]

Decay of Biological Material

Biological material is certainly not as resilient as geologic material, such as granite, and is especially susceptible to decay. In spite of the fact that researchers say DNA cannot survive in its natural environment for more than 10,000 years,[13] we have discovered it in places where it "ought not be!" One example is found in insects that were imbedded in amber.[14]

Scientists have even found some *Tyrannosaurus rex* bones with red blood cells and soft tissue![15] But dinosaur bones are supposed to be at least 65 million years old! How can that be? When these discoveries were made, the researching scientist, Mary Schweitzer (evolutionary paleontologist now at North Carolina State University) said she got goose bumps and stated that, "It was exactly like looking at a slice of modern bone. But of course, I couldn't believe it. . .the bones, after all, are 65 million years old. How could blood cells survive that long?"[16] Many scientists dismissed the evidence, because they believed it just couldn't possibly be true. Schweitzer stated, "I had one reviewer tell me that he didn't care what the data said, he knew that what I was finding wasn't possible. I wrote back and said, 'Well, what data would convince you?' And he said, 'None.'"[17] Since this original discovery, many others have been made (e.g., the discovery of the protein collagen[18]) and skeptics' criticisms have been answered. They have even discovered the protein osteocalcin in an Iguanodon that according to evolutionary stories is allegedly 120 million years old![19] Once again, these are all indicators that these bones cannot be millions of years old. However, paradigms are tough cookies and the "millions of years" paradigm is not likely to be reconsidered anytime soon. After all, if we don't have millions of years to work with, evolution isn't even a remote possibility.

Lastly, bacteria that is supposedly 250 million years old have been revived with completely undamaged DNA.[20] This is a huge conundrum for evolutionists, but fits very comfortably with a young Earth.

Rapid Layer Deposition

In the fairly recent past, most geologists believed that each individual sedimentary layer was laid down slowly and gradually by the same types of processes we observe today, thus requiring hundreds of millions of years to complete. However, further research argued strongly against this idea, forcing them to rethink their views. For example, it is now known that the sedimentary layers contain literally billions of fossils. But fossils generally only form under rapid, catastrophic conditions in which living things get buried quickly. If an animal dies, but does not get buried rapidly, it will simply decompose and there will be virtually no trace left whatsoever. The challenge was to come up with a new scenario without giving up their belief in millions of years for the origin of the sedimentary layers. So what did they do? They regrouped and proposed the following solution: Most of the layers truly were laid down catastrophically in a relatively short period of time, but then each one sat there for hundreds of thousands or millions of years before eventually being covered up by the next layer, which itself was deposited rapidly. So the time (millions of years) was just shifted from existing within the layers, to between the layers. That's a very creative idea. Regrettably for them, it's not a very credible idea, which is much more important when formulating scientific hypotheses. There are a number of lines of evidence that are contrary to this alleged scenario and we'll address a few of them here.

Polystrate Fossils: An interesting geologic anomaly is that of fossils (most often trees) that extend through multiple layers of rock that were supposedly deposited over hundreds of thousands or millions of years. We call these relics polystrate fossils ("poly" meaning *many* and "strate" referring to *strata* or *layers*). The issue here is that if those layers were truly laid down over such a long period of time, the trees would have rotted long before ever getting completely buried, thus, never turning into a fossil! Another critical observation is that when we find

these trees we do not find the root systems intact, meaning that these trees were not growing there! They were catastrophically uprooted from their original location and rapidly re-deposited elsewhere. These anomalies are strong evidence against the alleged millions of years that are assigned to the layers in the earth.

Folded Rock: Have you ever tried folding a rock? Probably not. I haven't either. However, that there are a number of places on Earth where we see great folds in solid rock (e.g., Tapeats Sandstone in Carbon Canyon and the Muav Limestone in the Grand Canyon, both in the United States). How did this occur? In most instances, if there is enough pressure, the rock will fracture, because of how brittle it is. Experiments have shown that if there is enough pressure and *heat*, rocks can fold to some extent. In each of these cases the rocks will show evidence of having experienced great amounts of heat. However, there are many instances where the rocks show no evidence of great heat while also yielding evidence that they were in a "soft and plastic" state when they were

Photo courtesy of Chris Budd (UK)

folded (not having had enough time to harden). This fits perfectly with a global flood, depositing the layers rapidly and then being uplifted and deformed by subsequent tectonic movements, all before they had time to harden.

Lack of Erosion, Soil and Bioturbation: A further anomaly is that we rarely see any evidence of erosion between these sedimentary layers and when we do, it appears to have occurred rapidly. If one layer sat there for a few million years before being covered by the next layer, we would expect to see a great deal of erosion. In addition, we would expect to see the development of soil and plant

growth during these periods of millions of years, but this is also mysteriously absent. We would also expect to see evidence of bioturbation, meaning the burrowing of animals or other creatures, tunneling into the layers. In reality, we don't see that either. Further evidence that the alleged grand amounts of time between layer deposits never actually existed.

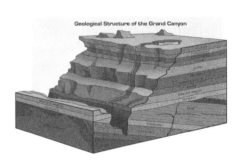

Geological Structure of the Grand Canyon

Oil and Coal: Millions of Years to Form?

We all *know* that it takes millions of years to form oil; right? And the same goes for coal; right? And don't forget diamonds —millions of years (maybe even a billion); right? WRONG!

Oil supposedly formed over millions of years from the breakdown of organic material buried within the earth. However, scientists today are able to produce oil in a matter of minutes in the laboratory.[21] All that is required is the right materials and conditions, not the magic of millions of years. The main ingredients are organic material, pressure, heat and water. This is exactly what the flood would have provided. Lots of water burying tons of organic material, forming huge layers of sediment, creating tremendous pressure, which in turn creates great amounts of heat. More recent studies have indicated that oil may even be forming today by abiotic (not derived from living material) methods. According to WorldNetDaily.com (February 01, 2008), "hydrocarbons are naturally produced on a continual basis throughout the solar system, including within the mantle of the earth. The advocates believe the oil seeps up through bedrock cracks to deposit in sedimentary rock."[22]

The same goes for coal. Argonne National Laboratories (Argonne, IL—USA) has proven that coal can be formed under natural conditions in a matter of weeks. Some laboratories have even produced it within hours under special conditions. [23]

Scientists have also been able to create diamonds indistinguishable from natural diamonds using carbon dioxide, metallic sodium, high pressure and a temperature of 440°C in just twelve hours![24] (Great last minute gift idea, by the way!) Keeping all of this in mind, millions of years are just not required!

Carbon-14 Dating

Since the subject of carbon-14 (^{14}C) dating comes up so often and because of the amount of misinformation that exits regarding this topic, we will delve into it a bit more thoroughly than the previous evidences.

I introduce you now to the all-powerful carbon-14 "trump card." Consider the following partial conversation between two hypothetical friends: Bill (a skeptic of Christianity) and Greg (a strong believer in the Bible).

Bill: "Of course the earth is billions of years old!"

Greg: "Well, the Bible says that God created everything in six days."

Bill: "The Bible is wrong, way wrong. I mean come on, haven't you heard of carbon-14 dating?"

Greg: "I don't know much about it; I just believe the Bible."

Bill: "Well you can have your 'faith;' but as for me, I live in the real world and I'm sticking with science!"

There you have it. Another battle has been won by the skeptic, and another Christian has been intimidated into backing down, mistakenly concluding that they just need to have "stronger faith" in light of all of the scientific evidence to the contrary. Many people walk around with this magical carbon-14 "trump card" and anytime a Christian brings up the subject of the Bible, creation or would even dare to speak of a young earth, they simply pull the trump card out of their pocket and the Christian is left defenseless.

Let's revisit the conversation, but change how Greg responds:

Bill: "Of course the earth is billions of years old!"

Greg: "Well, the Bible says that God created everything in six days."

Bill: "The Bible is wrong, way wrong. I mean come on, haven't you heard of carbon-14 dating?"

Greg: "Yes, I actually have heard of carbon-14, but I'm not exactly sure how it works or how it proves the earth is billions of years old. Could you help me out and explain it to me?"

Bill: "Well it's really complicated, but it proves the earth is billions of years old."

Greg: "I understand that it may be a bit complex, but could you explain in general how it works?"

Bill: "Like I said, it's just so complex. Science is like that, you know. It's not like the fairy-land of religion."

Greg: "Couldn't you just put it in laymen's terms so I had some idea of how it works?"

Bill: "It's just really complex and very scientific. You probably wouldn't understand."

Greg: "Alright, forget about explaining the dating method. Could you at least tell me where carbon-14 comes from?"

Bill: "Well it comes from, you see. . .it's like. . .well, I don't really have time for this right now."

Greg: "If you aren't able to describe carbon-14 dating in general terms and don't even know where it comes from, you must have a lot of faith in it, but it would actually be a blind faith, since it seems to me that you yourself don't really know much about it."

I have actually had similar conversations with a number of skeptics, as well as those who believe that God was involved in creation to some extent, but that the earth is truly billions of years old. In my personal version of this type of conversation, I do not say that I don't know anything about how carbon-14 dating works (because I do know a fair amount); I simply ask them if they can explain it to me. The revised conversation above was written with the assumption that the Christian at this point in their life really doesn't know much about carbon-14.

So What Exactly is Carbon-14?

[Note: If you just aren't interested in learning some of the technical details about carbon-14, you might want to simply skip to the section entitled "^{14}C Summary." It's alright—I won't tell anyone!]

Before we look at the actual dating method, let's briefly look at carbon-14 itself. Just allow me a little bit of "techie talk" and then we'll get right back to the laymen's terms. Carbon-14 (^{14}C, also called radiocarbon) is an "isotope" of carbon, which simply means a species or variety of the carbon element. In the case of the carbon element, carbon-12 (^{12}C) is a stable isotope (version), meaning that it stays ^{12}C throughout its entire lifetime. On the other hand, ^{14}C is an unstable (radioactive) isotope, which over time decays back in to what it originally was, nitrogen-14 (^{14}N).

Carbon-14 is created in our atmosphere when radiation coming from the sun produces thermal neutrons, which in turn, collide with and are absorbed by ^{14}N, converting it into ^{14}C. Because ^{14}C is unstable, it slowly decays back into ^{14}N. Scientists have measured the rate of decay and determined that it would take about 5,730 years for half of any particular amount of ^{14}C to decay back into ^{14}N. This is what is referred to as a "half-life." If all this is a bit too much, all you have to remember is that ^{14}C is created in our atmosphere by the sun and slowly decays away. Easy enough.

How does Carbon-14 get into Living Things?

You most likely have already heard of carbon dioxide (CO_2), especially with all the hype about global warming and global climate change, which is another subject for another time. It's just a combination of carbon and oxygen. Most carbon dioxide consists of stable ^{12}C and oxygen (and is therefore not radioactive). However, some carbon dioxide is created by the combination of unstable ^{14}C and oxygen, which is then radioactive. Both forms of CO_2 exist in our atmosphere. Carbon dioxide is absorbed by plants and trees in a process called photosynthesis. During photosynthesis, plants take in light energy, carbon dioxide and water. In return, they produce much needed carbohydrates (plant food) and give off oxygen back into the atmosphere. As you can imagine, some of the carbon dioxide taken in by plants is the radioactive form containing ^{14}C. As part of the normal life cycle, animals eat the plants and people eat the animals and the plants, so we all have some level of ^{14}C within our bodies. Therefore, all living things contain amounts of both stable ^{12}C and radioactive ^{14}C. Don't worry about the radioactivity, though. There's a lot less ^{14}C than ^{12}C in our world today. In fact, only about one in one trillion carbon atoms is ^{14}C, so I wouldn't be concerned just yet about glowing in the dark! Okay, so we all have some radiocarbon in us. What does that have to do with figuring out how old something is?

Carbon-14 can potentially be used to yield estimated ages, but we must consider a few limitations. First of all, the ^{14}C method can only be used on something that was once living, such as a bone or an animal hide. It cannot be used to date rocks directly. Therefore, when someone states that the earth is billions of years old and it has been proven by ^{14}C, the only thing that it proves is that they truly don't know much about this dating method. Secondly, because of its decay rate, there should be no detectable ^{14}C left after about 100,000 years. In fact, even if you had a ball of ^{14}C the size of the earth, there wouldn't be even one ^{14}C atom left after one million years![25] When an article in a magazine or a scientist on television claims that a certain bone is 1.5 million years old, they are not making that claim based on anything having to do with ^{14}C dating (even though the public often assumes they are). Here's something to keep in mind: just because this method could theoretically measure the age of something up to 100,000 years, it doesn't mean that anything actually *is* that old. It simply means that this method should be able to date something within that range. As an analogy, it would be like the markings on the speedometer in your car registering up to 100,000 miles per hour. It doesn't magically enable your car to travel that fast. It just means that if somehow your car could actually go 98,000 miles per hour, the speedometer would be capable of measuring it.

So How Does Carbon-14 Dating Work?

The carbon-14 dating method was developed by Willard F. Libby in the late 1940s, and for his development, he was awarded the Nobel Prize in Chemistry in 1960. Here's how it works. While an organism or animal is alive, it contains a certain ratio of ^{14}C to ^{12}C, somewhat similar to that of all other living organisms. Even though the ^{14}C in a living organism or animal slowly decays away, it is constantly taking in new ^{14}C (when it eats) replenishing the amount that decays. Once it dies, however, it stops eating and therefore stops taking in new ^{14}C. The ^{14}C that it contains at the time of death continues to decay back into ^{14}N (and this is when the "clock" starts ticking). Technically, scientists are not so much calculating how old an animal is, as they are figuring out how long ago it died (when it stopped taking in additional ^{14}C). Since they have determined that it takes about 5,730 years for half of the ^{14}C to decay away, if they find a bone with half the ratio of ^{14}C to ^{12}C that we observe today, then they say it must have died one half-life ago, or about 5,730 years. If they found just a quarter of the ratio (which equates to 2 half-lives: going from 100% to 50%, then from 50% to 25%), they would say it died about 11,460 years ago (5,730 years x 2).

It's Not Quite That Easy

Things often aren't as simple as they may initially seem and the radiocarbon method is no exception. There are a number of potential issues with this dating method. We will take a look at just a few.

One of the key assumptions about ^{14}C is that it has reached equilibrium. What does that mean? Picture a bucket with a few holes in the side. If you were to start filling the bucket with a hose, you would notice that initially the water would rise fairly quickly. When it reached the first hole, it would start to leak, but if the water ran fast enough out of the hose, it would still continue to fill the bucket, just not quite as fast as before the water reached the first hole. When it reaches the second hole, it will leak even faster, and fill even slower. Eventually, it will reach enough holes so that the amount of water leaking out is equal to the amount of water running in from the hose (meaning that the water level in the bucket is neither rising nor falling). This is the point of equilibrium. It is somewhat similar to our situation with ^{14}C. Even though it is being created in our atmosphere, it is also decaying away. Scientists have calculated that it would only take about 30,000 years for it to reach an equilibrium point (where the production rate and decay rate become equal). Libby, the inventor of this method, knew from his own measurements that this equilibrium had not yet been reached. This disturbed him greatly because he believed the earth was billions of years old and our atmosphere was at least millions of years old. He ignored this evidence and just assumed that equilibrium had been reached, stating that his own figures must have been in error. This shows us just how strongly our worldview or presuppositions can affect our evaluation of the actual data! Today's research shows that ^{14}C is being created in our atmosphere 30-32% faster than it is leaving. This fact, in and of itself, is evidence that our atmosphere has not been around for millions of years, but rather is actually less than 30,000 years old! The upper limit, according to these figures would be about 7,000-10,000 years.

Plants naturally discriminate against absorbing CO_2 that contains ^{14}C,—they are less likely to absorb ^{14}C than ^{12}C. This would mean that when we date the plants by this method, they would have less ^{14}C to begin with than expected, which would give the appearance of being older (appearing as though much time must have passed in order for the ^{14}C to have decayed away). Additionally, some plants absorb CO_2 at different rates than others, so two plants that died at the exact same time might yield significantly different "ages."

Another factor affecting this method is the earth's magnetic field, which acts as a giant shield, protecting us from a lot of harmful solar radiation. As we discussed earlier, this field is also slowly decaying, which means that it was much stronger in the past. How does that affect this dating method? With a much stronger magnetic field, there would be much less radiation from the sun reaching our atmosphere. With less radiation, there would be less production of ^{14}C. Anything that lived a long time ago (say 4,000 or 5,000 years ago) would have been living in an environment that had a lower $^{14}C/^{12}C$ ratio. When we dig up those fossils and test them today we typically say, "Hey, these don't have much ^{14}C in them at all. They must be really, really old; probably 28,000 years old!" In reality, it may only be 4,500 years old, having had less ^{14}C in it to begin with. In general, the farther back in the past you go, the less ^{14}C there would have been to begin with, giving it the appearance of being much older than it actually is.

Two additional factors affecting dates given by ^{14}C are volcanic eruptions and the Industrial Revolution. Both of these events are responsible for introducing great amounts of CO_2 into the atmosphere void of ^{14}C. Why does this matter? Once again, this method is completely dependent on the ratio of ^{14}C to ^{12}C. If we suddenly add a lot more ^{12}C, which is what happened during these events, then the ratio of ^{14}C to ^{12}C decreases dramatically, having even more ^{12}C than usual. The overall affect is that things living and dying during this time will give the appearance of being much older than they really are because of the method's assumption of a constant $^{14}C/^{12}C$ ratio throughout the past. Most ^{14}C dating does not take into consideration the effects of the Industrial Revolution which have been at least partially determined through the study of tree rings. The larger question is how do we know what it was like throughout history even prior to this period?

A Few Anomalies

Carbon-14 dating often yields ages that are in direct conflict with each other or with other dating methods. There are some instances where contamination can be legitimately detected (thus accounting for dates that are greatly in error), but many others instances where it is not possible. Occasionally, there are alternate ways to determine the approximate age of a specimen, usually through tree-ring dating or associated artifacts. In many of these cases, the carbon date is way off, which is a probable indicator of contamination or invalid assumptions. If the method can be significantly off when applied to objects of known ages, what makes anyone confident that the dates are accurate when testing objects of unknown age?

Numerous errors could be cited regarding dates that have been obtained using the radiocarbon method. In each case, scientists simply claim that there must have been "contamination," resulting in the unacceptable date. When they say "unacceptable" they mean not in accordance with what they were expecting, based on evolutionary assumptions or the traditional geological history of the earth.

Referring once again to the work done by the RATE Group, one particular study involved taking samples from ten different coal layers found in different alleged eras in the geologic column (Cenozoic, Mesozoic, and Paleozoic). Even though these layers supposedly represent millions and hundreds of millions of years, they found traceable amounts of ^{14}C in each sample, indicating that these layers are not millions of years old.

Diamonds present another anomaly for ^{14}C dating. They are the hardest natural occurring mineral known to man and are extremely resistant to any kind of contamination. Being anywhere from millions to billions of years old (according to the standard geological model), they should not contain any detectable ^{14}C. Interestingly enough, the RATE Group found ^{14}C in each of the diamonds they studied![26]

With all of this in mind, consider the following quote by anthropologist and archeologist, Robert E. Lee:

> Why do geologists and archeologists still spend their scarce money on costly radiocarbon determinations? They do so because occasional dates appear to be useful. While the method cannot be counted on to give good, unequivocal results, the numbers do impress people, and save them the trouble of thinking excessively. . ."Absolute" dates determined by a laboratory carry a lot of weight, and are extremely helpful in bolstering weak arguments. . .No matter how "useful" it is, though, the radiocarbon method is still not capable of yielding accurate and reliable results. There are gross discrepancies, the chronology is uneven and relative, and the accepted dates are actually selected dates. This whole blessed thing is nothing but 13th-century alchemy, and it all depends upon which funny paper you read.[27]

^{14}C Summary

While the ^{14}C dating method can in certain situations potentially yield fairly accurate estimated ages, it is fundamentally incapable of dating rocks or anything supposedly hundreds of thousands or millions of years old. There are a number of factors that need to be considered in any age determination. When these factors are properly accounted for, dates currently published in the range of 50,000+ years, fall within the biblical view of a recent creation and subsequent worldwide flood.

OVERALL CONCLUSION

Although virtually everything we hear from the scientific community would lead us to believe that the earth is roughly 4.6 billion years old, this conclusion is not well founded. In fact, even using evolutionists' own assumptions, including the historical constancy of decay rates, the vast majority (probably 90% or better) of the available potential chronometers yield ages far too young for the plausibility of evolutionary scenarios.

Science is fallible and ultimately based on the conclusions of men and women who do not know everything, were not there in the beginning, make mistakes, can be greatly subject to their own biases and who are studying a fallen world. There exists ample reason to doubt or reject altogether the conclusions of those who believe in the existence of billions of years. The Bible, on the other hand, is the infallible record of the One who was there in the beginning, is all-powerful, knows everything and does not lie. Subsequently, there exists ample reason to trust the straight-forward reading of the creation narrative, which conveys the idea of a recent, six-solar day creation.

The final word: it has been aptly said that, "Talking about the Rock of Ages beats talking about the age of rocks, anytime!" I heartily concur.

ENDNOTES

1.   www.icr.org/rate—*last accessed 9/13/10.*

2.   Humphreys, D. et al., "Helium diffusion rates support accelerated nuclear decay," www.icr.org/research/icc03/pdf/Helium_ICC_7-22-03.pdf, October 16, 2003—*last accessed 9/21/10.*

3.   "Radioisotopes and the Age of the Earth: A Young-Earth Creationist Research Initiative," edited by Vardiman, L., Snelling, A.A. and Chaffin, E. F., (Vol 1— 676 pages, Vol 2 – 818 pages), Institute for Creation Research and the Creation Research Society, El Cajon, CA, and St. Joseph, Missouri, 2000.

4.   *Thousands not Billions: Challenging the Icon of Evolution, Questioning the Age of the Earth,* DVD, Institute for Creation Research, 2005.

5.   Punkhouser, J. G., and Naughton, J.J., "He and Ar in ultramafic inclusions," *Journal of Geophysical Research,* Vol.73, 1968, pp. 4601-4607.

6.   DeYoung, Donald, *Thousands not Billions: Challenging the Icon of Evolution, Questioning the Age of the Earth,* Master Books, Inc., Green Forest, AR, 2005.

7.   www.icr.org/rate—*last accessed 9/13/10.*

8.   http://creation.com/the-way-it-really-is-little-known-facts-about-radiometric-dating—*last accessed 9/13/10.*

9.   Batten, Don, "101 evidences for a young age of the earth and the universe," 4 June 2009, http://creation.com/age-of-the-earth—*last accessed 9/24/10.*

10.   Humphreys, D. Russell, "The Earth's Magnetic Field is Young," http://www.icr.org/article/371/.

11.   Snelling, Andrew A., "Radiohalos: Startling evidence of catastrophic geologic processes on a young earth," *Creation* 28(2):46-50, March 2006.

12.   www.icr.org/rate—*last accessed 9/24/10.*

13.   Cohen, J., and Stewart, I., "Our genes aren't us," *Discover*, 15(4):78-84, 1994.

14.   http://www.amnh.org/exhibitions/amber/—*last accessed 7/19/12.*

15.   http://creation.com/dinosaur-soft-tissue-and-protein-even-more-confirmation—*last accessed 7/19/12.*

16.   Morell, V., "Dino DNA: The Hunt and the Hype," *Science*, 261 (5118): 160, 1993.

17.   Yeoman, B., "Schweitzer's Dangerous Discovery," *Discover* 27(4):37–41, 77, April 2006.

18.   Quinlan, M.E. et al., "Drosophila Spire is an actin nucleation factor," *Nature* 433:382–388, 2005.

19.   Wellington, A. et al., "Spire contains actin binding domains and is related to ascidian posterior end mark-5," *Development* 126:5267–5274, 1999.

20.   *Nature,* 407:897-900 (19 October 2000).

21.   *Discover*, May 2, 2003.

22.   "Discovery backs theory oil not 'fossil fuel'," *WND*, Feb 1, 2008, http://www.wnd.com/2008/02/45838/—*last accessed 7/19/12.*

23.   http://www.creationworldview.org/articles_view.asp?id=51—*last accessed 7/18/12.*

24.   *New Scientist*, July 26, 2003, p. 17.

25.   http://creation.com/ad-hominem—*last accessed 7/19/12.*

26.   DeYoung, Donald, *Thousands not Billions: Challenging the Icon of Evolution, Questioning the Age of the Earth*, Master Books, Inc., Green Forest, AR, 2005, pp.55-56.

27.   Lee, Robert E., "Radiocarbon: ages in error," *Anthropological Journal of Canada*, vol.19(3), 1981, pp.9-29.

Chapter Twelve

Intelligent Design:
The Good, the Bad and the Ugly

"The universe that we observe has precisely the properties we should expect if there is, at bottom, no design, no purpose, no evil, no good, nothing but pitiless indifference."[1]

 So states Richard Dawkins, one of the world's leading evolutionists and very outspoken atheist. Just in case you are wondering how Dawkins feels about God, take a look at another one of his quotes (or should I say "diatribes"):

The God of the Old Testament is arguably the most unpleasant character in all fiction: jealous and proud of it; a petty, unjust, unforgiving control-freak; a vindictive, bloodthirsty ethnic cleanser; a misogynistic, homophobic, racist, infanticidal, genocidal, filicidal, pestilential, megalomaniacal, sadomasochistic, capriciously malevolent bully.[2]

So, Richard; how do you really feel? I think he made it very clear. To be honest, even though I strongly disagree with his worldview and his occasional harshness, I appreciate his transparency. It's actually quite refreshing. He is at least being honest and you know exactly where he stands, as opposed to many others (Christians included) who are too worried about being politically correct.

Today, there are thousands of scientists who take exception to what Dawkins thinks, believing that the universe and life are not the random products of some fortuitous cosmic accident, but rather were purposely and magnificently

223

designed. These same scientists (and countless millions of other non-scientists) are convinced that this design is evident in the world around us and that will be the focus of this chapter. Biblically speaking, we would expect this design to be self-evident. Romans 1:18-20 (NIV) states,

> The wrath of God is being revealed from heaven against all the godlessness and wickedness of men who suppress the truth by their wickedness, since what may be known about God is plain to them, because God has made it plain to them. For since the creation of the world God's invisible qualities—his eternal power and divine nature—have been clearly seen, being understood from what has been made, so that men are without excuse.

ORIGIN AND BACKGROUND OF INTELLIGENT DESIGN

According to IntelligentDesign.org, the current concept of intelligent design (commonly referred to as "ID"), "holds that certain features of the universe and of living things are best explained by an intelligent cause, not an undirected process such as natural selection."[3]

The idea of "intelligent design" is one that has been around for quite some time. In fact, it dates back over 2,000 years ago to the ancient philosophers who were countering evolutionary ideas of their day. Fast-forwarding a bit to the eighteenth century, William Paley (1743–1805) wrote a book entitled, *Natural Theology*, in which he clearly elucidated the design argument. His central example was that of a man walking through the countryside and coming upon a watch. Paley claimed that no one would believe that the watch appeared on its own through a series of accidental occurrences until each of its complex parts were assembled in just the right place and just the right way. On the contrary, it is obvious that the watch was designed and hence, had a designer.

Of considerable interest is the fact that Darwin himself was quite familiar with (and very captivated by) Paley's book:

> I do not think that I hardly ever admired a book more than Paley's "Natural Theology." I could almost formerly have said it by heart.[4]

This, however, was while Darwin was studying theology at Cambridge (1828–31), approximately thirty years before writing *The Origin of Species*, which, of course, denies such design evidence. There were a number of events that occurred in Darwin's life that led him to reject his view of God as the creator and pursue only naturalistic answers for the world around him. He married his first cousin and they lost two children in infancy, but the most significant event was the death of his daughter Annie at the age of ten. Much could be said regarding Darwin's change in thinking (primarily his disdain for the God of the Bible), but it is not the intended focus of this book. (For further reading see, *The Dark Side of Charles Darwin,* Bergman, Jerry, Master Books, 2001.)

In more recent times, intelligent design has taken on a whole new character. Two of the more prominent organizations involved in this movement are:

The Discovery Institute

Seattle, Washington (US)

www.discovery.org

Access Research Network

Colorado Springs, Colorado (US)

www.arn.org

Here are a few of the more prominent spokespersons for the ID movement:

- William Dembski—research professor in philosophy at Southwestern Baptist Theological Seminary

- Stephen Meyer—founder of the Discovery Institute and its Center for Science and Culture

- Philip Johnson—retired UC Berkeley law professor, co-founder and program advisor of the Discovery Institute's Center for Science and Culture

- Michael Behe—professor of Biochemistry at Lehigh University and senior fellow of the Discovery Institute's Center for Science and Culture

WHAT IT IS AND WHAT IT AIN'T

Before we get into any example evidences of intelligent design, we need to discuss what ID is and what it is not. There's a lot of misinformation circulating regarding this subject.

Many people have the impression that intelligent design is basically the same thing as biblical creation. While they certainly do have a lot in common, they are not the same and many ID theorists make great attempts to distance themselves from anything having to do with the Bible. Why would this be the case? Further exploration will yield the answer.

Biblical creation teaches that God created everything in six days as specifically outlined in Genesis chapters 1-2. We know from the text: (a) who did it, (b) how it was done—to a certain limited extent, (c) approximately when it was done, and (d) why it was done. This view makes it very clear that the origin of life and the universe was certainly no accident.

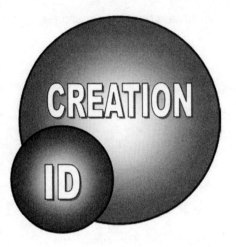

Intelligent design theorists heartily agree that our existence is no accident, but they do not wish to deal with the non-scientifically testable aspects of the "who" and "why" (and usually also steer clear of the question regarding "when"). They wish to extricate themselves from the discussion of anything overtly "religious." They are solely interested in evidence that shows design/purpose as opposed to 100% natural forces acting in a completely undirected manner.

A significant segment of evidence for biblical creation consists of the evidences that ID theorists promote. In that sense, you could say that ID is somewhat of a subset of the biblical creation model. More accurately, the two intersect significantly, but there many elements within the creation model that are not part of the ID model and there are even aspects within the ID model that to fit within the creation model.

It is important to realize that those within the ID camp come in all shapes and sizes. Since they (as a movement) are not concerned with identifying the "designer," there are many flavors of ID theorists.

Group 1: Strongly believe in the God of the Bible (and Jesus Christ) and view Genesis as an historical narrative, believing very firmly in the six-day creation account and the authority of Scripture as a whole.

Group 2: Strongly believe in the God of the Bible (and Jesus Christ), but do not view Genesis as an historical narrative. These still claim to believe very firmly in the authority of Scripture as a whole.

Group 3: Strongly believe in the God of the Bible (and Jesus Christ), but do not view Genesis as an historical narrative and also do not believe very firmly in the authority of Scripture as a whole.

Group 4: Believe in some type of god or supernatural force, but don't view the Bible as being inspired significant in anyway.

Group 5: Reject God and the inspiration of the Bible, believing that aliens are responsible for life here on Earth. Yes, aliens. . .very intelligent aliens!

Group 6: Believe most of what current evolutionary theory purports, but think that it is highly unlikely to have happened accidentally (evolution must have been directed somehow by some kind of intelligence.) Views regarding the Bible within this group vary greatly, but most reject its divine inspiration.

Each of the groups above, with the exception of the first, buys into most of secular astronomy and geology with its associated concept of millions and billions of years.

It is easy to see when ID theorists discuss evidence of design, it certainly fits with the biblical notion that God (*the* designer) created everything. Creationists are generally very excited about research that is being done by ID theorists and are encouraged by the growth of the movement.

However, the converse isn't always true. ID theorists are often reluctant to accept any evidence from biblical creationists that "goes too far." By going too far, I mean anything that would be supportive of the specific details found in Scripture, such as the "days" in Genesis 1 being actual solar days as opposed to millions of years each, or evidence for the global flood of Noah. This is all driven by the fact that most ID theorists work very hard at distancing themselves from creationists as a whole. They fear that if the distinction is not made by the scientific community the "excess baggage" of creationism will keep them from making progress within the public school and university settings. There is some justification for this concern. Most creationists that I am aware of are not bent on getting the Genesis account of creation taught in the public science classroom, because the entire account contains many elements that are outside the reach of true science and do not justifiably belong in the science classroom. (There are actually many aspects of evolution that also don't fall within the realm of science, but are strictly philosophical and even religious in nature. Unfortunately, they are currently being foisted on the public as "science.")

However, there are many aspects of the creation account that can properly be scrutinized by science and these are the very components that need to be included in any serious science curriculum, many of which fall into the category of intelligent design.

ID scientists are not focused on getting the teaching of evolution out of the school system, but simply wanting both sides of the scientific argument presented to the students so that they can formulate a well-informed opinion on the subject of origins. Even Darwin himself said that both sides should be considered, as we mentioned in chapter 1:

A fair result can be obtained only by fully stating and balancing the facts and arguments on both sides of each question.[5]

There are others today, however, who wish to censor information in the alleged interest of protecting the students. Eugenie Scott (executive director of the National Center for Science Education and ardent critic of both biblical creation and ID) made an interesting admission:

> In my opinion, using creation and evolution as topics for critical-thinking exercises in primary and secondary schools is virtually guaranteed to confuse students about evolution and may lead them to reject one of the major themes in science.[6]

In other words, if we let them hear scientific evidence for intelligent design, the students may end up not believing in evolution! How tragic that would be, in her mind. The marching orders are to teach the students what to think, instead of teaching them how to think (how to use their own critical thinking skills). We must indoctrinate them in evolution while they are young so that there will be much less of a chance that they will become apostates as they mature (through thinking for themselves).

While creationists are generally thankful for the inroads that the ID movement is making regarding public school science instruction (and doing some great research along the way), there are also inherent dangers related to the movement as a whole.

CONCERNS WITH INTELLIGENT DESIGN

One of the main problems with the concept of ID concerns the following logic: If intricate design is evidence of an intelligent designer, what does allegedly "bad design" indicate? Logically, you could say "a bad or deficient designer." Can we legitimately conclude that the designer isn't all that bright because of things we occasionally see that appear (at least in some minds) to be poorly designed? ID theorists have their hands tied to some extent at this point. They cannot give the same answer a biblical creationist can (and should) give. Specifically, that we are living in a fallen, cursed world; one that is far from how God designed it originally. God's original creation was perfect (Genesis 1:31). Nothing poorly designed; nothing run-down. It was Adam's sin that introduced the world-wide curse (Romans 5:12, 8:22) and things have been going down hill ever since. The current condition is not a reflection of the character of God or His creative abilities, but of the devastating effects of man's sin. Sin, however, is foreign to the concept of ID.

When the beautiful churches and synagogues in Europe were destroyed during World War II, no one thought "Those buildings were not designed very well; look at how run down they are!" In fact, in many cases their partial destruction revealed a level of internal intricacy and beauty not otherwise seen by the general public. It is often the same with the world in which we live. As decayed as it may be, there is still a high degree of beauty and sophistication beyond belief.

A second concern with the ID movement is that it doesn't go far enough. The only thing that is truly of eternal value is a personal relationship with the Creator Himself, through His son, Jesus Christ. Simply moving from an atheistic or agnostic viewpoint into group 4, 5 or 6 (from earlier in this chapter) will not change one's eternal destiny. A relationship with Jesus Christ only comes from understanding the "big picture," which not only includes God as the creator, but involves properly understanding our current fallen state and salvation through the shed blood of Jesus Christ, the Son of God. There is an eternal difference between the big picture and simply acknowledging God's existence. (See chapter 13 for further explanation.)

OBJECTIONS TO THE INTELLIGENT DESIGN ARGUMENT

The heated debate that currently exists regarding the validity of the intelligent design argument is not one that can be adequately addressed in a relatively short chapter within a single book. However, I do wish to touch on a few key points.

The biggest argument (from skeptics) is that ID does not qualify as true science. Some ID skeptics accuse ID scientists of being "closet creationists" or "biblical creationists in disguise." While there will always be people with hidden agendas in any particular camp, the tenants of the espoused viewpoint must be judged on their own merits, as opposed to the motivations of individual adherents.

You'll recall that back in chapter 2, we discussed how the definition of science itself has been changed to rule out God right from the beginning. (Dr. Scott Todd—"Even if all the data point to an intelligent designer, such an hypothesis is excluded from science because it is not naturalistic."[7]) So when we discover things that are so complex as to virtually eliminate a chance origin, and at the same time provide strongly supportive evidence of purposeful design, opponents will simply claim that since this conclusion entails supernatural involvement, it isn't science and cannot be considered as an argument within the science classroom. Just because a viewpoint has religious implications does not mean that it cannot be scientific. Evolutionary scenarios also have religious implications, but evolutionists are either unaware or they consciously choose to employ a double-standard. Some even admit that evolution is a religion. Michael Ruse (professor of zoology and philosophy, Florida State University) stated:

> Evolution is promoted by its practitioners as more than mere science. Evolution is promulgated as an ideology, a secular religion—a full-fledged alternative to Christianity, with meaning and morality. I am an ardent evolutionist and

an ex-Christian, but I must admit that in this one complaint. . .the literalists are absolutely right. Evolution is a religion. This was true of evolution in the beginning, and it is true of evolution still today. . .Evolution therefore came into being as a kind of secular ideology, an explicit substitute for Christianity.[8]

Today, court decisions seem to heavily favor the conclusion that ID is of a religious nature and not truly scientific. One of the most recently prominent cases involved Dover High School (in Pennsylvania). The Dover Area School Board had instituted a policy requiring ninth grade students to hear a statement about intelligent design as an introduction to their biology lessons on evolution. The brief statement informed the students that evolution is a theory, not a fact, and further told them that intelligent design (ID) is an alternative explanation regarding the origin of life. The book, *Of Pandas and People* (Foundation for Thought and Ethics, 1989), was also referred to the students for those wishing to learn more about the case for intelligent design. The ACLU (American Civil Liberties Union) and Americans United for Separation of Church and State, along with eight families of students at a Dover high school, complained that this policy violated the Establishment Clause of the First Amendment by promoting a religious doctrine. An official complaint was filed, leading to a court trial (Kitzmiller et al. v. Dover Area school District). The verdict was announced on December 20, 2005 by Judge John E. Jones III. He officially stated that "it is unconstitutional to teach ID as an alternative to evolution in a public school science classroom." In what certainly seems like "smoke and mirrors," Stephen Meyer (director of the Discovery Institute's Center for Science and Culture and a founder both of the intelligent design movement and of the Discovery Institute's Center for Science and Culture) stated that when pressed for a more detailed justification for this ruling the judge concluded that,

> the theory of intelligent design cannot be part of science, because it violates the principle of methodological naturalism. But that principle turns out to be nothing more than the claim that intelligent causes—and thus the theory of intelligent design—must be excluded from science. According to this reasoning, intelligent design isn't science because it violates the principle of methodological naturalism. What is methodological naturalism? A rule prohibiting consideration of intelligent design in scientific theories.[9]

This decision is akin to saying, "You can't teach intelligent design. . .because I said so." We are now deciding what science is and what it isn't in the courtroom, often by judges who have very little if any science credentials, but plenty of presuppositional biases that greatly affect the outcome of their rulings.

In their book, *Understanding Intelligent Design,*[10] authors William Dembski and Sean McDowell enumerate ten different objections to the concept of ID. We'll take a look at a few here (numbers 1-3 and 8).

Objection 1: ID makes no predictions

ID actually predicts that we should discover life forms and features that go beyond the limits of evolutionary explanations. Many such examples have been found, some of which we will explore shortly.

Objection 2: ID is religiously motivated

ID proponents come in all shapes and sizes, as mentioned earlier. Their particular individual religious beliefs do not disqualify their scientific experiments. Whether a scientist is an atheist, a theist or an agnostic, his or her science still has to meet with the same level of stringent critique as anyone else's.

Objection 3: ID argues from ignorance

ID does not merely point out short-comings in the evolutionary model, it highlights features that exhibit specified complexity within biological systems such as the blood clotting mechanism and the intricate structure of the human eye.

Objection 8: ID is Bible-based

Certainly, many of the conclusions of ID comport very well with biblical teachings, but the discipline itself is grounded in evidence from biology, astronomy, chemistry, physics and information theory.

THE ELEPHANT IN THE LIVING ROOM

There's an old saying regarding an "elephant in the living room." It refers to any obvious and significant issue that someone is not dealing with—acting as if it didn't exist, in a self-deluded manner. The following interchange from *The Ledger* (a Lynchburg, VA newspaper) was between one of their columnists (George) and a molecular biologist. It serves as an example of how even strong evidence for design can become an "elephant of design." These two men had just been discussing the incredible amount of information found in living systems.[11]

Columnist: "Do you believe that the information evolved?"

Biologist: "George, nobody I know in my profession believes it evolved. It was engineered by genius beyond genius, and such information could not have been written any other way. The paper and ink did not write the book! Knowing what we know, it is ridiculous to think otherwise."

Columnist: "Have you ever stated that in a public lecture, or in any public writings?"

Biologist: "No, I just say it evolved. To be a molecular biologist requires one to hold onto two insanities at all times. One, it would be insane to believe in evolution when you can see the truth for yourself. Two, it would be insane to say you don't believe evolution. All government work, research grants, papers, big college lectures—everything would stop. I'd be out of a job, or relegated to the outer fringes where I couldn't earn a decent living."

Columnist: "I hate to say it, but that sounds intellectually dishonest."

Biologist: "The work I do in genetic research is honorable. We will find the cures to many of mankind's worst diseases. But in the meantime, we have to live with the elephant in the living room."

Columnist: "What elephant?"

Biologist: "Creation design. It's like an elephant in the living room. It moves around, takes up space, loudly trumpets, bumps into us, knocks things over, eats a ton of hay, and smells like an elephant. And yet we have to swear it isn't there!"

This is an all too common occurrence among academics. Ben Stein's documentary, *Expelled: No Intelligence Allowed*[12] (which actually aired in many theaters across the country when it was first released), is a powerful testimony to this very phenomenon. The documentary was not intended to promote biblical creation or even all the great evidence for ID. Although it did cover a few arguments, its main focus was on the fact that if you are a scientist and you wish to continue to put food on the table, you had better not question the validity of the evolutionary paradigm or dare to say, "The emperor has no clothes!" If you have not seen

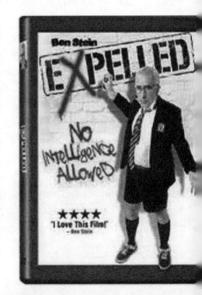

this documentary (and many Christians have not) I highly recommend renting it and watching it with your whole family.

EXAMPLES OF DESIGN

Of these two paintings, the one on the right is unmistakably designed. The one on the left might be designed, but it could easily be the result of an accident (e.g., the spilling of paint). Design is usually very easy to detect and most people recognize it instantly. The Golden Gate Bridge, a laptop computer and the space shuttle are just a few of the more obvious examples. There are also many examples

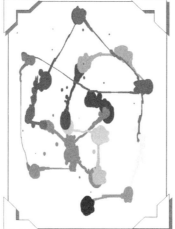

in the biological world as well, but how people react to them is more often based on their worldview and their openness to the truth than the actual science behind the evidence. For example, the design argument was powerful enough to lead Antony Flew (often referred to as "The world's most notorious atheist") to proclaim publicly that "There is a God." Flew reveals that his change of heart came,

almost entirely because of the DNA investigations. What I think the DNA material has done is that it has shown, by the almost unbelievable complexity of the arrangements which are needed to produce (life), that intelligence must have been involved in getting these extraordinarily diverse elements to work together. It's the enormous complexity of the number of elements and the enormous subtlety of the ways they work together. The meeting of these two parts at the right time by chance is simply minute. It is all a matter of the enormous complexity by which the results were achieved, which looked to me like the work of intelligence.[13]

Flew is just one example of someone who was "convinced by the evidence." This is not always the case, however. There are many other scientists who apparently are not at all fazed by the evidence and they merely explain it away, such as is evidenced by atheist Richard Dawkins, who stated:

Biology is the study of complicated things that give the appearance of having been designed for a purpose.[14]

He wants us to know that things just "seem" designed, but are not truly designed in reality. Another example is that of Francis Crick (Nobel Prize laureate and co-discoverer of the DNA helix). He warned that:

Biologists must constantly keep in mind that what they see was not designed, but rather evolved.[15]

Why would Crick (who is also an atheist) have to give this admonition to his colleagues? Can't they figure it out on their own? He seems worried that they won't. They apparently need a reminder. Perhaps it is because the evidence for design seems unbelievably obvious and overwhelming!

Are these men not intelligent enough to see the evidence? That would not be my conclusion. In a sense, I feel they might be "too intelligent" to see the evidence. By this I mean there is a very strong possibility that they are excessively proud of their own accomplishments and abilities, and their atheistic worldview will not allow them to see evidence for design. Ultimately, each person needs to decide if what they observe is better explained by unguided forces of nature, or by an outside intelligent cause. We need to constantly keep in mind that our worldview greatly influences the conclusions we make about what we observe.

George Lakoff (professor of linguistics at the University of California, Berkeley) offers his thoughts as they pertain to "facts":

People think in frames. To be accepted, the truth must fit people's frames. If the facts do not fit a frame, the frame stays and the facts bounce off.[16]

H.S. Lipson (professor of physics at the University of Manchester—UK) writes:

In fact, evolution became in a sense a scientific religion; almost all scientists have accepted it, and many are prepared to "bend" their observations to fit with it.[17]

The Human Eye

Darwin (writing in 1859) commented on the human eye:

To suppose that the eye with all its inimitable contrivances for adjusting the focus to different distances, for admitting different amounts of light, and for the correction of spherical and chromatic aberration, could have been formed by natural selection, seems, I freely confess, absurd in the highest degree.[18]

Don't be fooled into thinking that Darwin was admitting that the eye was actually designed, because he wasn't. In spite of this statement, he still believed the eye is nothing more than the product of a series of fortuitous accidents in nature. It just bothered him because it certainly gives the appearance of being designed. He has a similar reaction regarding a peacock feather:

> The sight of a feather in a peacock's tail, whenever I gaze at it, makes me sick![19]

The following segments were gleaned from Dr. Jonathan Sarfati's book, *By Design: Evidence for Nature's Intelligent Designer—the God of the Bible.*[20]

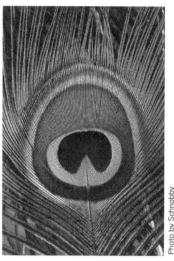

Photo by Schnobby

The Cornea: Imagine trying to make a transparent substance out of biological material. That is what you would need to do if you were going to construct an eye. In addition to imparting protection, the cornea also provides two-thirds of the focusing needed for our vision. There are no veins in the cornea (which would greatly impair our vision, blocking incoming light) so it must receive its nutrients another way through tears. It receives the oxygen it needs through direct contact with the air. Transparency occurs through principals described by diffraction theory, which (skipping the details) relates to the refractive index not varying over a distance of more than half a wavelength of light. The only way this can be maintained is through a complicated system of chemical pumps, supplying the precise amount of water.

The Retina: Sitting at the back of the eye is a layer of photosensitive cells, called the retina. This organ is so sensitive it can detect a single photon of light (which is the smallest amount of light possible.) Compared to typical photographic film (which has a dynamic range of 1,000 to 1), the range of the retina is 1,000,000,000 to 1!

In order for our eyes to adjust properly to different levels of light (particularly extremely bright light), there are a number of things that have to happen on a molecular level. We tend to just think of our pupils dilating, changing the amount of light admitted into the eye, but it's not at all that simple. Within the light-sensitive cell is a protein called arrestin, which is "called to duty" when needed. It rushes and binds in the location of the light-sensitive proteins to help "calm" them. These arrestin proteins don't simply "waltz on over" but are actually transported along what looks like train tracks by a motor protein called myosin. What would happen if all of these components were not all in the right place at the right time? They eye would be blinded by bright light. So how could this intricate system have evolved in a step-by-step fashion (one accident at a time)? The obvious answer: it could not and did not.

The retina also has some amazing processing capabilities. We think of the brain as doing all of the information processing, but the retina actually does some pre-transmission processing on its own which enhances the recognition of the edge of objects. It's been stated that it would take a minimum of a hundred years of Cray supercomputer processing time to mimic what happens many times in our eyes every second! There are specialized cells in the retina that send the brain different types of information regarding the same view. One focuses on line drawings of edges, another focuses on motion in a particular direction and a third set focuses on shadows and highlights.

Fovea: A small portion in the center of the eye, called the fovea, has extremely high resolution. The "information" that hits this area accounts for only 2° in the field of vision, yet more than 50% of the visual cortex is needed for processing this information. If the brain were bombarded with this much information from the entire field of view, it would have to be 50 times larger! (And you think your neck gets tired now!) We have just enough information regarding our peripheral view to make decisions as to whether or not we need to change our focus by moving our eyes, but not too much as to overload our brains. Sarfati (the author of the passage we are referencing for the eye) gives the analogy of tying to read a book if our brains were receiving the same amount of information about every word on the entire page, as it does regarding just the words we are currently looking at. That would probably send the reader to the funny farm!

Jitters: When you stare at a painting on a wall or a sunset, your eyes don't actually lock into a fixed position and simply send a snapshot of what you are observing to the brain. Our eyes actually experience the "jitters." They constantly move back and forth very rapidly, in all directions (undetectable to any observers). This motion actually accounts for a 16% improvement in resolution.

Color: Our eyes contain features called "rods" and "cones." The rods are located in the peripheral locations of the retina and do not need a lot of light to function, but also cannot perceive color. The cones on the other hand, need bright light and are primarily centrally located. Cones allow us to distinguish color. Three types of cones are involved in the perception of color. One set primarily detects the color red, another that detects green and a third set that detects blue. When the red-sensitive cones receive light within the red spectrum, they send signals to the brain, but there is nothing in the signal itself that contains information about the color red, only information about the intensity of the light. The way the brain "sees" red in this example is by the fact that the green and blue cones did not send any signal. In order to "see" yellow, both the red and green cones send signals.

Honey Bees

These highly advanced creatures come "fully loaded." According to Dr. Jonathan Sarfati (physical chemist and spectroscopist, Creation Ministries International—USA):

> Bees have airspeed gauges; gyroscopes; a "compass" that detects the polarization of sunlight; UV sensors to track the horizon to measure tilt; and two compound eyes, each with 7,000 hexagonal (six-sided) facets. These facets are windows to sub-eyes called ommatidia, which are tiny tubes containing their own lens and light-detecting cells. Each tube points in a different direction, enabling vision over a wide area. The hexagonal shape is ideal. It uses as little edge-cell material as possible (which is why the honeycomb is also hexagonal), has the least sharp corners needing less reinforcement, and is the most symmetrical structure. Such eyes are superb for detecting motion, since a small shift means different facets detect the image.[21]

These bees also posses an amazing ability to communicate.

> Scout bees need to communicate the location of the nectar they've found once they return to the hive. If the source is too far to see or smell, but less than about fifty-five yards) they do a circular dance. If the source is further away, then the scout does a figure-eight dance, occasionally cutting across the figure. Distance is determined by how many figure-eights are made in a given time period and also by the frequency at which the abdomen wiggles (lower frequency, greater distance). The direction is communicated by the angle of line that is made when cutting-across the figure.[22]

Monarch Butterfly

Most people are fairly familiar with the Monarch butterfly, but many have probably not thought very deeply about its origin. This amazing creature has one of the most interesting life cycles in all of God's creation. It begins with an adult male and female Monarch mating to produce an egg (usually on a milkweed plant). The egg then hatches and develops into a worm-like larvae, which in turn becomes a caterpillar. The caterpillar will eat its own egg casing for nutrition and then switch over to milkweed for sustenance. About two weeks later, the caterpillar will suspend itself from a tree branch or leaf, upside-down and encase itself in what is called a chrysalis. During this period (about another two weeks) it changes into

a butterfly through an incredible process we call metamorphosis. The chrysalis becomes transparent the day before the butterfly emerges. Once the butterfly leaves the chrysalis, it continues to hang on the twig, leaf, etc. until its wings are dry and is then free to begin the process all over again.

It is absolutely amazing that the caterpillar is able to melt all of its body components down into a "slimy goo," yet still be alive. Then, on top of that, be able to turn the "goo" into a completely different creature, and a very beautiful and delicate one at that! Another evolutionary challenge is that of "evolving" the ability to mate in its new form! Think about that for a minute. What would it mate with? Even if, just by dumb luck, another caterpillar has also accidentally morphed into a butterfly, they would have to be in the exact same spot on the earth at the same time and have complimentary plumbing, among a number of other challenges. If all of this did not come together the very first time, it would be done; an evolutionary dead-end. It could not afford to wait around for 300,000 or a million years until it "got it right." How would it reproduce in the meantime? It couldn't.

The Monarch also has the amazing ability to navigate during its 3,000 mile migration to a place it has never been before. You have to wonder, what was it in all that "goo" that is now telling it that it even needs to go anywhere at all? Even though the Monarch never met its parents, it is able to migrate not only to the same location (where they originated), but occasionally even to the exact same tree! If you are interested in learning even more about this fascinating creature, I would recommend that you watch *Metamorphosis: The Beauty and Design of Butterflies*, a new documentary (Illustra Media, 2011).

The Human Ear

It's been said that "Seeing is believing" and while that may be true, I think it is equally true that "hearing is believing"—at least when it comes to looking at what is all involved in how we hear.

We don't think much about it; someone speaks, and we hear. What's the big deal? After reading this section, you will look at it

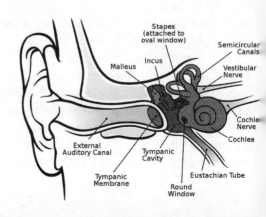

much differently. We will only be discussing some of what goes on when our ears carry out their normal function. I highly recommend that the reader view the video entitled, *The Hearing Ear and the Seeing Eye*,[23] by Dr. David Menton. This is a stunning video and the graphics greatly help to appreciate how complex the human ear truly is. I will share a few highlights from the video.

The ear is composed of three sections: the outer, the middle and the inner ear. These sections work in perfect harmony with one another.

Sound is nothing more than alternating compressed and rarified (expanded) air. When someone speaks, they are causing air molecules to bump into each other like pool balls lined up on a pool table. The first one moves a very small distance, pushing the second one slightly into the third and so on. This motion of air molecules eventually reaches your outer ear, which is shaped in such a way as to amplify the sound and channel it into the auditory canal. The size of the canal is also optimal for the frequency range of sounds we hear on a normal basis. This air, which contains varying pressures, eventually reaches the tympanic membrane (the ear drum). Hearing essentially works by detecting differences in air pressure. Your ear is so sensitive to changes in pressure that it can detect a change in pressure as little as 1×10^{-10} atmospheres! Some of you are saying, "Great, I have no idea what that means, but I guess I'm supposed to be impressed." Written a different way, that's 0.0000000001 atmospheres. Alright, you still may not have any idea what that means.

Dr. Menton (in the video) compares this to changes in altitude, which most people can relate to. We all know that when you climb a mountain or go up in a plane, you notice the change in atmospheric pressure, because the air is "thinner" at higher altitudes. You're ears might "pop" as the plane you are in climbs, or even while in an elevator going to the top floor of a sky scraper. Climbing to the top of a mountain that is one mile high would effectuate a difference in pressure of about half an Atmosphere, or roughly 7 lbs/in.^{2} However, your ears are so sensitive that you don't have to climb that high to sense a change in pressure. All you have to do is go up 1/30,000th of an inch (which is less than the thickness of a sheet of plastic wrap used in a kitchen) and your eardrum can detect the change! Imagine laying a piece of "Gladwrap" on the floor and then stepping up onto it; you're eardrum would say, "Hey, the air's a bit thinner up here!"

Then there's the challenge of "keeping it clean." We don't want foreign objects getting into this canal and impeding our ability to hear. Fortunately, the ear produces a waxy substance that captures dust and other particles that enter. This, however, presents another problem. Wouldn't this just continue to accumulate and eventually block the entire canal? It would, if the cells in our inner ear grew outward like normal skin cells. It just so happens that they grow sideways, towards the outer ear, moving the debris along like a conveyor belt!

This wax also happens to be noxious to many bugs, so that they are naturally turned away from entering your ear.

As sound travels from the source through our ears, it goes through three different mediums: air (outer ear), bone (middle ear) and fluid (inner ear). When it reaches the middle ear, it is transferred from air to bone through some tissue called the tympanic membrane. This membrane is sensitive to movements of just 1/10 of the width of an atom! That's an incredibly small movement. This is the movement that is transferred into the bones. Consider this. While this tiny, miniscule movement is going on, blood cells are flowing through the living tissue of the membrane, which are huge in comparison to the movement of the membrane. Dr. Menton said it is like comparing baseballs (tympanic membrane movement) to the Rocky Mountains (blood cell size). Imagine trying to detect these tiny movements in the midst of all the "pushing and shoving" caused by the gigantic blood cells! This requires an incredible "noise filtering" system to weed out the extraneous signal and transmit movement representative of the sound from the original source.

The sound is then transferred into the middle ear where it meets the ossicle bones, which are the smallest bones in the entire body. One function these bones provide is amplification. When the sound enters the labyrinth (inner ear), the fluid greatly dampens the sound. In fact, (for you "techies") it has an impedance of 99.9%. It's similar to standing above a pool and trying to hear someone talking to you from underwater. These ossicle bones increase the signal by 120 decibels, which helps compensate for the impending dampening that will occur in the inner ear fluid. In those instances when our brain perceives that the sound is too loud, it actually controls a set of muscles attached to these bones in a manner to dampen the sound, thus reducing the amount of damage that could potentially occur.

From the middle ear (and the set of bones) the sound travels into an elaborate maze in the inner ear. Included in the inner ear are three semi-circular tubes that work to give us our sense of balance. Opposite these tubes is an area called the cochlea, which is where the signal from the middle ear gets translated into something the brain can decipher. The motion of the fluid causes another membrane to slide back and forth on top of cilia (hairs) which are embedded in cells. When these "hairs" bend, tiny gates are opened up allowing ions (atoms with a positive or negative charge) to flow into the cells, creating an electrical signal that is sent to the brain. These gates are controlled by a molecular spring and have to be able to open and close up to 20,000 times per second! The brain has to be able to interpret these electrical currents as meaningful messages and act accordingly (such as moving the body out of the way if we hear a train coming!).

To put this into a more practical perspective, consider the following real-life situation. You are sitting in a restaurant, eating dinner with some friends. The following sounds are hitting your ears all at the same time:

• Background music playing over the speakers in the ceiling.

• One of your friends placing his order with the waiter.

• Another friend talking with the babysitter on their cell phone.

• A third friend telling you about their day.

• All the conversations at the other tables in the room.

• All the noise from the silverware being used throughout the restaurant.

• Noise coming from the cooks in the kitchen.

• A baby crying at the table behind you.

• The sound of pouring rain as it hits the roof of the restaurant.

• Traffic driving by, splashing water and an occasional horn honking.

• A police siren half a mile across town.

Picture all of this, which is ultimately just pressurized air, entering your ears. It is absolutely amazing that your brain can receive these signals, through all those mediums (air, bone, fluid) and sort it all out, allowing you to respond in the appropriate manner. You also have to consider that we have two of these things called ears. Each one is hearing it own sets of sounds, slightly different than the other. The brain has to "sync" these two signals in addition to interpreting them. And then there is the multiplied millions of signals the brain is receiving visually (which it has to match up with the all of the audio). Oh yes, and all this just happened to evolve accidentally one piece at a time over millions and millions of years!

The Anthropic Principle

Another line of evidence indicating that we are not "living in an accident" has to do what is known as the "anthropic principle" which states that the universe appears to be designed for the express purpose of the existence of life. Robert Jastrow (theoretical physicist and founding director of NASA's Goddard Institute for Space Studies) commented that the anthropic principle seems to say that science itself has proven, as a hard fact, that this universe was made, was designed, for man to live in. It's a very theistic result.[24]

Here's a simple analogy. Let's say that you went to visit a friend who had recently moved into a new home. You enter their living room and notice how stunning it is. You say, "Wow, what a beautiful home! Did you guys hire a professional decorator?" They respond in a begrudging tone, "No, we are actually very upset. When the movers unloaded all of our belongings, they literally threw everything into the living room and this is how it turned out!" Would you believe them?

Movers might throw things around once in a while, but would it have resulted in the sofa and love-seat being situated at a 90° angle to one another, bordering the floor rug which just happens to be perfectly centered under the coffee table? The lamps are on the end tables, the pictures hung nicely on the walls, etc.? Obviously, no one would believe that. It is the same situation with our universe, only trillions upon trillions of time more unlikely. Let's take a look at a few examples of these "astronomical coincidences."

Earth's Delicate Balance: The earth appears to be in just the right place, possessing just the right attributes in order to sustain life. There are so many critical factors (about twenty or so), that "chance" is neither a sufficient nor reasonable explanation of our fortuitous circumstance. The following partial list of factors comes from the video, *The Privileged Planet* (Illustra Media, 2004):[25]

- It is within the Galactic Habitable Zone.

- It is orbiting a main sequence G2 dwarf star.

- It is protected by giant gas planets.

- It is within a circumstellar habitable zone.

- It has a nearly circular orbit.

- It has an oxygen-rich atmosphere.

- It has the correct mass.

- It is orbited by a large moon.

- It has a magnetic field.

- It incorporates plate tectonics.

- It has a proper ration of liquid water and continents.

- It is a terrestrial planet.

- It has a moderate rate of rotation.

Each one of these factors is necessary for our existence. We'll take a look at just a few of these in detail.

Galactic Habitable Zone: Our solar system exists within the Milky Way galaxy, in just the right position. If it were much further away from the center of our galaxy, we would not have enough heavy elements as a source of energy. If we were much closer to the center, we would be detrimentally affected by high-frequency radiation.

Circular Orbit: If the earth were in a significant elliptical orbit, part of the year we would be too far away from the sun (and freeze), and another part of the year we would be too close (and fry!).

Giant Gas Planets: Planets such as Jupiter help protect the earth from being bombarded by asteroids, acting as a giant cosmic vacuum cleaner. Without the planets, the earth would not be a safe place to live.

Large Moon: Our moon is considered to be fairly large, being one-quarter the size of the earth. It stabilizes the tilt of the earth on its axis, which in turn ensures temperate climates. It also is responsible for the ocean tides, which play an important role in our ecosystem. It is currently believed that if we didn't have our moon, life would not be possible.

Rate of Rotation: The earth rotates on its axis roughly once every twenty-four hours. If it rotated much slower, it would be way too hot half the day and way too cold the other half. If it rotated much faster, the winds and climate change would be too dramatic.

There are approximately thirty different factors on a cosmological scale that are also finely-tuned, such that if they weren't right where they are today, life wouldn't be possible on Earth. We'll take a look at just two of within this category.

There are a number of fairly common formulas used in physics, such as $F=ma$ and $e=mc^2$. Another formula that is fairly common is Newton's law of universal gravitation ($F=G \cdot m_1 \cdot m_2 \div r^2$). This formula calculates the gravitational force between two objects such as the earth and the moon. The capitol "G" represents the Gravitational constant (6.6720×10^{11} m^3 kg^{-1} s^{-2}). This particular constant is very finely-tuned, such that any deviation from its current value would be disastrous. If there truly was a big bang that subsequently created our universe, this constant could have been just about any value. In fact, scientists tell us that if you had a ruler that was so long it could reach from one side of the universe to the other, every inch on the ruler would

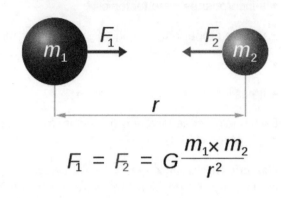

$$F_1 = F_2 = G\frac{m_1 \times m_2}{r^2}$$

represent a different possible value for this particular constant. So what would happen if the gravitational constant were some other value? How would that affect us? For illustrative purposes, picture a pointer located somewhere on this cosmologically long ruler and pretend it represents where this constant actually is today. We could move our pointer half way across the universe to see how that affects us, but we're not going to be so aggressive. Let's move it just one inch. What happens? For starters, animals anywhere near the size of people would be instantly crushed! Insects would need very thick legs to support themselves and animals much larger than insects would not even be able to survive! And that's just messing with this constant a tiny, tiny bit! So did we just get lucky, having this constant turn out to be right where it needs to be? Probability (and rationality) says "no."

The Cosmological Constant: This second example relates to the energy density of empty space. The what? Don't worry about the details, just know that this is another one of those finely-tuned constants that has to be right where it is or we wouldn't be here. Scientists have determined that due to the astronomically wide range of potentially possible values, the probability that this constant turned out to be right where it needs to be by pure coincidence is equal to one chance in—not one million, not one billion, not even one trillion, but one chance in one hundred million billion billion billion billion.[26] Just in case you do not have a background in science, that's a big number!

It gets even worse! We need to figure out what the chances are that both of these constants just happened to be correct by sheer coincidence. Well, they've calculated that, too. The probability is one chance in one hundred million trillion trillion trillion trillion trillion trillion![27] Yes, you could still choose to believe it happened by chance, but you'd have to have an extremely strong faith—much stronger than mine. (In fact, it would be a very unreasonable faith, as opposed to Christianity, which involves a very reasonable faith.)

This is just a small sampling of the numerous factors that are so precisely-tuned that they defy naturalistic explanations and point directly to a causal agent, which in my mind, is clearly the God of the Bible.

Quick side story. I was speaking at a state university a few months ago and shared some of this information as part of the presentation. Afterwards, during the Q&A time, an atheist in the audience spoke up in protest. He stated that although I was claiming this information proves that God created everything, in reality it doesn't, because there are actually millions of universes. His point was that while it might seem very unlikely here in our universe, because there are so many other universes (maybe even an infinite amount) it is bound to happen somewhere. It just so happens that we are living in the universe where it did happen. In fact, if it didn't happen here, we wouldn't be even around to discuss it! Setting aside many aspects related to this question for the sake of brevity, I graciously corrected him and said that I had not claimed that these probabilities prove anything. In fact, probabilities don't and can't prove anything. They simply give us a good idea of whether a certain belief or hypothesis is extremely likely, extremely unlikely or somewhere in between. I then asked him if he was a student at the university to which he replied, "Yes." Then I asked him to consider the following scenario. Let's say you have an exam later today and it's an all-essay exam—no multiple choice and no true or false questions. Let's also say that you complete the exam and walk away feeling it went very well. The next day, you return to class and the professor hands you your exam. . .marked with a big fat zero on it! You are in complete shock. You say, "Hey prof, what's going on here? I thought I did very well on this!" He says, "Well, I've been teaching at the university for over nineteen years and I don't know that I've ever seen a better exam." Even more perplexed, you ask, "Then why did you give me a zero?" He replies, "Because your exam was 100 percent identical to Steve's who was sitting right next to you. In fact, you even had the same spelling and grammatical errors that Steve had on his exam. One or both of you cheated, so I gave you both a zero!" Still stunned, you look up at the professor and say, "But you don't understand. I know the chances of our exams being identical is too much of a coincidence if this were the only universe in existence, but there are actually millions and millions of universes out there. It was bound to happen somewhere, sometime. It just so happened that it occurred in this universe, in your classroom, yesterday afternoon!" Finishing this scenario, I then asked the skeptic if he would expect his professor to say, "Wow, I never thought about that. Good point. Here, let me give you an A." He looked at me, smiled and said, "No, he would give me a zero." I said, "That's how we use probabilities." By the way, the multiple universe concept is just a metaphysical construct that was dreamt up in an attempt to counter the staggering improbability of the chance origin of the our universe. It has no actual evidence and has nothing to do with real science.

Irreducible Complexity

As a sub-topic of the larger "design argument," the principal known as "irreducible complexity" provides powerful evidence of purposeful design. Dr. Michael Behe (professor of biochemistry, Lehigh University and key player in the intelligent design movement) formulated this principal and defines this concept in the first sentence of the following quote:

> By irreducible complexity I mean a single system which is composed of several interacting parts that contribute to the basic function, and where the removal of any one of the parts causes the system to effectively cease functioning. An irreducibly complex system cannot be produced gradually by slight, successive modifications of a precursor system, since any precursor to an irreducibly complex system is by definition nonfunctional. Since natural selection requires a function to select, an irreducibly complex biological system, if there is such a thing, would have to arise as an integrated unit for natural selection to have anything to act on. It is almost universally conceded that such a sudden event would be irreconcilable with the gradualism Darwin envisioned.[28]

Behe's now famous example of a mouse trap serves as a great visual illustration. The mouse trap consists of five individual parts:

1. hammer or bar

2. spring

3. latch

4. trigger

5. wooden base

All five of these parts are necessary in order for the mouse trap to carry out its intended function. If we remove the spring, for example, there would be nothing to bring the bar over to trap the mouse. If we remove the latch, there's nothing to hold the bar back. If we remove the wooden base, there's nothing to hold the pieces together, and so on. (You get the picture.) How could the mouse trap "evolve" slowly, one piece at a time? How would it "survive" while waiting hundreds of thousands or millions of years for the remaining parts to accidentally evolve in the right place and be able to function properly in association with all of the other parts? Obviously, mouse traps don't evolve, but there are many examples in the living world that yield the same type of challenge when it comes to explaining their naturalistic origin.

In light of the concept of irreducible complexity, it is interesting to note a quote from Darwin himself:

> If it could be demonstrated that any complex organ existed which could not possibly have been formed by numerous, successive, slight modifications, my theory would absolutely break down.[29]

Irreducible complexity serves to demonstrate quite admirably that complex organs do exist and they defy slow, gradual development, thus rendering Darwin's theory scientifically implausible, even by his own admission.

Bacterial Flagellum

One of the most prominent examples of design being discussed in ID circles today is that of the bacterial flagellum. This biological structure consists of a hair-like structure and a miniaturized motor that provides locomotion for the cells of many living organisms. Dr. Behe further explains the functioning of this intriguing feature:

> The rotary nature of the bacterial flagellar motor was a startling, unexpected discovery. Unlike other systems that generate mechanical motion (muscles, for example) the bacterial motor does not directly use energy that is stored in a "carrier" molecule such as ATP. Rather, to move the flagellum it uses the energy generated by a flow of acid through the bacterial membrane. . .The bacterial flagellum, in addition to proteins already discussed, requires about forty other proteins for function. . .In summary, as biochemists have begun to examine apparently simple structures like cilia and flagella, they have discovered staggering complexity, with dozens or even hundreds of precisely tailored parts. . . As the number of required parts increases, the difficulty of gradually putting the system together skyrockets, and the likelihood of indirect scenarios plummets.

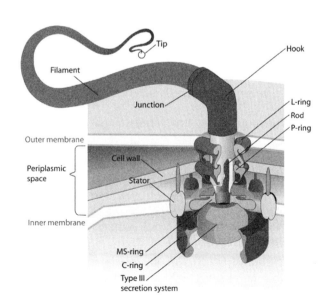

Darwin looks more and more forlorn. New research on the roles of the auxiliary proteins cannot simplify the irreducibly complex system. The intransigence [stubbornness] of the problem cannot be alleviated; it will only get worse. Darwinian theory has given no explanation for the cilium or flagellum. The overwhelming complexity of the swimming systems push us to think it may never give an explanation.[30]

Consider some of the features of this miraculous miniature motor:[31]

• Self assembly and repair

• Water-cooled rotary engine

• Proton motive force drive system

• Forward and reverse gears

• Operating speeds of up to 100,000 rpm (1,667 rotations per second!)

• Direction reversing capability within ¼ of a turn

• Hard-wired signal transduction system with short-term memory

• Clutch to disconnect filament from motor when required

And just how big is this powerful motor? Only about forty-five nanometers in diameter! (A nanometer is one billionth of a meter.) Approximately 8,000,000 of these motors could fit within the cross-section of a human hair![32] How's that for miniaturization? All these features enable the bacteria to move up to thirty-five cell lengths per second, which might not sound all that impressive, but on a human scale, it would be like a six foot tall man swimming 143 mph! And all this happens very efficiently. A typical internal combustion engine has an efficiency of about 20%. Electric motors, being generally much more efficient, range up to 75-95%, but the efficiency drops off as the size of the motor decreases. However, these tiny flagellar motors are almost 100% efficient![33]

Our mouse trap consisted of only five components and yet we could easily see how impossible it would be for it to assemble itself by chance, one piece at a time. The flagellar motor is constructed from more than forty different kinds of proteins! Some critics claim that the individual components exist in other extant systems and they could have simply been "co-opted" to form the flagellar motor. (This would be like going through your garage and grabbing miscellaneous parts from your car, lawn mover, snow blower, bicycle, shovel, rake, etc., and bringing them together to form something new, except, of course, you can't use any intelligence; it all has to be random.) However, there are a number of problems with this "just-so" story. One major problem is that only ten of the forty components are found elsewhere—the other thirty are brand new! Another problem is that you need instructions (a blueprint) to tell the components exactly where to go. Even if one of these existing parts fortuitously shows up from another system, the "foreman" reading the "blue-print" would say "I don't know what this part is, where it's supposed to go or what I am supposed to do with it!" And that's just for one new part; try guessing correctly for all thirty new parts!

Even if these "parts" somehow fortuitously fell together in the exact necessary positions, that would only produce one motor and would not enable the bacteria (via its genetic code) to produce another motor when the cell replicates itself. The "blue-print" (genome/DNA) would have to be permanently modified with all the appropriate information in order to be of use in any future motor assembly.

Blood Clotting

If you've ever had a small cut on your skin that caused you to start bleeding, you appreciated your body's ability to stop the bleeding on its own. This is due to the phenomenon of blood clotting; a process in which your blood thickens, closing off the opening in the blood vessels, restricting the loss of blood. This is no simple event, even though it may not seem very complex from our vantage point. However, it is actually an amazingly complex process.

Courtesy of Manfred Maitz (Germany)

There are numerous steps involved, each of which is necessary to successfully clot your blood. The $64,000 question is how did this process slowly evolve over time, when each step is necessary to carry out this function? Since Michael Behe published his initial work, *Darwin's Black Box*[34] in 1996, there have been a number of attempts to explain how this could possibly happen, but each one has missed the point, or amounted to nothing more than creative story-telling. Blood clotting still remains a strong example of irreducible complexity.

DID HE REALLY SAY THAT?

We will start to wind down this chapter with another interesting remark from atheist Richard Dawkins, made as he was interviewed during the filming of *Expelled: No Intelligence Allowed.*[35] At the end of the documentary, we hear the following dialogue between Ben Stein and Richard Dawkins:

Stein: "What do you think is the possibility that intelligent design might turn out to be the answer to some issues in genetics or in evolution?"

Dawkins: "It could come about in the following way. It could be that at some earlier time somewhere in the universe a civilization evolved by probably some kind of Darwinian means to a very, very high level of technology and designed the form of life that they seeded onto, perhaps this planet. Now that is a possibility, and an intriguing possibility. And I suppose it's possible that you might find evidence for that if you look at the details of biochemistry, molecular biology, you might find a signature of some sort of designer. And that designer could well be a higher intelligence from elsewhere in the universe, but that higher intelligence would itself had to have come about by some explicable or ultimately explicable process. It couldn't have just jumped into existence spontaneously. That's the point."

Let's think this through for minute and discuss a few points. Dawkins admits that we might actually find evidence of intelligence. The first point would be that he is admitting that it is theoretically possible to detect evidence of design, which actually goes against what many of his evolutionary colleagues claim (and what our court systems are ruling is not possible on a scientific level).

Why would he admit to design at all? Because of the amazing complexity of the living world, indicating that someone or something "higher" than itself must have been necessary. The cause of an affect must always be greater than the affect itself (intrinsic to the law of cause and effect).

Dawkins resorts to invoking "some earlier time somewhere else in the universe." In doing so, he's taken us beyond the reach of science, being somewhere that we can't observe, in a time in the distant past when no one else was around to observe (i.e., pushing the origins dilemma back another level).

Even though this "higher intelligence" supposedly existed in the distant past in some other sector of the universe, Dawkins is adamant that it must have come about by a slow evolutionary process. Here's another paradoxical point. If life on Earth must have been intelligently designed because of its enormous complexity, and its "designer" must necessarily be even more complex, would not this "higher intelligence" also had to have been designed, as opposed to having evolved naturalistically? If the "higher intelligence" is sure to have evolved (as Dawkins claims so ardently), why wouldn't he just stick to saying that life here on Earth also evolved, rather than resorting to invoking a "designer"?

Simplifying it a bit, it is like saying that because "Life form A" is so complex it must have been designed by something like "Life form B," which is even more complex than "A." However, we believe the "Life form B" happened accidentally. In reality, if "Life form B" could evolve by accident, then why couldn't "Life form A" which is allegedly not as complex? Their rationale is that they are both incredibly complex, but the conditions here on Earth (even billions of years ago) are not sufficient to allow life's accidental arrival. They would go on to surmise that perhaps the conditions somewhere else in the universe, billions of years ago, were sufficient enough to produce a highly advance form of life that could in-turn, create additional life and seed it on this planet. Do you see how far we've strayed from true science, into a world of endless metaphysics and hypothetical, *ad hoc* situations? These types of ideas apparently warrant a place in the public school science classroom, but anything involving the intelligence is labeled "religious myth."

WRAPPING IT UP

In summary, intelligent design is a scientific research program that specifically seeks to find evidence of design in nature, while not concerning itself with any details about "who" or "what" the designer is/was. It does not have a religious agenda, but there are definite religious ramifications related to its logical conclusions, just as there are religious ramifications related to Darwinian evolution.

A considerable amount of excellent research has been conducted within the ID movement by highly trained scientists. ID theorists have made some significant headway regarding challenging the exclusive and dogmatic teaching of evolution within the public school system and hopefully will continue to do so. We also saw, however, that ID theory is not capable of providing answers for all that we observe, such as apparent "bad design." These types of observations are more thoroughly and consistently addressed within the context of a biblical worldview, specifically with the Genesis creation account, subsequent fall of man and resultant curse. We would all be better served if we not only knew and understood a few of the evidences for intelligent design, but also had a much better handle on God's Word! (A very wise person once said "You are in error because you do not know the Scriptures or the power of God."—Jesus, in Matthew 22:29, NIV)

We'll close with a few quotes from various scientists; from yesteryear and today.

Lord Kelvin (British mathematical physicist and one of the pioneering founding fathers of modern science. He entered Glasgow University at the age of ten and published over 600 scientific papers. He became president of the Royal Society in 1890.):

> Overwhelming strong proofs of intelligent and benevolent design lie around us. . . The atheistic idea is so nonsensical that I cannot put it into words.[36]

Sir Isaac Newton (arguably the greatest scientist who ever lived):

> This most beautiful system of the sun, planets, and comets, could only proceed from the counsel and dominion of an intelligent Being. . .This Being governs all things, not as the soul of the world, but as Lord over all; and on account of his dominion he is wont to be called "Lord God," or "Universal Ruler". . .The Supreme God is a Being eternal, infinite, absolutely perfect.[37]

Cosmologist Alan Sandage (winner of the Crawford prize in astronomy):

> The more one learns of biochemistry the more unbelievable it becomes unless there is some type of organizing principle – an Architect for believers.[37]

George Greenstein (astronomer, department of astronomy at Amherst College):

> As we survey all the evidence, the thought instantly arises that some supernatural agency—or rather Agency—must be involved. Is it possible that suddenly, without intending to, we have stumbled upon scientific proof of the existence of a Supreme Being? Was it God who stepped in and so providentially crafted the cosmos for our benefit?[39]

Edward Harrison (cosmologist, University of Massachusetts, Amherst, and University of Arizona):

> Here is the cosmological proof of the existence of God. The fine tuning of the universe provides *prima facie* evidence of deistic design. Take your choice: blind chance that requires multitudes of universes or design that requires only one. Many scientists, when they admit their views, incline to the theological or design argument.[40]

Robert Griffiths (physicist at Carnegie Mellon University, winner of the Heinemann Prize in mathematical physics):

> If we need an atheist for a debate, I go to the philosophy department. The physics department isn't much use.[41]

Frank Tipler (professor of mathematical physics, Tulane University):

> When I began my career as a cosmologist some twenty years ago, I was a convinced atheist. I never in my wildest dreams imagined that one day I would be writing a book purporting to show that the central claims of Judeo-Christian

theology are in fact true, that these claims are straightforward deductions of the laws of physics as we now understand them. I have been forced into these conclusions by the inexorable logic of my own special branch of physics.[42]

ENDNOTES

1. Dawkins, Richard, "God's Utility Function," *Scientific American* (vol. 273, November 1995), p. 85.

2. Dawkins, Richard, *The God Delusion*, BantAm Press, 2006, p. 31.

3. www.intelligentdesign.org—*last accessed 7/28/09.*

4. Darwin, Charles, *Life and Letters of Charles Darwin,* Francis Darwin, ed. (New York: D. Appleton & Co., 1911).

5. Darwin, Charles, *Origin of Species*, Introduction, 1859, p. 2.

6. Cited in Larry Witham, *Where Darwin Meets the Bible*, p. 23, Oxford University Press, 2002.

7. Todd, Scott C., correspondence to *Nature* 410(6752):423 (30 September 1999).

8. Ruse, M., "How evolution became a religion: creationists correct?" *National Post*, pp. B1,B3,B7 May 13, 2000.

9. Meyer, S.C., *Signature in the Cell: DNA and the Evidence for Intelligent Design*, Harper One Books, New York, 2009, p.434.

10. Dembski, William, and McDowell, Sean, *Understanding Intelligent Design*, Harvest House Publishers, 2008, pp.190-192.

11. "The Biologist," 2/17/2000, in *The Ledger* (Lynchburg, VA).

12. *Expelled: No Intelligence Allowed* (2008) Produced by Ben Stein—presidential speech writer, syndicated columnist and author. http://www.discovery.org/expelled—*last accessed 9/21/10.*

13. Flew, Antony, *There is a God: How the World's Most Notorious Atheist Changed His Mind*, Harper Collins, New York, 2007, p.75.

14. Dawkins, R., *The Blind Watchmaker*, W.W. Norton & Company, New York, USA, p. 1, 1986.

15. Crick, Francis, *What Mad Pursuit*, Basic Books (1990), p.138.

16. Lakoff, George, *Don't Think of an Elephant!: Know Your Values and Frame the Debate—The Essential Guide for Progressives*, Chelsea Green Publishing, 2004, pp. 16-17.

17. Lipson, H.S., "A Physicist Looks at Evolution," *Physics Bulletin*, vol. 31, May 1980, 138.

18. Darwin, Charles, *The Origin of Species*, J.M. Dent & Sons Ltd, London, 1971, p. 167.

19. Darwin, Charles, *The Life and Letters of Charles Darwin*, Francis Darwin, ed., Vol. 2, (New York and London: D. Appleton and Company, 1911) pp. 90-91.

20. Sarfati, Jonathan, *By Design: Evidence for nature's Intelligent Designer—the God of the Bible*, Creation Book Publishers, 2008, pp 23-39.

21. Sarfati, Jonathan, "Can it bee?" http://creation.com/can-it-bee—*last accessed 8/4/09.*

22. Doolan, Robert, "Dancing Bees," http://creation.com/dancing-bees—*last accessed 8/4/09.*

23. Menton, David, "The Hearing Ear and the Seeing Eye," DVD, 2003, available from www.Creation.com.

24. Jastrow, Robert, "A Scientist Caught Between Two Faiths," Interview with Bill Durbin, *Christianity Today*, August 6, 1982.

25. This video is very professionally produced and contains some very powerful evidence; however, a number of the scientists interviewed generally accept the big bang along with its billions of years—they just don' believe it could have been completely accidental.

26. Strobel, Lee, *The Case for a Creator*, (Zondervan, 2004). p.133

27. Ibid., p.134.

28. "Molecular Machines: Experimental Support for the Design Inference," *Access Research Network,* website: http://www.arn.org/docs/behe/mb_mm92496.htm—*last accessed 9/15/10.*

29. Darwin, Charles, *Origin of Species,* 6th ed, (New York; New York University Press, 1988), p.154.

30. Behe, Michael, *Darwin's Black Box*, Free Press, 1996, pp. 70-73.

31. Sarfati, Jonathan, *By Design: Evidence for nature's Intelligent Designer—the God of the Bible*, Creation Book Publishers, 2008, pp 136.

32. Brown, Walter, *In the Beginning: Compelling Evidence for Creation and the Flood*, 7th ed., Center for Scientific Creation, Arizona, USA, pp. 17-18, 2001.

33. Ibid.

34. Behe, Michael, *Darwin's Black Box*, Free Press, 1996.

35. *Expelled: No Intelligence Allowed* (2008) Produced by Ben Stein, http://www.discovery.org/expelled—*last accessed 9/21/10.*

36. Lord Kelvin, "Proceedings of the Victoria Institute," No. 124, p. 267.

37. Newton, Isaac, *Principia*, "General Scholium," 1713).

38. Sandage, Alan, "A Scientist Reflects on Religious Belief," *Truth*, Vol. 1 (Dallas: Truth Incorporated, 1985), p. 54.

39. Greenstein, G., *The Symbiotic Universe*, New York: William Morrow, 1988, p.27.

40. Harrison, Edward, *Masks of the Universe*, New York, MacMillan, 1985, p. 248.

41. Robert Griffiths quoted in Robert Jastrow, *God and the Astronomers* (New York: W. W. Norton, 1978), 116.

42. Tipler, F.J., *The Physics of Immortality*, "Preface," New York, Doubleday, 1994.

Chapter Thirteen

The Most Important Chapter

So what's with the title of this chapter? Why did I not come up with a title that gives the reader a better idea of what it covers? I felt that using this title would yield the highest probability of it being viewed by most readers. Who wouldn't take a look at what is supposed to be the most important part of an entire book? Maybe I'm thinking of my own tendency to skip around through books, not always having time to read them in their entirety. I also knew that the most important message isn't directly related to wading through all of the nuts and bolts of the creation/evolution controversy, although we certainly have done a fair amount of that and it can be very interesting along the way. Ultimately, it's not about evidence for the existence of the Creator, but about your relationship with Him! For many of you, this will hopefully be just a refresher. For others, I truly believe that it is the most important message you will ever receive in your entire life. That's a very bold claim, but I think you will see why as we head into the remainder of the chapter.

DEATH AND TAXES

It's been said that two things are certain in life: death and taxes. Realizing both of these are unavoidable, it just makes sense to be as prepared as possible to deal with each in the best way possible. Since I'm not interested in giving out tax advice, I will stick to focusing on the issue of death and the afterlife.

Stephen Wright, a comedian known for his very dry sense of humor, relates a story about two men. He said that these unrelated men were both born on the exact same day, in the same city, in the exact same hospital in the exact same ward and were placed on tables lying right next to each other. They soon separated, each going their own way, living completely independent lives. Seventy-two years later, by some strange act of fate, they were each involved in a freak accident and ended up at the same hospital, in the same emergency room lying next to each other on their deathbeds. One turned to the other and said, "So whadya think?" I know; very dry sense of humor, but I thought it was funny. It also made me think of a more serious question. What's next for these guys? If that were you, what would be next?

Even though many people don't spend very much time thinking about what might happen to them when they die, virtually everyone has some opinion about the subject. The less certain people are of what will happen when they die, the less likely they are to spend time thinking about it. On one hand, that makes sense, because people feel uneasy not knowing, so why spend time doing something that is generally uncomfortable. On the other hand, considering how crucial this issue is, it would make sense to learn all you possibly can in order to make decisions in life that would lead to the most favorable outcome when life is all over. There is also a correlation between one's age and the seriousness of thought given to life after death. The younger a person is, the more they tend to feel immortal and are therefore less likely to sense a need to take this issue seriously. As we age and our health declines, our mortality becomes much more apparent and like it or not, we wonder a lot more about our own eternal destiny.

Here are three questions that everyone should be able to confidently answer:

1. What do you believe is required to go to heaven when you die?

2. Where did you get that idea?

3. How do you know you can trust your belief?

Responses to the first question usually consist of a laundry list of different types of "good deeds" such as believing in God, going to church, being kind, giving money to the poor, etc. Answers to the second question vary somewhat, but are typically something like, "That's just what I believe," "That's what my parents told me," or "That's what my church teaches."

The third question is usually the most uncomfortable for people to answer, because even though they may have some type of response, deep down inside, they sense that their answer is not very solid. Let's take a look at each one of these questions a bit closer.

Question #1—(What do you believe is required to go to heaven when you die?)

Regarding the responses to the first question, I always ask people, "How many good works do you have to do?" Going to church sounds like something God would consider honoring, but how many times do you have to go? I often ask "What if you miss going to church one time, because you were very tired and felt like sleeping in?" They always say, "Well, missing one time out of your whole life wouldn't be enough to keep you out of heaven!" Then I ask, "What if you miss ten times?" "Still," they reason, "that isn't all that many when you consider a whole lifetime." I then continue by asking, "What about 75 times, or 118 or 392 or 1,105?" Their confidence starts to diminish quickly. They feel that missing a few Sundays is not a problem at all, but that almost never going is probably not going to cut it. What they don't know is "Where's the cutoff?" How many church services *can* you miss and still get to heaven?

The same thing goes for giving money to the church. Giving five dollars over a lifetime doesn't seem like it would qualify, but giving half of all you own should just about be a guarantee, right? Again: where's the cutoff? In this system of thought, there will be a number of people getting into heaven with no problem at all and many others who don't have the slightest chance. There would also be numerous situations where people are "standing at the pearly gates" and God looks at them, hangs His head and says, "I dreaded this moment. You were so close to getting in. So close! You missed it by two church attendances! If you would have gone just two more times, you would have made it. I would have even accepted an extra one hundred dollars in the offering to make up for the missed services, but I have to draw the line somewhere, and you just missed it. Sorry!"

Can you imagine what that would be like? This scenario is not very comforting to us. We would probably all be wondering if we would be one of those people who "just missed it." That's scary! When you think about it, we have three options to consider:

• God doesn't actually have any standards and doesn't care at all what you do with you life. (This is kind of a bizarre, illogical view of God).

258 LET THERE BE LIGHT

- He does have standards, but has not clearly defined the criteria for getting into heaven, in which case, it seems unfair for Him to judge us by standards that we don't really know.

- He does have standards and has conveyed them to us. Therefore, He is completely justified in judges us by these criteria.

This leads us into question number two.

Question #2—(Where did you get that idea?)

Where do people get their opinions on what will happen to them when they die? It is human nature to think we need to do the right things in order to earn a reward or be considered worry. That's what religion is all about: doing the best we can in order to earn some kind of cosmic eternal reward. Why are there so many different religions in the world today? Because "religion" is man's idea of God, as opposed to God's idea of God. There are so many different religions, because there are so many different people. Everyone has their own ideas about who God is, why He created us and what He wants from us. They all ultimately have their origin in the mind of man. Someone, somewhere along the way, decided to proclaim what truth was and others later chose to attempt to follow those standards.

God either has to let everyone decide for themselves what is best, which standards they like and which they don't, or God has to tell us what His standards truly are.

The Bible declares itself to be the inspired word of God (II Timothy 3:16) and it tells us exactly what His standards are. God tells us, in no uncertain terms, that His standard is one hundred percent absolute perfection! (For example, keeping all of the Ten Commandments, all of the time.) Wow! There's no way we could achieve this! We've all messed up somewhere along the way and we continue to do so. Does that mean it is hopeless

for us? No. How can that be? It is because God loved us so much that He was willing to pay the price for our sins (something we are unable to do) by sending His son, Jesus, to die in our place, thus paying the penalty for us:

For Christ also suffered once for sins, the righteous [100% absolute perfection] for the unrighteous, to bring you to God. He was put to death in the body but made alive in the Spirit (I Peter 3:18, NIV).

What must we do in order to apply Christ's payment to our personal debt? Religion would love for us to think that we have to work very hard and earn it, but this is not what the Bible teaches.

> . . .know that a person is not justified by the works of the law, but by faith in Jesus Christ. So we, too, have put our faith in Christ Jesus that we may be justified by faith in Christ and not by the works of the law, because by the works of the law no one will be justified (Galatians 2:16, NIV).

This passage tells us that it is not by our good works (keeping the law) that we are justified or have our sins forgiven. It is only by faith in Jesus and what He did for us. A very important question would be: "What exactly does faith in Jesus mean?"

Let's first look at what it does not mean. It doesn't simply mean believing that Jesus existed and that He was the Son of God. That's just head knowledge, believing a fact, and is not what is meant here. If you lost your job, simply believing that Bill Gates is the chairman of Microsoft wouldn't help your situation. On the other hand, if you had a personal relationship with him, that could change everything. You could call him up, tell him your situation and he would be able to help you, because of his connections and personal wealth. It's the personal relationship that makes the difference, not just believing a set of facts about someone.

How do we get this personal relationship with Jesus Christ? By sincerely repenting of (turning from) our sins and asking for His forgiveness, believing that He is the Son of God and that He died on the cross to pay for our sins and rose again three days later.

> By this gospel you are saved, if you hold firmly to the word I preached to you. Otherwise, you have believed in vain. For what I received I passed on to you as of first importance: that Christ died for our sins according to the Scriptures, that he was buried, that he was raised on the third day according to the Scriptures (I Corinthians 15: 2-4, NIV).

> For it is with your heart that you believe and are justified, and it is with your mouth that you confess and are saved...for everyone who calls on the name of the Lord will be saved (Romans 10:10, 13; NIV).

This leads us to the last question.

Question #3—(What gives you confidence in your belief?)

If your answer to the second question was more along the line of "That's just what I think," or "That's what my parents told me," you most likely don't have all that much confidence in what you believe. If you were in a courtroom setting and were asked to take the witness stand to defend your belief, there might be a lot of crickets chirping! As a Christian, I have confidence, not in my own wisdom and philosophy, but in God's Word. The message of how someone gets to heaven may be clear in the Bible, but how do we know the Bible is true? We covered this in a fair amount of detail in chapter 8, so I won't repeat it here. Please revisit that chapter for a refresher, especially with an eternal view in mind.

PERSONAL CHALLENGE

Here's the personal challenge: before the day is over, ask yourself this question:

If I were to die tonight and find myself standing before God, and He asked "Why should I let you into heaven?" what would my response be?

The Bible tells us in no uncertain terms that it is only by faith specifically in Jesus Christ (our Creator) that anyone can enter into heaven:

Jesus answered, "I am the way and the truth and the life. No one comes to the Father except through me" (John 14:6, NIV).

Salvation is found in no one else, for there is no other name under heaven given to men by which we must be saved (Acts 4:12, NIV).

Is there any rational reason that you would not confess your sins and place your faith solely in Jesus Christ for the forgiveness of your sins and securing eternal life? Don't put it off. I tell you, now is the time of God's favor, now is the day of salvation (II Corinthians 6:2 NIV).

Don't put it off another day. And I'll say to myself, "You have plenty of good things laid up for many years. Take life easy; eat, drink and be merry." But God said to him, "You fool! This very night your life will be demanded from you. Then who will get what you have prepared for yourself?" This is how it will be with anyone who stores up things for himself but is not rich toward God (Luke 12:19-21, NIV).

Once you've committed your life to Christ, rest in His protection!

For I am convinced that neither death nor life, neither angels nor demons, neither the present nor the future, nor any powers, neither height nor depth, nor anything else in all creation, will be able to separate us from the love of God that is in Christ Jesus our Lord (Romans 8:38-39, NIV).

MAKE IT PERSONAL!

Perhaps you are realizing you don't know for sure what would happen to you if you were to die today. You may also sense you truly need to commit your life to Christ, but aren't quite sure "how" to do it. It's not by chanting some magical phrase and doing something highly mystical, but simply by honestly and sincerely praying something similar to the following:

Dear God, I know that you created me and that I have not lived according to your standards. I also realize that I cannot possibly try to be good enough to earn your favor. Because of your great love for me, you sent your son (Jesus) to die on a cross to pay the penalty for my own sins, so that I don't have to spend eternity separated from you in judgment. I am asking today for you to forgive my sins and am accepting the free gift of eternal life that you are offering to me, through your son Jesus Christ. Help me to live the rest of my life in a way that is honoring and pleasing to you. When I do sin in the future, help me to confess those sins and thank you for the fact that they, too, are also forgiven in Jesus. Amen!

If you sincerely pray a prayer similar to the one above, you can have peace today knowing where you will spend eternity! That beats knowing anything about DNA or carbon-14 dating! It doesn't mean that everything else in your life will be easy, but that you can have confidence in your own eternal destiny (and you have a new-found relationship with the Creator of the universe who cares for you!).

Very truly I tell you, whoever hears my word and believes him who sent me has eternal life and will not be judged but has crossed over from death to life (John 5:24, NIV).

I give them eternal life, and they shall never perish; no one can snatch them out of my hand. My Father, who has given them to me, is greater than all; no one can snatch them out of my Father's hand (John 10:28-29, NIV).

Cast all your anxiety on him because he cares for you (I Peter 5:7, NIV).

I am the LORD, the God of all mankind. Is anything too hard for me (Jeremiah 32:27, NIV)?

I can do all things through Christ who strengthens me (Philippians 4:13, NKJV).

Chapter Fourteen

Wrapping Things Up: Some Practical Advice

We have covered a lot of ground and you may be asking yourself, "So now what?" The answer to this question completely depends on your response to what we have already discussed.

DON'T QUITE BUY IT

If you find yourself still struggling with much of what was discussed, at the risk of sounding arrogant, I would highly recommend praying and re-reading the book. I would suggest that when you do, make a list questions and comments. You may then contact our ministry so we can assist in helping you work through these issues. We'd be more than happy to do so.

READY FOR THE NEXT STEP

It may be the case that you are in general agreement with much of what you've read and are feeling very encouraged regarding your faith in the authority and reliability of God's Word. In this case, I would recommend four action steps:

1. Start or continue an in-depth study of Scripture so that you have an even better personal understanding of God's Word and what it truly says, as opposed to simply believing what others tell you it says. That includes me as well, meaning that you should not even take for granted what I am sharing is true! You need to have your own faith based on your own understanding of the Bible through the power of the Holy Spirit. This is the safest course to take because the Spirit of God will not lead you

astray. I am not saying you cannot learn from others, just that you need to check everything they say against God's written, inspired, inerrant Word.

2. Study a few of the key apologetic arguments for the defense of the Christian faith. These would include evidences from archaeology, history, science and prophecy. This will primarily serve to strengthen your own faith and better position you to share the gospel message with those around you. We covered some of these evidences in chapter 8. We don't use these evidences to "prove" anything, but simply to show that Christianity does provide answers to life's toughest questions and challenges. It's the only worldview that provides answers that are "consistently consistent." For a biblically-driven defense of the existence of God, please see appendix B.

3. Mentor those believers who are within your sphere of influence, whether they be your children, grandchildren, friends, etc.

4. As God grants you the opportunity, share your faith with unbelievers, including family members, friends, neighbors, co-workers, classmates, etc.

As an additional detail regarding this last point, I would suggest starting with your own personal testimony of how you placed your faith in Jesus Christ for the forgiveness of sins. Along with this, I highly recommend giving them an overview of the bigger picture, meaning discussing God as our Creator, mankind's subsequent fall through sin and God's plan of redemption through His son, Jesus Christ. Too often, we jump right into the middle of the story, telling people they need to "accept Christ" or they will go to Hell. This is fairly confusing to people and also understandably inflammatory. You are telling them to do something they do not quite understand (i.e., "accept Christ") regarding someone they know very little about. You are also telling them that they are so bad they deserve to go to Hell. (I realize that biblically speaking we are all guilty and deserving of judgment, but that is most likely not part of their current worldview.) Should we be surprised that they most often do not respond well? Most people do not normally feel all that bad about themselves, because they all know others who are much worse than they are. It is human nature to establish and live by a standard that is reasonably obtainable and not self-incriminating. Therefore, according to their way of reckoning, they are doing fairly well so who are we to tell them otherwise? To the unbeliever, it sounds very arrogant, judgmental and intolerant. And even if they sense they might be lacking something spiritually, why should it be Jesus? Why not Muhammad or Allah or Buddha? In fact, why do they need anyone at all? Why can't they just be "good"? Why are we Christians so bent on making sure everyone does things our way? Those are very good questions. I feel the only way to even begin to properly answer them is to share the "big picture" starting with the Genesis creation account. It is foundational to the gospel message which is ultimately what matters most.

Even if you understand the importance of all of this, you may also be feeling a bit overwhelmed. Occasionally, after reading a compelling book or listening to a powerful lecture, I find myself thinking "That was great, but there's no way I'm going to remember all of that." You may be thinking something similar regarding this book. So what are you to do with all of this information? The balance of this chapter briefly shares a number of suggestions regarding where to go from here. We will cover some simple and practical advice that I typically share during Q&A sessions at the end of our speaking engagements, particularly in response to questions from audience members who want to know how to handle specific situations. My advice falls into various categories based on whatever particular life stage in which you find yourself. (Much of what I will share in the next section related to children in grade school also applies to other levels of education, so I recommend everyone read the following segment, independent of who you are.)

CHILDREN IN GRADE SCHOOL

I am often asked questions regarding how parents should handle controversial teaching that their children are exposed to in grade school. My advice is for them to focus on making sure their children know God's Word, as opposed to trying to teach them many apologetic arguments to be used to combat what they are hearing from their teachers. They need to have a solid understanding of God's Word and they need to hear from you that it can be trusted in all matters, whatever it addresses, from cover-to-cover. When apparent conflict arises between what the Bible teaches and what they are hearing at school, you can simply tell them that their teachers may have a different way of looking at things, but because they were not around at the very beginning to observe what happened, they certainly don't know everything and sometimes even make mistakes in their judgments. Because of this, it is easy to see how they might be wrong about things that happened in the unobserved past. They may wonder (and you may also),

"But doesn't all of this apply to Christians as well?" Yes, it does. The important difference is that we actually have the word from the One who: (a) was there in the beginning, (b) knows everything, (c) does not make mistakes, and (d) does not lie. That's the only reason we as Christians can be so confident about our views. (In case you missed it, see chapter 8 for more information regarding evidence for the inspiration of the Bible.)

For the most part, they will not be learning all that much about evolution while in grade school. It will mostly come in the form of indirect comments, rather than focused attention on teaching evolution as a whole. One of the most common topics to arise is the issue of dinosaurs. Our ministry offers a DVD and a booklet[1] on this particular subject. I chose to leave it out of this book to keep the length more manageable.

I would highly recommend telling your child (or children) that their teachers are not "bad" or "evil" and they are certainly not consciously trying to lie to them. They are sincerely teaching what they have been taught themselves and what they also believe is mostly likely true. Unfortunately, most of them have never heard any evidence to the contrary and whatever religious background they may have probably allows them to be fairly comfortable with evolutionary scenarios. As alluded to earlier in this book, most teachers have attended public schools all the way through high school and received their college education in a state university or some other non-Christian institution. Considering this, it comes as no surprise that the majority of teachers themselves believe in evolution. They generally don't see anything harmful in teaching evolution or see it as being all that controversial, other than they are aware that those who are more fundamental in their religious beliefs seem to object. However, even in those cases, they believe rejecting evolution is purely driven by issues of faith, as opposed to anything based on science.

STUDENTS IN JUNIOR HIGH AND HIGH SCHOOL

Much of what I shared regarding children in grade school applies here, too, so you want to make sure you don't skip over the previous section as you might have done if you don't have children in that age group.

One major difference is that from eighth through twelfth grade they will hear more and more about evolution and will need training on how to respond. It is not unheard of that in some classes the teacher will actually directly ask, "Who in this class believes in creation and the Bible?" If anyone is actually brave enough to raise their hand the teacher may promptly respond with, "Well, you won't anymore once you've finished this course!" It seems harsh and extreme, but I personally know of two cases where this occurred right in my own home town and I know our city is not unique.

So how should they respond to the presentation of evolution? I believe we should let them learn as much as they can about it, because they will be in a much better position to see where the faults are, as well as gain more credibility from skeptics they will interact with in the future. Too often, we shelter our kids completely from the idea of evolution, but this does more damage than good. At some point in their life they will be challenged regarding their belief in the Bible and presented with arguments for evolution that seem very powerful. If we don't help them work through these issues while they are still under our roof, we are in a sense "throwing them to the wolves" when they move out on their own. As was mentioned earlier in the book, 50-75% of Christian students walk away from their faith before they finish college, and the attack on the validity of the Bible is arguably the biggest factor in this trend.

Here's my advice for responding to the teaching of evolution in the classroom. I suggest that at the beginning of the semester they respectfully let their teacher know that they personally do not believe in evolution, but they clearly understand the teacher will be covering this topic as a standard part of the course. Make sure they also define what they mean by "evolution," because as we discussed in chapter 1, the student has in mind "molecules-to-man" evolution, but the teacher might simply be equating evolution with any kind of change. In this case, the teacher will understandably feel that the student is speaking out of ignorance and letting their faith greatly impede their ability to understand and accept science. Once this has been made clear, it becomes a lot easier to respond to specific questions on exams. For example, let's say a question on an exam asks, "How many years ago did chemicals react together to form the first single-cell living organism?" The student should not write, "Chemicals did not spontaneously react to form a living cell. This is a myth and I do not believe it. The Bible says God created life and that's what I believe!" Yikes! In addition to annoying the teacher and getting the answer marked as being wrong, you can imagine how much longer it would take to finish the entire exam, especially if half the questions were ones having to do with controversial evolutionary concepts!

Here's how I suggest they respond. They should succinctly write "3.8 billion years ago." That's it. Nothing more is needed. First of all, that would be the correct answer according to what was being taught (or something very close to it, depending on which textbook is being used). Secondly, the teacher already knows that the student does not necessarily personally believe it, but it does show respect for authority (i.e., the teacher) and it also shows that they are a good student and that they were listening in class. The student will also be in a much better position to engage in a conversation with the teacher if they do wish to question a particular issue. I will offer further suggestions that work for both this age group and college students in the section titled, "Just Ask Questions."

COLLEGE STUDENTS

Again, much of what was just covered (junior high—high school) applies equally as well to the college scene. There are, however, a few major differences once you get to this level:

- Students are generally out from under the protection of their parents, usually for the first time ever.

- They may feel an innate sense of freedom and also a desire to be rid of some of the "rules and regulations" imposed on them by their parents or church.

- They truly need to "think for themselves" more now than ever.

- They often are trying to figure out what it is that they personally believe, as opposed to having existed under the cloak of their parents' set of beliefs.

- They are often under the impression that they are embarking on a journey in which they will now learn about the real world from professors who actually know what they are talking about, as opposed to the simple and naïve wisdom of their parents and church leaders. Because of the naturally rebellious sin nature that affects us all, they are often looking for reasons to reject their parent's authority and frequently use what they learn from their humanist and/or fairly liberal professors to argue with their parents and justify their confrontational attitude.

- There will be much greater peer pressure to accept a more humanistic worldview along with its associated lifestyle and morals (or lack thereof).

- The attack on their faith will be much more direct, dogmatic, intimidating and potentially devastating.

Quick question: are you sleeping right now? If so, this next quote will wake you up. Regarding the last bullet point, consider the following citation from Dr. Richard Rorty (philosopher, University of Virginia):

Secular professors in the universities ought to arrange things so that students who enter as bigoted, homophobic religious fundamentalists will leave college with views more like our own. Students are fortunate to find themselves under the [benevolence] of people like me, and to have escaped the grip of their frightening, vicious, dangerous parents. We are going to go right on trying to discredit you [parents] in the eyes of your children, trying to strip your fundamentalist religious community of dignity, trying to make your views seem silly rather than discussable.[2]

If that doesn't wake you up, nothing will! They have a very definite agenda and unless we prepare our children, we are in essence playing russian roulette and the stakes are much, much too high for that. One of the biggest challenges that parents face is that they cannot impart to their children what they themselves do not possess (i.e., answers to tough questions). Too many parents are struggling with the authority of God's Word (i.e., just when can it be trusted and how serious do we take it) and therefore, are not in a good position to aid in strengthening the faith of their own children. Too often we consciously or subconsciously tell our children, "You just need to believe the Bible, because we're Christians and that's what we believe. Don't ask me why, just obey." That sometime works when our children are younger, but as they mature and start thinking more for themselves, it becomes more and more untenable for them to live with that philosophy, especially when immersed in a highly advanced academic environment such as college. Our work as parents is definitely cut out for us. Are we up for the task? Are we willing to do the hard work and not take the easy, passive road? I am particularly concerned about the male leadership in the home. We have dropped the ball for many years and I believe it is time that we step-it-up, ask for God's forgiveness and pray that He strengthens us for the task set before us. Wow—getting off on another topic! That will have to wait for another book.

We've been talking about how easy it is for our children to be led astray in college, but what about those who do have a fairly strong faith and good head on their shoulders? How are they to respond to the continual attack on their beliefs? Well, I just happen to have some advice on this as well. In addition to making sure they answer test questions according to what is taught in class, even when contrary to what they personally believe, there is one additional tactic that works quite well.

JUST ASK QUESTIONS

Let's consider a typical confrontation that might occur between a Christian and a skeptic. (Note: Even though we have been talking about a college setting, this strategy works well in all situations.)

Skeptic: "Evolution is a fact and the Bible is just mythology!"

Christian: "I don't believe that. I think creation is true and the Bible is the inspired Word of God."

Skeptic: "Prove it! Give me one fact that proves creation is true or that the Bible is actually from God."

Christian: "Well, I don't know that I can prove it, but that's what I believe."

Skeptic: "Just as I suspected. Well, you can have your faith, but I live in the real world and I'm sticking with science!"

This type of conversation results in the Christian feeling very defeated and dejected, being much less likely to share any comments about their beliefs with a skeptic in the future. I realize that there are a number of Christians that can handle themselves just fine in a situation such as this, but they are admittedly more the exception than the rule. Let's revisit this conversation, but this time we'll have the Christian strategically change their response by simply asking follow up questions (something anyone can do).

Skeptic: "Evolution is a fact and the Bible is just mythology!"

Christian: "What do you mean by 'evolution'?"

Skeptic: "That life arose from chemicals billions of years ago and slowly evolved into every life form that we see today."

Christian: "How do you know evolution is a fact?"

Skeptic: "Well, all the scientists believe it!"

Christian: "How do you know that all scientists believe it?"

Skeptic: "Well, all real scientists believe it!"

Christian: "How do you define a 'real' scientist?"

Skeptic: "Ummm, anyone who believes in evolution."

Christian: "Isn't that circular reasoning?"

Skeptic: "Well, you believe that God created everything magically out of nothing in six days and made Adam and Eve in some mystical garden. Yeah, that's really believable!"

Christian: "You know, I actually haven't said anything about what I believe. You, however, have made some very serious claims and I'm just asking you to give me reasons for why you believe they are true. So why do you believe the Bible is just mythology?"

Skeptic: "Because it's full of errors and contradictions!"

Christian: "Could you give me some examples?"

Skeptic: "Well, there are tons of them!"

Christian: "Great, then it should be fairly easy to share an example or two."

Skeptic: "Well, I can't think of them right now."

Christian: "Could you tell me what the general story line of the Bible is from beginning to end. . .just a one minute overview?"

Skeptic: "Well, it's been a while since I've looked at it."

Christian: "Tell me, if you can't think of any actual errors or contradictions and you don't even know what it is all about, why do you have such a strong opinion against it? Are you sure that you are not simply reciting someone else's view as opposed to your own, well thought out opinion?"

A much different scenario and it didn't even require the Christian to "have all the answers." In fact, they didn't have to give any answers! What we just observed is that the skeptic was making what are called "truth claims"—general or specific statements about the world that they contend are valid. The Christian, on the other hand, was not making counterclaims, in which case he or she would need to be able to back them up, but simply asking for reasons as to why the truth claims are valid. Greg Koukl, from Stand to Reason ministry[3], calls this the "Columbo tactic," after the famous 1970s television series, in which actor Peter Falk played a brilliant, but bumbling-in-appearance homicide detective, named Lieutenant Columbo. He was always asking questions and did so in a very powerful way. It just requires that we truly listen to what others are saying, and not simply just wait for them to finish talking so we can give them an earful of our so-called brilliance!

Now I am not at all suggesting that we don't need to have answers. On the contrary. I am simply pointing out that there are ways to handle conversations even in situations where you are not well-prepared to answer the skeptic's tough questions. But what if within this scenario the skeptic *does* know a few examples of alleged errors or contradictions? How do we respond then if we don't know the answer? Surprise, surprise, I have a few thoughts on this, too.

The best response you can give when someone asks a question to which you do not know the answer: "I don't know." Why? It's honest and it's the truth! Actually, I would suggest saying something more like: "I'm not sure I know the answer to your question, but that's a good one and I will certainly look into it and get back to you." An important follow up question for them is, "If I am able to get back to you with an answer that is at least plausible, would you be willing to listen to more of what I have to share about the Bible?" With this question, you are qualifying them to see how sincere they really are. If they say "No," then you really aren't under any significant obligation to getting back to them, because they are clearly telling you that it won't matter either way. You would have to pray about it, but there's a good chance that you would just be spinning your wheels with this person and not using your time wisely. Whenever I encounter someone who by all indications is not open to hearing the truth, I picture in my mind a long line of people standing behind them, desperately wanting someone to answer their questions. They are sincerely skeptical, but also sincerely seeking. That makes it much easier for me to wrap things up with the current individual so that I can focus my time, talents and energy on those who are eager to have a healthy dialog and deep down are seeking to know God, even though they are currently struggling. By the way, this is not always just something I picture in my mind. I have to confront this fairly often in a very real way (with literal lines of people) when answering questions after my lectures. I always rely on the Holy Spirit to let me know when to move on and when to hang in there a little longer. I suggest you do the same.

Here's another word of advice regarding questions from skeptics. It is very important to find out if the questions they are asking are somewhere in the top five or so on their list. If not, you may not be spending your time very efficiently. I've had it happen to me before, where I do a fair amount of research in finding an answer to a question, only to have the skeptic later reply with something like, "Well, what I really want to know is. . ." In essence, they were telling me (after the fact) that the question I just answered wasn't really all that critical and there are other questions that are much more important.

Once you've figured out what their most crucial questions are, the ball is in your court. Be diligent in researching an answer in a timely manner and get back to them as soon as possible. There are a number of great apologetic ministries that would be more than capable of assisting you with an answer, including ours. One note of caution: There are a number of ministries, while having some very solid material on evidence for the resurrection of Christ, the inspiration of the Bible, defense of the Trinity, etc., they also somewhat blindly buy into the big bang and possibly other secular concepts regarding the origins issue and it manifests itself in their resources. It always pays to find out where they are coming from before naively assuming that everything they produce is biblically solid. I even know of one ministry that was very reliable for years and years, but all of a sudden, starting buying into a number of secular views regarding origins. I was greatly saddened by this and could no longer financially support them or even take for granted the validity of what they taught in other areas. We enjoy helping people with answers to their puzzling questions, so feel free to contact us anytime through our ministry website: www.CECwisc.com.

In the case where the questions are coming from a school teacher or college professor, here's how I would suggest you handle the situation. Once they've conveyed their questions (from their "Top Ten" list), express your thanks without attempting to argue or downplay what they presented, and let them know that you will be taking some time to think about what they shared. Once you've found the answer(s), get back to them by saying something like, "Dr. Johnson, the other day we were talking about evolution and you shared a few questions that at the time were difficult for me to answer. I appreciated you taking to time to talk with me and I did some research, because I felt the questions you asked were very challenging. I found some information that I thought was very interesting and it made a lot of sense to me, but I would really be interested in getting your opinion on it, because you probably know much more about the subject than I do. Would you be willing to read this at your leisure and get back to me sometime with your thoughts?" This is a very gracious and humble approach and will potentially lead to a response much better than "being in their face" which I never recommend, not with anyone.

Even though you handle the situation as cordially as possible, there's no guarantee they will respond in like fashion. As a reminder, this ultimately is not an issue of science, but rather of worldviews and pride. The teacher/professor may become very emotional in their response and not even agree to look at your materials. In this situation, they will probably verbally attack you and imply that you are very naïve and uneducated, so be prepared ahead of time not to take it personally, but be willing to thank them for their time and walk away without retaliating. If they do ultimately agree to read what you are presenting (and I always recommend having it be something relatively brief—no one has time to read a 500 page book just to get an answer to a couple questions), you also need to be prepared for a less than cordial response from them, if they do get back to you. Once in a while a professor may indicate that what they read was very interesting and does seem to adequately address the question, but more often than not, your conversation may look something like the following:

Student: "Were you able to take a look at the article I gave you?"

Professor: "Yes, I kind of read it over a bit."

Student: "What did you think?"

Professor: "Well, it's all pretty much garbage."

Student: "What made you think that?"

Professor: "Well, the whole thing is just off, way off."

Student: "What was in it specifically that makes you feel that way?"

Professor: "These creationists. . .they're not real scientists. They just want to get their religion into the schools and force everyone to believe in the Bible."

Student: "I don't remember them saying anything about the Bible or religion in the article. It was just about amino acids and proteins. So what did they say about those things that you are convinced is wrong? They were actually citing secular journals in doing so."

Professor: "You know, I really don't have time to get into a discussion about religion. You're not going to change my mind, so don't bring it up again!"

There you have it; a typical conversation, of which I've had many. In fact, here's an actual story from my own college experience. (This is the story I alluded to in the beginning of the book.) It is the recounting of the very first time I confronted a professor regarding something that was taught in class. Keep in mind that I was a junior, studying physics at a state university and that I had just started researching evidence for the validity of the creation account, so I knew very little at the time. In addition, I was also very shy and fairly intimidated

by college professors. I always approached my professors after class, in their offices, so as not to come across as trying to discredit them or humiliate them in front of their students. That will not win you any Brownie points and will certainly make them a lot less open to what you have to say.

One day, in my geology class (very early on in the semester) my professor told the class that all of the planets in our solar system rotate the same direction. In my initial research, I read that two rotate backwards; Venus and Uranus (Uranus actually rotates sideways)[4]. Why would any of this matter?

Well, according to the nebular hypothesis (the most commonly accepted theory of the origin of our solar system), our entire solar system formed from a swirling cloud of gases. If this were the case, we would expect that all of the planets would spin in the same direction—the same direction as the original spinning cloud of gas. The fact that there are anomalies is evidence against this origin scenario. I approached my professor in his office after class to discuss this issue. At this point, he didn't know who I was and certainly did not know that I was a Christian or a creationist. I was just another one of his many students. I knocked on his door, which was open, and he told me to come in. I introduced myself, only mentioning my name and that I was a student in his geology class. I then told him that although he instructed the students that all of the planets rotate the same direction, two in fact rotate backwards, Venus and Uranus. He angrily retorted, "No they don't, they all rotate the same direction!" I respectfully told him that I could bring him the documentation if he would be interested, to which he replied, "Yeah, you do that!" I walked out of his office feeling terrible that he was so mad at me, especially when I was trying to be so respectful. I was also intimidated, because, after all, he was my professor and I had to sit under his teaching for the rest of the semester (and accept whatever grade he chose to give me).

I went out and found the reference for what we discussed, which was from *Science* magazine, a highly respected secular journal, and brought it back to his office two days later. Once again I knocked on his door and kindly reminded him, "A couple days ago, we were talking about the rotation of the planets in our solar system and I mentioned that two rotate backwards. You said you would be interested in seeing the documentation, so I brought it with me today." Sitting in his chair, he took hold of the article and started nervously reading. About ten seconds later, he handed it back to me and said, "Well, I guess I wasn't keeping up with the latest findings." I responded, in a very respectful tone, "That was from sixteen years ago." Interestingly, he never went back to the class to correct his error. I also felt it was not my place to prompt him in front of the students to explain to them what he and I had discussed. But wait, it gets even better.

Skipping numerous other stories regarding the rest of my time at the state university, I graduated the following year with a degree in physics and was also inducted into the National Physics Honor Society. Approximately three or four years after entering the working world, I was invited by InterVarsity Christian Fellowship to return to the University of Wisconsin-Whitewater and speak to their group on campus. There were about one hundred twenty-five students in attendance and I spoke for about an hour, followed by an hour long question and answer session. After the meeting was over, quite a few students stayed to ask further questions. During this time, one of the students said something that prompted me to share the story about the geology professor and the planet rotations, which I had not shared with the entire group, wishing to be respectful to my former professor, even though I did not know if he was still teaching at the university. After I recounted the story, one of the students looked at me in utter shock and said, "I can't believe that! I have him for geology and just yesterday he told us that all the planets rotate the same direction! I have it in my notes—I wish I could show you!" He indeed was still teaching at the university and apparently was still promoting ideas that he knew to be fallacious. I do not imagine that this is a unique occurrence restricted only to this university.

On a related note, while I was conducting some research for this book, I stumbled upon an interesting *Discover* magazine article. It was titled, "Wrong way planets screw up our perfectly good theories."[5] The sub-caption read, "Stupid reality, always mucking about with our ideas. How dare it!" It was about the recent discovery of planets that orbit their stars in the wrong direction. Of course, it is only the wrong direction if you choose to hold on to your belief in the nebular hypothesis!

RESCUING DEVICES

As a logical continuation of presenting evidence to skeptics, one important point to note is you will rarely sway someone by the evidence you present. As mentioned in chapter 2, I believe this is much more of a spiritual issue, a battle of worldviews, than a matter of scientific debate. An evolutionist worth their salt will always come up with a way to explain away contrary evidence. Before I comment on this further, I would like to mention that this is not necessarily wrong. In fact, it is a fairly natural response. Christians do the same thing. The action itself should not be the cause of concern, but more so, the logic behind the counter-response.

In his book, *The Ultimate Proof of Creation*, astrophysicist Dr. Jason Lisle refers to these kinds of retorts as "rescuing devices," which he defines as being, "a conjecture designed to save a person's view from apparently contrary evidence."[6] The point being, that no matter what evidence you present, the skeptic can potentially define a scenario in which what you presented comports with their views. As an example, say you were to use the first law of thermodynamics to "prove" your point that you cannot get something out of nothing, and therefore claim that God must have created the universe since it could not create itself. The skeptic might respond by postulating the possibility of some unknown laws of physics that existed billions of years ago that enabled matter and energy to be created from some uncertainty in the quantum fluctuation of the great cosmic void. A *what* in a *where*? They are appealing to an "unknown factor" in an attempt to counter what *is* "known." Can you disprove the "uncertainty in the quantum fluctuation of the great cosmic void?" No, but there is no reason to

WRAPPING THINGS UP: SOME PRACTICAL ADVICE 277

believe in it either, other than simply choosing to because it would be allegedly help them explain away evidence to the contrary.

An additional example comes directly from Lisle's book, on page 23.[7] According to evolutionists, our solar system is billions of years old. A perplexing phenomenon, however, is the observance of short-period comets. As the hypothesis goes, these objects should only last, at most, for approximately 100,000 years, being made of silicate and ice (dirty snowballs). Each time they orbit, they burn off some of their mass. This is the fascinating comet tail we often see. If these comets could only last a maximum of 100,000 years and the solar system is allegedly billions of years old, why do we still see comets? When presented with this logic, an evolutionist may invoke a rescuing device by referring to the Oort cloud hypothesis, named after Dutch astronomer, Jan Oort (1900-1992). The Oort cloud is assumed to be a massive object filled with comets somewhere outside the reach of our telescopes (conveniently beyond detection) that occasionally spits out a new comet, thus addressing this apparent enigma. The weakness of this particular rescuing device is that not only has there been a complete absence of observations of the Oort cloud, but it is theoretically "out of reach," meaning that we could not see it even if we wanted to. It is not a testable hypothesis. Evolutionists may respond by saying that maybe some day we will have telescopes powerful enough to allow us to detect the Oort cloud. This is nothing more than wishful thinking and is no more of a convincing argument than a creationist saying maybe some day we will have telescopes powerful enough to allow us to know for sure the Oort cloud *does not* exist! Science should be focused on what can be observed now, not what it hopes to someday observe. In fact, science has no mind of its own, desiring or favoring anything. Only people do.

The main point with rescuing devices is that they are plentiful and generally considered to be satisfactory responses in the mind of those who employ them. Therefore, while presenting evidence certainly has its place in discussions with evolutionists, it is not an end-all tactic. We keep getting back to the concept of one's worldview, which is the basis for how we interpret evidence. We need to focus on showing the weaknesses of the evolutionary-naturalistic worldview if we are to make any headway in our discussions.

DEFINE YOUR TERMS

Another important point relates to defining and refining the debate. Rather than letting your opponent wander off in all directions, it is important to stick to one point at a time, preferably the most important points as previously mentioned. In doing so, you will maximize your effectiveness and lessen the chance of the evolutionist changing subjects to avoid tough questions. In this process you may also want to ask the following critical question: "What would you accept as evidence for creation?" I can almost certainly guarantee they will respond by asking, "What do you mean?" Explain to them that if they have not determined what type of evidence would qualify as being supportive of the creation model, how would they recognize it when presented to them? They cannot have a rational, respectable discourse on the subject if they are unable to define what does and does not constitute legitimate evidence. If they are unable to address this adequately, you would be best advised to discontinue the conversation, at least until a later date when they are better prepared, otherwise there is nothing to gain. In reality, this will be very difficult for them to answer. They could justifiably turn the question back on you, asking, "What would you accept as evidence for molecules-to-man evolution?" You should be prepared with a response or you will be guilty of evoking a double standard. As an example, I might share that if we find evidence of an animal with a truly transitional feature such as one that is part scale, part feather, that would be supportive of the evolution model. Not a creature having both scales and feathers, but something in between. I would also say that if scientists ever demonstrate that chemicals can form living cells in a natural environment without the aid of intelligently-directed influences, that too, would be supportive of evolution's origin of life hypothesis. A third supportive example might be that if they ever discover that mutations can consistently create significant amounts of new, biologically useful information. In reality, none of these occurrences would constitute proof, but they would be very significant in making a scientific case for evolution.

START WITHIN THE CHURCH

Many people ask me if I've every debated an atheist, assuming that it would be interesting to observe. "Interesting" would probably be an appropriate word, but not necessarily "effective." It would almost certainly not transpire the way they would expect. I have debated many atheists in small group settings and individually, but not in the context of an official public debate. Apart from the fact that I have never been invited to do so, I would not personally be very interested, for a number of reasons. The most significant being that these debates are most often a battle of whit and generally serve to determine who is the better public speaker and who is quicker with the come-backs, getting the audience to laugh in support, and to the embarrassment and humiliation of the opponent. This situation is not limited to debates with atheists, but applies equally as well to evolutionists and skeptics in general, and in reality, for any topic that might be deliberated. Also, both sides, Christians included, are fully capable of resorting to personal attacks and name-calling, as opposed to sticking to the issue at hand (an all too common occurrence). I have seen very, very few effective debates and most people in attendance do not have their views affected in any truly significantly way. I did, however, take part in a forum this past year which featured myself along with a theistic evolutionist. It was hosted on a Christian campus and the theistic evolutionist was one of the PhD biology professors. This particular college taught evolution, which is shamefully becoming more and more common among Christian universities. I believe a forum is a much better setting for discussions of controversial issues. Instead of pitting one speaker against another (which often engenders personal attacks), each speaker simply gives a defense for their view and does not comment directly on the other speaker, for the most part. Obviously, if there is a Q&A period to follow, responses are to be expected, but they can be handled more graciously.

When I first began speaking on creation many years ago, I was focused on talking with evolutionists, atheists and skeptics in general. However, after a few short years, I felt God leading me to change my focus to those within the church. To be honest, I was excited, because I was getting just a bit burned out and frustrated talking with people who for the most part, rarely seemed to respond in a positive way. I couldn't wait to begin dialoging with those who were naturally sympathetic to what I had to share and would be very eager to listen. And then reality set in! I found that in many cases I received more resistance and argumentation from various Christians than I did with the skeptics! I was completely taken by surprise and was very discouraged, to say the least. I have since gained a much better understanding of why this was (and still is) the case. It is largely due to the powerful affects of the secular worldview on Christians within the church. It's part of what is known as syncretism, in which various concepts from a mixture of beliefs are combined. In this case, it would be secular views on the origin of life and the universe being mingled with God's Word, resulting in all types of perspectives on what Genesis really means, as we have briefly covered earlier in this book. I have actually had countless Christians become very offended and angry that I would dare convey confidence in the idea that God created everything in six solar days, just like it says in Genesis. "Who am I to say that God could not have created everything over billions of years, using the big bang?" and "How can all the scientists be wrong?" In response to a lecture I gave to college students at a Christian university, I actually had a professor of Old Testament history tell me, "What you are doing is damaging to the students!" He also asked, "How can all the scientists be wrong?" Not to dwell on this particular instance too long, but in response I asked, "Do you think that most scientists believe the Bible is the inspired Word of God?" to which he confidently replied, "No." I then respectfully asked him a familiar question, "How can all the scientists be wrong?"

Here is one of the main reasons why I primarily focus on ministering within the church. Let's say, that by God's grace and the power of the Holy Spirit, I am able to speak to an atheist and eventually the light bulb comes on. He gets it. It makes sense. He now believes in God. We talk further about the Bible and Jesus and he actually repents and places his trust in Jesus Christ for the forgiveness of his sins. Wonderful! This former atheist is now a Christian. He asks me one day, "Hey, can I come to church with you sometime?" to which I reply, "That would be great! How about this Sunday?" The weekend rolls around and he shows up, just like he promised. He is excited to be there and everyone is so friendly, especially excited to hear about his recent conversion. However, it doesn't take long before he senses that many people there don't really believe what he is now so excited about: that you can trust the Bible from cover-to-cover in all that it addresses, the Genesis creation account included. He starts to become disillusioned, naively thinking that the reason everyone got together on Sunday was because they all believe what was presented to him, which is what changed his entire life. Now he is discovering that many within the church don't really buy into the whole "creation in six days" thing or the flood of Noah, and maybe are not so hot on a few of the other miracles in the Bible, but they sure seem to love Jesus. He's not quite sure how they can be so confident regarding all the Bible states about Jesus when they seem to question its reliability in so many other areas. They also don't seem too concerned about thinking it through too deeply or taking it too seriously. They just want him to lighten up and enjoy the music and fellowship. Sadly, it is not always limited to members of the congregation, but also involves many in leadership positions, including pastors. The final "nail in the coffin" comes when the senior pastor himself tells our new convert that you really can't take the Bible "that way" and it ultimately doesn't even matter. He is often also told that he is still very young in his Christian life and will certainly become more comfortable with this more relaxed viewpoint as he matures.

This is why I feel very strongly that our first and foremost priority is to make sure that the church is biblically solid and has the proper view of, and respect for, God's Word. We can make concerted efforts to witness to the lost (and we most certainly should), but if the church isn't healthy, the converts will flounder. It is even a very strong possibility that we will produce many false converts if we don't have our message straight. I am certainly not focusing on the age of the earth when stating this, but to the bigger issue of understanding the authority of God's Word.

WRAPPING UP THE WRAP UP

I sincerely hope you feel that you have benefited from the time spent reading this book, and trust that God will use it in your life to affect the change that He truly desires—for you to be conformed to the image of His Son, Jesus Christ (Romans 8:29). It is ultimately not about science and certainly not about how to win an argument, but about our personal relationship with Jesus Christ, who being our Creator, is honored when we seek to know more about Him and His creation.

Be confident, knowing that God will honor your efforts in your journey to deepen your relationship with Him. For we know that, "the eyes of the LORD range throughout the earth to strengthen those whose hearts are fully committed to him" (II Chronicles 16:9a, NIV).

Don't hesitate to contact our ministry if there's anything we can help you with. We would love to schedule an engagement at your church, school, camp or any other group. Visit our website for more details: www.CECwisc.com. We look forward to hearing from you!

ENDNOTES

1. www.CECwisc.com

2. D'Souza, Dinesh, "The Atheist Indoctrination Project," October 22, 2007.

3. Stand to Reason, www.str.org—*last accessed 9/24/10.*

4. Sarfati, Jonathan, "Slipshod logic in Creation for Kids? When did evil begin, and is retrograde planet motion still a good argument?" http://creation.com/slipshod-logic-in-creation-for-kids—*last accessed 9/22/10.*

5. "'Wrong way planets screw up our perfectly good theories'—Stupid reality, always mucking about with our ideas. How dare it!" (*Discover* online, April 13th, 2010) http://blogs.discovermagazine.com/badastronomy/2010/04/13/wrong-way-planets-screw-up-our-perfectly-good-theories/—*last accessed 9/22/10.*

6. Lisle, Jason, *The Ultimate Proof of Creation*, Master Books, 2009, p.22-25.

7. Ibid., p.23

So Where Did God Come From?

"Alright, mister smart guy. If God created the universe, then tell me, who created God?"

 There's a good chance that you have either been asked that question or may have even asked it yourself. This is actually a great question and a very logical one for skeptics to ask. In fact, if I were a skeptic, this is probably the first question I would ask. The problem is that too many Christians do not have a very well thought out response. Since we are commanded in Scripture to, "Always be prepared to give an answer" (I Peter 3:15, NIV), we'll tackle this question head on.

The scenario that often brings on such a question is the claim is made that God must have created the universe, because nothing can create itself. "Fine," says the skeptic, "then if God created the universe, and nothing can create itself, then who created God? Gotcha." If the skeptic does not receive a reasonable response, they will frequently not want to listen to anything else the Christian might have to say, and I completely understand that reaction. It is my desire that what follows will aid in establishing enough of an answer to allow for additional dialogue.

THE WRONG QUESTION

It's not surprising that a skeptic would ask this question, but in reality, a lot of Christians have the same question. For the Christian, however, this is actually the wrong question to ask. Many questions actually have hidden assumptions buried within them. For example, let's say a man who absolutely loves animals and would never do anything to hurt them was on trial one day. The judge asks him, under oath, "Have you stopped beating your dog?" How does the defendant answer? If he says "no," he is admitting that he beats his dog. If he says "yes" he is admitting that at some point in the past he was beating his dog. The intrinsic assumption within the judge's question is that the man has in the past beaten his dog, which in this case, is a false assumption. In our question, the implied assumption is that God was created (He had a beginning). Is this a valid assumption?

We will address this question from two angles; first from a biblical perspective and then from a purely logical/scientific perspective. (I do not wish to imply that the Bible is not logical or scientific, just that the second approach will be without making reference to Scripture.)

A BIBLICAL RESPONSE

There are certain attributes that the Bible ascribes to God.

- His omniscience, referring to His infinite knowledge.

- His omnipresence, referring to His being everywhere at the same time.

- His omnipotence, referring to the idea that He is all-powerful.

- His existence in general. Psalm 90:2, for example, tells us that God is "from everlasting to everlasting," meaning that He had no beginning and will have no end.

Most of us can picture God existing in the present, as well as imagining Him existing on out into the infinite future. No real problem at least grasping this concept. However, when it comes to looking in the other direction and trying to imagine Him having always existed, we run into a mental roadblock. We have nothing to relate this concept to. Everything else we know of has a beginning.

It's similar to envisioning a one-dimensional object—a straight line (not considering the actual width of the line). No problem. A two-dimensional object—a surface area. Again, envisioning this is no problem. Three dimensions; a simple cube. Piece of cake. (Actually, a piece of cake is also 3-dimensional and much more appealing than a simple cube!) Now how about a 4-dimensional object? That's where our minds come to a screeching halt. (Yes, some consider "time" to be the fourth dimension, but for our example, we are strictly talking about special dimensions.) Does that mean that 4-D objects don't exist? Not necessarily. It's just that we are not able to envision them. So just because we cannot personally envision God having always existed, it doesn't mean that He hasn't or couldn't have.

AN ELEMENT OF FAITH

Believing something that we cannot prove requires a certain amount of faith. Even though the idea of "faith" sometimes seems like the plague to a skeptic, in reality, they live their lives exercising a lot of faith, in many different areas. They just aren't always aware of it. For instance, every time they get into a car or board an airplane to travel somewhere, they are exercising faith that the engine will not explode killing them along the way. They do not personally go through numerous vigorous procedures before each trip, proving beyond the shadow of a doubt that there won't be any life threatening incidences during their trip. They simply trust (have faith) that their journey will indeed be safe. While it may be true (and hopefully is) that others (engineers and technicians) may have performed many rigorous tests, even those people have not truly proven that there won't be any issues in the future, but the passenger is in essence relying on (trusting in, having faith in) those who performed these tests, who themselves are exercising a certain amount of faith. They also have faith that they can trust their own logic when reasoning through all of these issues. (See appendix B for more along these lines.)

On the other hand, let's say someone believes tomorrow they will receive a check in the mail from an anonymous donor for $1,000,000. You ask them why they believe this to be true and they respond by saying there's no particular reason. It's never happened before and no one gave them any indication that it would ever happen. They just believe it. This would truly be a case of "blind faith." Faith without reason (and sometimes, in spite of reason).

Christianity is not an example of blind faith. On the contrary, it is a reasonable faith, based on actual events in history and has a myriad of support from disciplines such as archaeology, literature, science and prophecy. For the Christian and skeptic alike, it isn't a matter of whether or not one has faith, it's a matter of what that faith is based upon (whether it is closer to a "blind" faith, lacking evidence, or a very reasonable faith, firmly grounded in history, reason and logic, etc.).

Hebrews 11:6 (NIV) tells us, "And without faith it is impossible to please God, because anyone who comes to him must believe that he exists and that he rewards those who earnestly seek him." Nowhere in God's written Word does He try to prove His existence. He merely states that He exists and always has. This segment does not focus on whether or not God exists, but simply on the question of His origin. Nonetheless, a few pertinent comments are in order at this point.

An atheist is one who claims that there is no God. However, if God is a non-physical, invisible entity (which is how the Bible describes God), how could anyone prove that He does not exist? In fact, the only way to truly know that God does not exist, would be to have all knowledge of all time and space in order to know that God does not exist anywhere in the universe or beyond. The only way to have this kind of knowledge would be if that person were actually God. Another way of looking at this is to ask the skeptic, "Do you know everything?" Their reply would be "No" (more likely, "No—and neither do you!"). Then ask, "Do you know a tenth or even a thousandth of everything?" The reply again would be "No." Then you could ask whether or not it is possible that the knowledge or evidence for God might exist somewhere in large percentage of information that they just admitted not knowing. This approach is not one I generally use or recommend to others, but it does make a point. (If you do take this approach, I would strongly caution you not to do it in a condescending manner, or with any arrogance. We need to be Christ-like examples in all we do.) I would also advise that before one gets too far into a discussion on God's existence, they ask the skeptic what evidence they would accept as being supportive of God's existence. If they are unable to answer that question, there isn't much hope of them recognizing any real evidence even if it were clearly presented to them.

Most arguments against the existence of God are not centered on the existence of God in general, but on the unlikelihood of there being a God who would under no circumstances ever allow something "bad" to happen (which is what many mistakenly assume the Christian God is supposed to be). We will have to save that discussion for another book!

Science is limited to testing things of a physical nature; things that typically have mass, dimensions, color, temperature, etc. It is by definition, unable to comment on things of a non-physical nature. It would somewhat be like if I set before you two cartons of ice cream (chocolate and strawberry), then gave you a ruler and asked you to determine which one is colder. Apart from using the ruler as a spoon (trying to taste both to see if you could tell any temperature difference), that object is incapable of directly making that kind of judgment.

In the same sense, science is incapable of proving there is no God. What about going the other way? Can science "prove" God does exist? Many Christians would say "yes." I used to be one of them. As I have thought through the issue of the proper use of science and the nature of the existence of God, I would say that I don't believe science itself is actually capable of yielding "absolute proof" of God's existence, but it can comment on phenomenon that can only be reasonably explained by the existence of God. This should not at all be a disappointment for Christians, but rather very exciting. If the tool (science) was capable of proving God's existence, but had not done so, that would be disappointing. In reality, science only deals with matter, energy, time and space, but God, by definition, is outside of matter, energy, time and space. It can measure the "effects" of God's actions, but not God directly. Science can and has given us sufficient evidence to make belief in God a most reasonable conclusion. This, again, is strictly looking at what science can and cannot do. I think a more robust defense for the existence of God comes from logic and reasoning. See appendix B for a further discussion of a defense for faith.

LOGIC AND SCIENCE

There are many aspects of our world that only make sense if there actually is a God. Space precludes going into great detail, but just the fact that there exists anything at all, is evidence for God. (We'll explore that in a bit more detail in the next section.) The great order in our solar system and universe actually speaks of God's existence (as opposed to sheer randomness). The existence of information also only makes sense if God exists. Matter and energy can "store" information, but they are completely incapable of "creating" information to begin with. Compact discs, DVDs, hard drives, books, and catalogs all *contain* information, but the materials that each is made from did not create the information to begin with. No one would think that all of the information contained within a set of encyclopedias arose from the wood pulp (paper) and ink of which the set consists. Just a pinhead's volume of DNA is equivalent to stack of books 500 times the distance from the earth to the moon![1] DNA can store tremendous amounts of information, but it cannot create the information. Information only comes from pre-existing intelligence. Science knows of no exceptions. . .none![2]

But what about God's *eternal* existence? Is there anything in science or logic that sheds light on this question? You may have heard of the "Kalām cosmological argument," regarding the existence of our universe, although it is not commonly known in most social circles. This system of logic is of Arabic origins and posits the following:

- Everything that begins to exist has a cause.

- The universe had a beginning.

- Therefore the universe has a cause.

Although many scientists in the past believed the universe was eternal (primarily to avoid having to explain how it could have "begun without a beginner") most today now accept that it did have a beginning. The "big bang" is a theory which attempts to explain the origin our universe, but in reality, it does not actually address the issue of getting something from nothing—only how "something" allegedly evolved over time into "everything." (For further information, please refer back to chapter 3 of this book.)

Since the universe did have a beginning, it follows logically that it also has a cause; a sufficient cause that would logically have to lie outside of itself, for nothing can create itself.

If it were true that God had a beginning, it would also logically follow that He had a cause as well, which again, would have to be outside of, and greater than Himself. The Bible claims, as mentioned earlier, that God *did not* have a beginning. Therefore, His existence would not require a cause. This sounds simple, but is there anything to backup the Bible's claim that God is eternal? I believe that science and logic not only indicate that God exists, but that He *must* be eternal.

Consider the following line of reasoning:

Question: If there was ever a time in the past (no matter how far back you wish to go—100 million years, 100 billion, 100 trillion, 100 gazillion) when *absolutely nothing* existed, what would be here today? The answer should be clear: *nothing*. If there truly was a time when nothing existed, what could that "nothing" do? Nothing, because nothing is nothing but nothing! It could not be acted upon by anything else, because nothing else exists. It could not slowly or abruptly change from one thing to another; from nothing into something. In fact time itself would not even exist, if there really was absolutely nothing in existence.

Observation: There actually is a lot of "stuff" here today, a whole universe full. One of the reasons that the universe is so vast is that God had so much stuff and needed a place to put it! (I know that's bad theology, but it's just my feeble attempt at humor.)

Conclusion: There could never have been a time when absolutely nothing existed. In other words, there has always been *something* around.

Most sensible people would not argue with the previous line of reasoning. Still, we are left with trying to determine what this eternal "something" might be. On a very fundamental level, everything we can think of falls into one of two categories: (a) matter and energy or (b) mind. The physical world around us is made up of combinations of matter and energy. Einstein taught us that matter and energy are interchangeable. Matter can be converted into energy and vice versa. His famous equation equates the two: $e=mc^2$ (where "e" = energy, "m" = mass [of matter] and "c" = the speed of light).

On the other hand, if I told you that my favorite color was teal, that idea would be part of my "mind." You can't go into the lab and take the concept that teal is my favorite and chop it up into five pieces and give each one of your friends a sample. It is a non-physical entity, but it is part of reality. So our two choices are either some combination of matter and energy, or mind. Let's first take a look at "matter and energy" as a potential candidate for this "eternal something."

As mentioned earlier, some scientists used to believe that matter (and the universe) was eternal. With advancements in scientific discoveries, this view has become untenable. There are two laws that arguably are the best, most well established laws in all of science, namely, the first and second law of thermodynamics. Without getting into the technical details, thermodynamics is the study of heat, energy and work within a given system. The particular law that most directly relates to our question is the second law. Simply put, this law states that every system, left on its own, always tends to move from order to disorder, its energy tending to be transformed into lower levels of availability (for work), ultimately becoming totally random and unavailable (useless).

The famous science fiction writer Isaac Asimov put it in even simpler terms:

> Another way of stating the second law then is: "The universe is constantly getting more disorderly!" Viewed that way, we can see the second law all about us. We have to work hard to straighten a room, but left to itself it becomes a mess again very quickly and very easily. Even if we never enter it, it becomes dusty and musty. How difficult to maintain houses, and machinery, and our bodies in perfect working order: how easy to let them deteriorate. In fact, all we have to do is nothing, and everything deteriorates, collapses, breaks down, wears out, all by itself—and that is what the second law is all about.[3]

This being the case, if the universe (and the matter within it) were infinitely old, there would be no energy or order left! It would have "run out of gas," so to speak, long, long ago. The fact that we do see high levels of order and great concentrations of useful energy (such as our sun) indicate that it is not infinitely old and in fact, cannot be infinitely old.

The second law of thermodynamics rules out one of our "eternal candidates" (matter/energy), thereby leaving only one alternative: that of "mind." We know from biblical descriptions that God is a spirit (John 4:24), not a physical being. The concept of spirit is basically the same as that of "mind." Therefore, we can conclude logically and scientifically that there has always been something in existence and that "something" is an eternal mind (God)—just like the Bible tells us!

CLOSING THOUGHTS

Ultimately, the issue of God's existence is a spiritual issue, not a scientific or logical issue. By this I mean that those who wish not to believe in God (or

His self-existence) are going to do so no matter what evidence or reasoning is presented to them. God will nonetheless hold them accountable for their choices. Romans 1:19-20 (NIV) states:

> since what may be known about God is plain to them [the godless], because God has made it plain to them. For since the creation of the world God's invisible qualities—his eternal power and divine nature—have been clearly seen, being understood from what has been made, so that *men are without excuse* (emphasis added).

The passage goes on to say,

> For although they knew God [were inwardly aware that He does truly exist], they neither glorified him as God nor gave thanks to Him, but their thinking became futile and their foolish hearts were darkened. Although they claimed to be wise, they became fools and exchanged the glory of the immortal God for images made to look like mortal man and birds and animals and reptiles. Therefore God gave them over in the sinful desires of their hearts to sexual impurity for the degrading of their bodies with one another. They exchanged the truth of God for a lie, and worshiped and served created things rather than the Creator—who is forever praised.

The Bible tells us that God has always existed and we find that true science and sound logic are consistent with His self-existence and eternal nature. The evidence is all around; we must simply humble ourselves and acknowledge His authority:

> The heavens declare the glory of God; the skies proclaim the work of His hands. Day after day they pour forth speech; night after night they display knowledge. There is no speech or language where their voice is not heard (Psalm 19:1-3, NIV).

> Has not my hand made all these things, and so they came into being?" declares the Lord. "This is the one I esteem: he who is humble and contrite in spirit, and trembles at my word (Isaiah 66:2, NIV).

For a more thorough discussion regarding "proof" that God exists, see appendix B (Presuppositional Apologetics).

ENDNOTES

1. Gitt, Werner, "Dazzling Design in Miniature," *Creation*, 20(1):6, 1997.

2. See also Gitt, Werner, *In the Beginning Was Information*, Master Books, 2005.

3. Asimov, Isaac, *Smithsonian Institute Journal*, June 1970, p. 6.

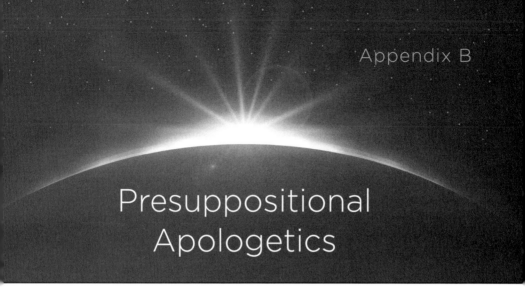

Presuppositional Apologetics

I am taking my chances addressing this topic in an appendix. Certain things in life are best approached with a motto of "Do it right or don't do it at all!" It could be that this topic is one of those things, but I am going to throw "caution to the wind" and take a chance by giving you a relatively brief overview of this subject matter. Even though the title may seem intimidating, I think you will find this topic fascinating and not all that hard to grasp. It doesn't require you to know anything about science! How's that for easy? By way of a quick definition, a presupposition is something you assume to be true to begin with. All other arguments are built upon this belief or set of beliefs. With this brief introduction, let's dive right in.

THAT'S THE WAY WE'VE ALWAYS DONE IT

You are most likely already aware of the fact that "apologetics" has to do with defending the Christian faith. The word itself is derived from the Greek word, *apologia*, which is found in 1 Peter 3:15 (KJV), "But sanctify the Lord God in your hearts: and be ready always to give an answer [apologia] to every man that asketh you a reason of the hope that is in you with meekness and fear."

Traditionally, apologetics has involved defining the Christian faith (including the existence of God, creation, the deity of Jesus, the inspiration of the Bible, etc.) and then sharing various evidences to demonstrate its validity. There certainly is a place for sharing evidence (as I have done throughout this book), but we need to be careful how and when we use it. You shall soon see why.

Appendix B

Within the intended scope of this brief appendix, I will narrow my focus to one topic (the existence of God) and one general audience (atheists and/or agnostics). As a Christian, I am committed to believing that the Bible is the inspired, infallible Word of God. I do not feel, as a fallen human being, that I am in a position to tell God what parts of the Bible He actually inspired and which ones He didn't. I accept as my starting point (my presupposition) that God exists and all of Scripture is inspired, as is indicated in II Timothy 3:16. Therefore, all that the Bible conveys is true. I know the atheist does not accept this, but this is my starting point and everything that I personally believe must be rooted in, and consistent with, God's Word. It is important to note that this starting point is not completely arbitrary, as some may suppose. By this, I mean that some might say I just happen to choose this set of beliefs where others choose something different. My choice is not arbitrary, but driven by the fact that God has revealed Himself to me through the Holy Spirit. That is why I personally have this starting point, as opposed to atheism, Buddhism or any other belief.

With that in mind, what does it tell us about the atheist? After all, what I might personally think about atheists may be of some interest to others, but ultimately my own opinions and philosophies really don't matter; only what God tells us can be trusted with any real certainty. Here are a few things God says about the atheist:

- "The wrath of God is being revealed from heaven against all the godlessness and wickedness of people, who suppress the truth by their wickedness, since what may be known about God is plain to them, because God has made it plain to them. For since the creation of the world God's invisible qualities—his eternal power and divine nature—have been clearly seen, being understood from what has been made, so that people are without excuse" (Romans 1:18-20, NIV). These verses tell us that everyone knows God exists, including the atheist, because God has made it plain to them. However, they have chosen to suppress the truth. We could read every philosophy book that exists on atheism and conduct survey after survey in an effort to determine what the atheist really believes and why, but God Himself is telling us that they know He exists. This should be our starting point. I'm not saying they admit He exists (they obviously don't), but God says they actually do know.

- "The fool hath said in his heart, There is no God" (Psalm 14:1, KJV). This is not name-calling. God is simply stating that those who say there is no God are thinking foolishly. Yes, they claim that God does not exist, but we just learned from Romans 1 that they know the truth—they are simply suppressing it. This verse is obviously in reference to moral character and not intellect, as evidenced by the fact that many atheists are highly intelligent academically.

- "Professing themselves to be wise, they became fools" (Romans 1:22, KJV). They claim great enlightenment, but truly are foolish.

- "For the wisdom of this world is foolishness with God" (I Corinthians 3:19, KJV). Even the most brilliant scientist on the earth knows nothing compared to God.

- "But the natural man [unsaved] receiveth not the things of the Spirit of God: for they are foolishness unto him: neither can he know them, because they are spiritually discerned" (I Corinthians 2:14, KJV). The skeptic cannot on his own understand the things of God, because they are spiritually discerned. That's why I keep mentioning throughout this book that this is ultimately a spiritual battle and not simply an academic argument.

- "The fear of the Lord is the beginning of knowledge, but fools despise wisdom and instruction" (Proverbs 1:7, KJV). If appropriate reverence for God is the beginning of knowledge, then the atheist hasn't really even begun to learn anything yet. If they are also fools (which is what Scripture states) then we also learn from this verse that they "despise wisdom and instruction."

There are many other verses in the Bible that further describe the skeptic and the atheist, but these will suffice for now. Again, the point is not to denigrate them or resort to name-calling, but simply to see how God views their situation. This is critically important for us to understand as we consider engaging them in conversation.

USING EVIDENCE

When you think about it, where do we most often hear people presenting evidence? In a courtroom. And to whom is the evidence presented? The judge, and in some cases the jury, as well. In this situation, the judge and/or jury sit in authority over the case in dispute. They weigh the evidence and get to determine what constitutes reality or truth.

Let's turn back to our traditional apologetics strategy. We present evidence to an atheist, then sit back and say, "Now you get to decide." We are letting him (or her) sit in authority over God's existence (and His Word). Not a good thing to do; certainly

not biblical. When you take into account what the Bible says about their inability to reason correctly and their lack of wisdom, how in the world can we expect them to come to the right conclusion? Even if somehow it appears that they do conclude that God actually does exist, they may still not believe in the God of the Bible, just that there must be "a god." In fact, it doesn't necessarily even have to be "a god," maybe it's just a super intelligent, super powerful alien! To make matters worse, if they come to the point of belief (even in the God of the Bible) through their own reasoning of the "facts," they could just as easily reason away from God later, if they hear new facts or other information to which they had not previously been exposed. On a personal note, I believe that if someone is truly saved, in reality, they cannot "reason away" from salvation, because it ultimately is a spiritual transformation and not just an intellectual decision. However, there are certainly cases of apostasy by those who gave the appearance of being a Christian, but were not actually saved.

> They went out from us, but they were not of us; for if they had been of us, they would no doubt have continued with us: but they went out, that they might be made manifest that they were not all of us (I John 2:19, KJV).

A BETTER APPROACH

If you were to enter into a discussion with an atheist, you might try asking if they expect you to be logical in stating your case for the existence of God. They would certainly say, "Yes, of course." They would probably even think that it was a very odd question. Then you could ask them *why* they think you should be logical. If they've never had anyone ask this question before (which is very likely) they may stammer a bit for an answer (which is very understandable), but eventually they would convey to you that it is the only way to really have a meaningful conversation. Let's convert all of this to a sample conversation which will make it easier to follow.

Christian: "Do you expect me to be logical in stating my case for the existence of God?"

Atheist: "Yes, of course! That's a very odd question."

Christian: "Why should I be logical?"

Atheist: "It's the only way to really have a meaningful conversation."

Christian: "I completely agree, but in your atheistic worldview, where does it state that everyone has to be logical? How do you even know you can trust your logic? And whose logic do we use? Are there different types of logic? Where does logic come from in your worldview? Can different types of logic exist that contradict each other? If so, how and why? If not, why not?" [Note: These are not easy questions for most people, atheist or otherwise, so don't expect them to be extremely eloquent when responding.]

Atheist: "No, one set of logic cannot contradict another, because that would be illogical. I trust my logic because of my own personal experience. It has shown itself to be reliable."

Christian: "So there's only one set of laws that define logic. And apparently, these laws are pragmatic in nature, meaning that they are true because they seem to work well according to your reasoning. How do you know you can trust your own reasoning?"

Atheist: "Again, because of my own experience."

Christian: "So you use your reason to determine that you can trust your reason. That sounds very circular. It also seems like the laws of logic are subjective, because different people have different reasoning and different experiences. You have yours, I have mine, others have their own. Where did the laws of logic actually come from?"

Atheist: "The laws of logic are simply mental constructs that reflect reality."

Christian: "But mental constructs are products of our reasoning, and if different people have different reasoning (which you and I certainly do) doesn't that mean there would be different laws of logic which could at least potentially contradict each other? How would we determine which set of laws are correct? How would we even know there was a 'correct' set?"

Atheist: "No, the laws of logic are not subjective. There aren't numerous contradictory sets of these laws."

Christian: "So you believe that the laws of logic are universal, meaning they are the same everywhere for everyone?"

Atheist: "Yes."

Christian: "Do you believe these laws are unchanging, meaning they are the same today as they were yesterday and as they will be tomorrow? If not, could you tell me why?"

Atheist: "Yes, I believe they are unchanging."

Christian: "Are the laws of logic physical entities? Can we observe them under a microscope? Do they have weight, size, mass, color, etc?"

Atheist: "No, they are immaterial, non-physical. They are abstract."

Christian: "Then I ask again, where did the laws of logic come from? If, according to your atheistic worldview, the physical universe is all that exists, where did these immaterial, universal, unchanging laws come from? Can matter and energy produce non-physical things? If so, can you give me an example? If not, then where did the laws of logic come from?"

Atheist: "They just exist. They are properties of matter."

Christian: "I've never heard any scientists say they have measured the laws of logic before. All other properties of matter can be measured; length, width, height, mass, temperature, etc. Could you give me some documentation regarding the laws of logic being properties of matter? And since different types of matter have different properties (densities, electric charges, etc.), do they each have their own laws of logic?"

This type of a conversation can go on and on, but it quickly degenerates to the point where the atheist has less and less of a defensible "logical" response and it often will produce more and more emotion and anger.

Here's the main point in all of this. An atheist certainly uses the abstract, universal, unchanging laws of logic when attempting to make his case, but he is completely incapable of rationalizing why they should be used and where they came from in the first place. Furthermore, there is no ultimate rationale for why they can truly trust their own logic.

On the other hand, a Christian believes in the God of the Bible who is Himself: abstract (immaterial), universal and unchanging. It makes perfect sense that He created a universe that would operate under the laws of logic which themselves are also immaterial, universal and unchanging (a reflection of His own character).

Therefore, in order for an atheist to make their case that God does not exist, they actually have to assume He does! It certainly seems bizarre, but it is logically very solid. If an atheist wants to use logic in his argument, he must first defend why this should be the case. Why should there even be laws? Where did they come from? Why can we trust them? What were they like in the distant past? How do we know they won't change? What would keep them from changing? As we have just seen, the atheist will not be able to rationally answer these questions. If he doesn't wish to use the laws of logic (or not require others to do so), then the conversation is already over.

WHAT DO YOU KNOW YOU KNOW?

Here's another interesting question to ask an atheist: "Is there anything you know for sure?" The reply often comes, "You can't really know anything for sure—not with one hundred percent certainty." I would then follow up by asking, "Are you sure about that? Are you one hundred percent certain?" They just said it's not possible to know anything for certain, so to be logically consistent, they can't say, "Yes." However, if they say, "No," they are admitting that it really is possible to know something for certain. Within the atheist's worldview, they can't even know for sure that they can't even know anything for sure! Is your head spinning yet? If not, then maybe I am not doing a very good job of explaining things! I know, it gets kind of crazy here, but hang in there. You are starting to see how illogical the atheistic worldview is when played out to its logical end.

A typical response from the atheist to all of this is to simply retort by saying, "Well, you can't know anything for sure, either!" Once again, you can ask them, "Are you sure about that?" Once again, to have any credibility, they would have to admit that they don't know for sure that a Christian can't know anything for certain, meaning that it is possible that a Christian could know something with absolute certainty.

So how is it different for a Christian? How would a Christian rationalize being able to know anything for certain? Are Christians just so much smarter than everyone else? That's certainly not the claim being made. Here's the rationale. Ask the skeptic if it is possible that an immaterial, universal, unchanging, all-powerful, all-knowing God exists. If they say, "No," you could ask them how they know that for sure, since they've already admitted they can't know anything for sure. If (and more likely "when") they say "Yes, I suppose so," then you can ask, "Is it possible that this all-knowing, all-powerful God could convey some absolute truth to us in such a way that we could know and understand it for certain?" Again, the skeptic cannot justifiably say they know for certain this is impossible, so they would have to say, "Yes, it's possible."

Putting all of this together—this is Christianity (at least partially) in a nutshell. We believe there is a God who is immaterial, universal, unchanging, all-powerful, all-knowing and has communicated absolute truth to us in such a way that we can know for certain. That is our starting point. That is our presupposition. We don't subsequently seek out evidence with which to "prove" our presupposition, we use our presupposition to show that it is the only one that makes sense of the real world in which we live. You may arbitrarily start with a different presupposition (for example, that God does not exist), but you will quickly see that it will not allow you to make sense of our daily experiences, including the rationale for why the laws of logic exist and why anyone should be bound to using them.

In summary, when discussing the existence of God with an atheist, it's really not a matter of sharing some evidence from science to show that He most likely exists, but that if you don't start your thinking with the assumption that He does exist (which is what the Bible posits), it's impossible to prove anything at all!

BE NICE, NOW. . .

Simply being in the right is not a justification for lording it over anyone or being condescending and disrespectful. We need to always "speak the truth in love" (Ephesians 4:15, KJV). If you've ever been caught in a lie before (and don't say you haven't or you'll be lying) you know how awkward it can be. You may feel "cornered" and may start to squirm and get angry inside.

Mother: "Why are you late getting home?"

Son: "Because I had to stop at the grocery store."

Mother: "Did you get the milk like I asked?"

Son: "No."

Mother. "Why not?"

Son: "Because I forgot you asked me to get some."

Mother: "How could you forget? I asked you three times and even texted you before you left Grandma's."

Son: "Well, I was at the store, looking at the milk and I couldn't remember what kind you wanted, so I decided not to get any, because I didn't want to buy the wrong one."

Mother: "I thought you said you forgot that I asked you to get milk?"

Son: "Ummm, well, yes, I did."

Mother: "But you just told me that you were trying to figure out what kind of milk I wanted. So which is it? Did you forget or did you just not know what kind I wanted? And why wouldn't you have just texted me to find out? You text everyone else all the time!"

Son: "Well, no, I didn't forget to buy milk. . . I. . . I meant that I forgot what *kind* you wanted, and I didn't text you, because I didn't want to go over our monthly limit."

Mother: "But you know we have unlimited texting. It's been that way for the past year and a half!"

Son: "Well, I knew it was unlimited, but I thought maybe it was only for a certain amount of unlimited minutes each month. . . those were unlimited."

Mother: "That makes no sense at all!"

The more you say, the worse it gets and you start to feel a lot of inward turmoil (conviction that you know you are not being honest, whether you want to admit it or not). Why did I bother with this lengthy exchange? I think it is important to keep in mind that the skeptic may feel somewhat similar at some point in your conversation. I am not saying they are consciously lying to you (because they usually think they are right and that you are the one who is wrong). I am simply saying that they may very well be sensing the conviction of the Holy Spirit at some point and we need to let them see Christ in us in a very real way. We should be focused on helping, rather than just trying to win an argument. You may indeed win the argument (and if you present all of this properly, you will). However, if this isn't done in love, you will lose the relationship and the opportunity to share the gospel message if you are not gracious in your approach.

ULTIMATE AUTHORITY

It truly all comes down to the idea of "ultimate authority." One of the most basic questions you can ask anyone (whether an atheist, a skeptic, a humanist, a Mormon, etc.) is, "What is your ultimate source of authority? What do you rely upon for determining ultimate truth?"

Amusement parks often have minimum height requirements for various rides. You'll see signs that state something like, "You must be at least 52 inches tall to ride on this roller coaster." A child might think they can handle it even though they don't meet the requirement and perhaps even the parents are in agreement, but does that really matter? Does that change the rules? Who is the ultimate authority? You could say the parents, but even though they have a certain amount of authority over their own children, they don't have authority over the rules of the amusement park. Maybe it's the person in charge of the ride. Actually, he or she is only enforcing what is written on the sign. Is the sign the ultimate authority? No, it is just conveying what the owners of the park have established. They must be the ultimate authority, right? Actually, they cannot enforce anything that goes against state law. In that case, maybe the state politicians are the ultimate authority. Not really. The state cannot enact any policies that are contrary to national law. So maybe the national law makers are the ultimate authority. Within our simple example, they truly do represent the ultimate authority. There are no "world laws" governing amusement parks; not yet anyway! Ultimately, this law is in force, because the national powers that be, said so. Why do they get to set the rules? Because they get to set the rules! It sounds kind of like circular reasoning, but that's only because it is! That's the way it works. (No analogy is perfect, so if you try hard enough, you may be able to poke holes in this, such as discussing the fact that the citizens of the United States elect our national officials, but let's just leave it as is for simplicity sake.)

The main point here is that all ultimate authority is circular in its defense, and must be by nature. If there were further reasoning or justification for a particular source having authority, then whatever source we were considering does not actually constitute final or ultimate authority. What I mean by this is that in our defense of why a particular source has ultimate authority, we would be appealing to an even higher authority to do so. For example, if we said the national law makers are the ultimate authority because the European Union grants them authority to rule over the United States, then the European Union would actually be the ultimate authority. We then would either have to say that the European Union has ultimate authority because they just do (circular in nature) or they do because the "Council of Twelve" (or whatever group) has granted them authority (in which case, the "Council of Twelve" would the be the ultimate authority, unless they received their power from yet another agency). Therefore, the defense for all ultimate authority is always circular in nature. If not, then you are not really talking about an ultimate authority! It may seem strange, but this is a very important concept to understand.

For a Christian, the ultimate source of authority is the Bible. The Bible is true because the Bible say is it the inspired Word of God. This is actually more than just saying that the Bible is true because the Bible says so. It not only evidences its truthfulness internally, but rejecting it as truth leads to all sorts of logical absurdities. It could also be stated that while the Christian's presuppositions seem circular (which is unavoidable when dealing with ultimate authorities), the atheist's presuppositions are "viciously" circular and self-destructive. Author and Christian apologist Greg Bahnsen explains:

> In the Christian worldview, however, the Christian is not engaged in viciously circular argument, a circular argument on the same plane. We appeal above and beyond the temporal realm. God's self-revelation in nature and in Scripture informs us of the two-level universe. God is not a fact like other facts in the world. He is the Creator and Establisher of all else. His existence alone makes the universe, and reason, and human experience possible. . .The "circularity" of a transcendental argument is not at all the same as the fallacious "circularity" of an argument in which the conclusion is a restatement (in one form or another) of one of its premises. (*Pushing the Antithesis*, American Vision, 2007, p.124)

Skeptics often say, "You can't use the Bible to prove the Bible; that's circular reasoning and you can't do that!" However, the atheist believes (whether they admit it or not) that *their* reasoning is the ultimate authority. They believe their reasoning tells them that they can trust their reasoning. That's circular, too, but it lacks any explanatory power. Some might say that skeptics actually rely upon scientific experiments and such, but ultimately they are using their own reasoning to evaluate the experiments and interpret the results. The problem isn't actually with circular reasoning, but rather with the explanatory power of anyone's particular set of presuppositions (or ultimate source of authority). The Christian's presuppositions make sense of the world we live in, including the existence of immaterial, universal and unchanging laws of logic. The atheist's presuppositions do not. At this point, it truly is a matter of choice (which presupposition you will choose for yourself). However, until the atheist will humbly bow in reverence to God, Scripture tells us that their thinking will remain futile, and all the logic and facts in the world will not change their mind.

It is only by God's grace that they will even be able to make the right decision. It is not our job to "convert" or "save" anyone. We can't! That's the job of the Holy Spirit. It is, however, our responsibility to share the truth of the gospel message with a lost and dying world.

> for, everyone who calls on the name of the Lord will be saved. How, then, can they call on the one they have not believed in? And how can they believe in the one of whom they have not heard? And how can they hear without someone preaching to them? And how can anyone preach unless they are sent? As it is written: "How beautiful are the feet of those who bring good news!" (Romans 10:13-15, NIV).

How all this works (salvation and God's grace), I truly do not fully understand. Thankfully, God does not ask me to. He simply wants me to be obedient by being a faithful witness. It actually takes all the pressure off.

CONCLUSION

In summary, when discussing the existence of God with an atheist, we have learned the truly biblical approach teaches us a few very important points:

- The atheist already knows God exists, but is suppressing this knowledge by his unrighteousness.

- Their rejection of God has caused their thinking to become darkened and foolish.

- We should not approach this issue by sharing evidence and facts, because that puts the atheist in a position of authority over God and His Word, letting them be the judge of God.

- Even if the atheist considers the facts and reasons that God does exist, he may just as easily use his own logic to reason away from God if he later is exposed to additional facts that he considers to nullify what he previously heard.

- An atheist wants to use the laws of logic in making their case for atheism, but they cannot explain the existence of these laws nor why anyone is obligated to follow them. In fact, in order for those laws to exist, you must first assume that God exists, which is the whole point they are trying to refute!

You may still have one burning question left: So where does typical, traditional apologetic argument fit? Should we abandon it altogether? The answer is, "No." It can be used in a very powerful way as an encouragement to the believer, to help them see the depth and breadth of the inspiration, authority and trustworthiness of God's Word. Not as ultimate proof, but as confirmation. Paul admonishes us in I Thessalonians 5:21 (KJV) to, "Prove all things; hold fast that which is good." The Greek word used for "prove" (*dokimazō*) conveys the concept of testing, examining, scrutinizing to see whether or anot something is genuine. This assumes that there is some standard against which everything can be judged: God's Word. We can often use traditional apologetics to evaluate things we hear from those around us (including other Christians) to see if they "truly are true," meaning how they conform or don't conform to what we know from Scripture.

Traditional apologetic arguments can also be shared along the way with skeptics and even atheists to demonstrate that Christianity does have answers to the various alleged challenges to Scripture. Again, we don't use them as proof, but we often do need to have some type of reasonable response, whether it is a question about carbon-14 dating, or "missing links," or whatever is being posed as a challenge to our faith. That's largely what this book has been all about. So yes, there is a place for traditional apologetics, we just need to be careful to use them appropriately with the right audience for the right reasons!

I know much of this has been a bit heavy and maybe not the easiest concepts to follow, but that's partially because it is probably fairly new to you. I am still working through all of this myself. I would encourage you to pray about this and allow God to refine you in the process (and I will do the same).

CREATION
EDUCATION CENTER
CECwisc.com

If you have further questions regarding our ministry or would be interested in discussing a potential engagement at your church, school, conference, camp or other organization, please contact us:

Web: **CECwisc.com**

Email: **info@CECwisc.com**

We do not charge for our engagements, but simply accept freewill offerings, honorariums or whatever the hosting organization deems appropriate. We just ask that any actual expenses be covered in addition (such as travel and lodging).

Our presentations are always very encouraging and graciously presented, strengthening the faith of those within the body of Christ, while compassionately challenging the sincere skeptic.

We also encourage you to visit our website to check out all our great resources (DVDs, books, booklets, video clips, audio, articles, etc.).